LIFE AFTER HOCKEY

When the Lights are Dimmed

Michael A. Smith

Codner Books

Grateful acknowledgement is given for permission to reproduce a portion
of *"Circle"* by Harry Chapin, Copyright 1971, Harry Chapin Foundation.

Codner Books

4449 Lynx Ct.

St. Paul, MN 55123

Printed in the United States of America

First Printing, October 1987

ISBN 0-9619033-0-9

. . . for my parents.

Table of Contents

Preface

This is a study of former hockey players, their transitions from the hockey world to the "real world", and their post-playing careers. It evolved from a conversation between Bill Lesuk and me. Bill scouts for the Winnipeg Jets and we often have philosophical talks about the game. This was one of those "hockey is going to hell in a handbasket" guys. We agreed that youth hockey was heading in the wrong direction with the advent and growth of traveling all-star teams. It seemed to us that many programs were being run by the parents for the parents. The kids were playing the game for their parents wish fulfillment. We wondered why today's youth teams play a 100 or so games, if Gordie Howe, Bobby Orr, Jean Beliveau and hundreds of other professionals never played in such programs. Bill suggested I write something about this.

I gave it some thought and came up with the interview project that led to this book. The interviews started with the assumption that there is more to life than hockey. I thought that having players who made it to the top talk about their experiences would shed some light on the subject. Between August, 1986, and June, 1987, I interviewed 22 former players. The study soon became more than just one for only those involved at the youth hockey level. The scope of the study was expanded by the people interviewed. It became a project to educate people at all levels of the game.

This is a book about people, not hockey. Hockey is just their common denominator. They are frank, candid and honest about their experiences on and off the ice. These are stories of people who reached the top of their profession as athletes, then moved on to the "real world."

This book became, for me, a testimonial to human character. I was astonished by the way some of these players opened up to me. It was as if we had been lifelong friends. To a man, they offered their help. That, in itself, has been rewarding to me.

The 22 former players we interviewed are good men. They share a sense of humility. Their stories made this project what it is.

I need to thank several people who helped in many and different ways. Without their assistance, this project would not have been completed. My sincere thanks and appreciation go out to Bill Lesuk, Dennis MacDonald, Gene Rosa, Ted Green, Don Baizley, Barry Shenkarow, Mary Jane Lesuk, Kathy Page, John Cunniff, Jerry Rodrigues, Sarah Remon, Dave Peterson, Tom Savage, Bill Hefferman, Alpo Suhonen, Jack Stouffer, Pat MacDonald, Murray Costello, Brian O'Neil, Ken Fried, John Gilbert, David Corr and Tony Biegun. Special thanks go to the Winnipeg Jets Hockey Club who permitted me to work on this book while under their employment.

My wife, Judy, deserves a lot of credit. She did the bulk of the typing and transcribing of interviews. She made sound suggestions, offered encouragement, and added determination to the project.

West Tisbury, Ma.   *June, 1987*

Introduction

All my life's a circle
Sunrise and sundown
Moon rose though the night time
Till the daybreak comes round

All my life's a circle
But I can't tell you why
Seasons spinning 'round again
The years keep rolling by

        Circle -- Harry Chapin

Is there "life after hockey?" This book is an attempt to look at what "life after hockey" is like. The former hockey players interviewed call upon their actual experiences to see how they handled the transition to post-playing careers. The interviews take place during a period defined as "after hockey" to permit the players to reflect on those experiences.

The Project

This study attempts to reveal behavioral patterns drawn from common experiences among the people interviewed: former hockey players. A number of hypotheses were established at the outset. The group of people selected had to give the study a good balance. The initial impetus for the study was to show young players, their parents and coaches that there is more to life than hockey. However, it quickly became more. It is an educational awareness study for those athletes who either strive for or have reached the elite playing level. It offers insights from the experiences of those who played. It shows that the real life of the former "star" athlete is not much different than that of the normal person.

The time frame of the players' careers for the study ranges from the 1950's to the 1980's. The only requirement is that the person interviewed is beyond his immediate transition period, so that the transition period, rough or smooth, is viewed from a historical perspective. The difference between the transition period and the "life after hockey" period is that the first can be defined in terms of time, while the second is on-going.

The Sample

This is an interview book. The people who are interviewed are the source for both the data and for any conclusions that may be drawn. The people selected are former hockey players who played a number of years beyond high school or junior age level. Professional and amateur players are included. One does not have to have been a professional to have had a hockey career.

To give the study a good balance, we chose a cross section of players - Americans, Europeans, and players from across Canada, and players from a broad spectrum of talents. Some played in the minor leagues and were, at best, marginal National Leaguers. Others were considered among the best of their era, maybe an all-star or a Hall of Famer. Former players of different ages tell stories from the different eras. A sub-group in the study consists of people who were considered elite players but either decided not to pursue a hockey career or to abandon the playing career and get on with what they felt was their real career. This is done for two reasons. The first is to show that players who have an alternative can decide not to play. The second is to offer a comparison between the career player and the sub-group in terms of "life after hockey." In this group are Joe Cavanaugh, a lawyer in Providence, R.I.; Roger Bourbonnais, a lawyer in Vancouver, B.C.; Jerry Kruk, a businessman in Winnipeg, Man.; and Fr. Les Costello, a Catholic priest in northern Ontario.

A committee of four selected the players to be interviewed, so that the names did not come from one person and that they brought objectivity to the study. The people on this committee were: John Cunniff of Boston, MA., Dennis MacDonald of Ottawa, Ont., and Don Baizley and Bill Lesuk, both from Winnipeg, Man.

The Hypotheses

The hypotheses proposed at the start of this study are:

1. Personal achievement is measured in terms of team championships. Hockey is

a team sport and an individual's level of achievement is perceived as directly related to the success of one's team.

2. Formal education is perceived as important in "life after hockey". Once outside the hockey world, the player becomes like everyone else. He comes to realize the importance of education both as a means to a livelihood and as a measurement of status.

3. Some players would regret having spent so long playing the game, and would wish that they had not played professionally. The experiences would not all be good and some would say, "My life would be a lot better if I had not played."

4. The money earned as a player is not as significant a measurement of achievement as reaching the top of one's profession. The money is inherent when one arrives there.

5. The effective use of the off-season during the career, either for education or employment, would lead to a smooth and short transaction. Specific skills needed in the world outside of hockey and a feeling of self-confidence in one's ability would be enhanced with success in off-season activities.

6. A player's fondest memories, other than his athletic achievements, are of teammates and people met through hockey.

The Methodology

A list of questions acts as a guide for the interviews. The sessions were more conversational than question and answer. The questions presented a central focus for the interviews.

The questions are:

I.   **Perception of playing career.**

    1. Looking back, how do you view your career?

    2. What do you think you achieved during your career?

    3. What kind of player were you?

    4. What were your high and low points of your career?

    5. What good and/or bad memories do you you have?

II.   **Transition period.**

    1. Can you define your transition period in terms of time?

    2. What about employment during the transition?

    3. Did anyone, in particular, help you with the transition?

    4. Would you do anything differently if you were to do if over?

    5. Would you characterize the transition as smooth or rough?

III.   **Life After Hockey.**

    1. What about jobs and a career?

    2. Any personal or professional problems you care to talk about?

    3. Can you evaluate your personal and professional status?

    4. How do you now view yourself and your life?

    5. To what extent has hockey been a force in your life?

The process for each interview included a telephone conversation explaining the project, its goals and reasons, and then a letter with the list of questions. The interviews were conducted in person. The time span for the interviews varied between 30 minutes and two hours. They were taped and then transcribed. The edited interview was then sent back to the person for his comments. Either a second meeting was held or several phone calls were made to complete the interview. This assured that each person would know what was included in the final text.

"Disengagement Theory"

The subject matter of this study is a phenomenon few people experience. Most people's careers end through the normal aging process. The athlete ends his career at a relatively young age, and must find and develop a second career. Following retirement, the athlete lives on. Employment and a career can make this life enjoyable. In terms of a life span, an athlete does not really retire but disengages.

Professionals who go through a similar disengagement process are jet fighter pilots. A normal retirement comes after 20 years, when the pilot is in his early forties. In essence, he is still capable of flying but chooses to leave the service. There is external pressure to make room for younger pilots. A retiring pilot leaves the service, say the Air Force, where everything is directed to help him fly. The pilot is the star performer, he is a special person. The retiring pilot moves into the real world. No longer does his world exist to help him fly and treat him differently. He has become a citizen in the real world. He really has to disengage, not retire. This disengagement process brings with it personal and psychological problems that few people experience.

The professional athlete, meanwhile, leaves the sport at an age considered young for normal retirement. He then moves into the real world, and finds he no longer is a special person in a special world. This new world places a different set of obligations and responsibilities on the athlete. He needs to reengage into another profession and career.

The Life of a Player

The life of a professional hockey player is less glorious than it may appear to the public. It brings tremendous highs and the potential for severe lows -- interwoven with a high potential for insecurity. He can make good money. He has a lot of free time. The travel is hard, and the pressure of playing, both real and imaginary, brings stress. The main attraction for the player is the chance to satisfy the competitive drive by playing the game with the best, at the highest level. The dream of playing in the National Hockey League has been lifelong and is compelling.

What is a typical day? Practice lasts one to one-and-a-half hours. Added to the locker room time before and after practice, time at the rink totals between two and three hours. The rest of the day is usually free. A home game day has a morning skate and meeting which lasts, with the locker room time, about 90 minutes. The afternoon is geared toward rest and individual preparation for the game. Players arrive around 5:30 for a 7:30 game. Players leave the rink after a game around 11:00 p.m. and may spend another two or three hours unwinding. It is a long day.

For travel, each player receives an itinerary which, in detail, lays out the schedule for a trip. Everything revolves around the games and practices. It is not uncommon for a team to leave the hotel for the airport at 6:30 a.m. the morning after a game to meet an early morning flight. The western teams have more demanding travel schedules, but all teams go through periods of difficult travel. On road trips, players make few, if any, personal decisions. Team buses carry them between the airport, hotel and arena. Curfews are set, dress standards are established, and times are set for intra-city travel. The club makes all decisions so the players can concentrate on playing the game. The hockey season is a long merry-go-round that starts with training camp in September and ends with the season, in April or May. Such a schedule allows few stretches of 7 to 10 days at home.

What kind of money can be made? The financial potential for a 24-year-old is much greater playing hockey than working. The average salary in 1987 for a National League player is about $155,000, usually in a one-way contract that guarantees the player a salary whether he plays in the major or minor league. However, many players have two-way contracts, one of which may call for $145,000 in the major league and $30,000 in the minor league. Despite great potential for going from the minors to the majors, many players feel real pressure of going from the majors to the minors.

What about free time? There is a lot of it, and over the years, players have perfected ways of wasting it. Hockey imposes peer pressure to be one of the guys, to spend a lot of time at unofficial team-related activities -- historically involving alcohol and bars. It is difficult to take a college course or to work afternoons for a company because of the travel schedules. The average career lasts 4.5 years. All that free time lasts for a short period.

What about the off-season? For many players the off-season is a time for relaxation and training. The tendency is to play golf, visit friends, go to the cottage, enjoy the good life. Most teams now have demanding off-season training programs, at which players spend a lot of time and energy. The off-season is short, and the successful player can easily fall prey to this life. A 24-year-old earning $175,000 may be tempted to say, "Why work?" The money can be seductive. The career usually ends sooner than one expects, and when it does, there are no more off-seasons.

In many ways it is a fantasy life, playing the game of boyhood dreams and love, getting paid for it, traveling, having the summer off, making friends and sharing experiences, locker-room humor and camaraderie. But it does not last forever.

MARK HEASLIP

Mark Heaslip was born on December 26, 1951, in Duluth, Minnesota. He grew up there and attended the Duluth schools. He attended the University of Minnesota - Duluth for four years. During this time he accumulated enough credits to remain about one year shy of graduation. A member of the UMD hockey team, he was able to earn his first professional contract with the Los Angeles Kings organization in 1973. After three years with Kings farm teams at Springfield, Oklahoma City and Fort Worth, Mark spent the next two years, 1976-77 and 1977-78, in the New York Rangers organization. The 1978-79 season was spent with the Kings. His last season as a player was spent with the Tulsa Oilers, a farm team for the Winnipeg Jets. In six seasons as a professional hockey player, he had sporadic stints in the NHL until spending the 1978-79 season with the Kings.

Duluth has remained Mark's home since his playing career ended. His work career has consisted of a variety of jobs. He currently is employed as a consultant with Hazelden, the drug and alcohol rehabilitation center. Married during college, Mark is divorced and his former wife, Barbara, has custody of their daughter, Courtney.

* * * * * *

Roger Svendsen, Program Development Manager, Hazelden Cork Sports Education Program:

"Initially Mark comes off as a professional athlete. But beneath the surface is one of the more caring and compassionate people I have met. He wants very much to help people who are having trouble. He brings with him the enthusiastic and hard-working attitude that he demonstrated in his playing days. He attempts to apply the same attitude with people and their problems here at Hazelden."

Parker MacDonald, Mark's coach with the New Haven Nighthawks:

"A nice guy, one of the better guys you could coach, he worked like hell when he was on the ice. He was captain of the team both years here. Always gave 100 percent, wanted to win. He really hated to lose. A team guy, got along with everyone, and his teammates looked up to him because he worked so hard. Mark wanted to play in the National League in the worst way. I coached against him when he played with Springfield and he was a real sparkplug. Played the same way here. I was surprised when I later heard about his chemical dependency problem. He was never a problem here."

* * * * * *

I met Mark for the first time during his first year in the New York Rangers organization in 1976. A marginal player at the NHL level, his upbeat attitude was always noticeable. One incident will always stand out. He was called up from New Haven in February, 1978, for a game. He played exceptionally well and when I told him so after the game and said there was a good chance he would stay up, I asked him how everything was going. He replied with a big smile, "Great, really great. Well, my house in Duluth burned to the ground last night, but other than that, just great." His last season was in Tulsa where I was coaching. His year was a big disappointment and I told him at the end of the year the Jets would be buying him out of the last year of his contract. When we were talking about doing the interview, he reminded me that I had spoken to him during that season about some of his problems. I remembered and said that he was actually incapable at times of even performing in practice. Mark said that he later came to learn during his treatment that the recovering alcoholic is told about his problems about 40 times before he actually realizes it himself and that I was the first. Of all the players interviewed for this book, I knew of Mark's playing career perhaps better than any other. That, plus the odyssey of his post-playing career made him a natural for a starting point. His interview was the first.

We did the initial interview in Duluth with a follow-up at my house. Never a shy person, Mark talked easily about his experiences with the same upbeat attitude that he displayed when playing. It became apparent during the interview that he had taken on a more realistic view of himself and why he had ended up where he did. He never showed any signs of not wanting to talk about anything. Actually, his approach was realistic, saying "This is what happened, I can't change the facts, only the future."

* * * * * *

Q. How do you view your career?

I perceived myself as a hard-working hockey player. I knew my role. I knew I was not a superstar. I knew I had to do certain things well if I wanted to play. I knew if I did not do these things consistently that there would not be a place for me on the team. The team is made up of a couple of superstars and a lot of hard-working players. I was a hard-working player. I think it kind of amazes me how far I got just on my hard work.

I think I achieved a lot as a player. I was not supposed to make my high school team. I went to the University of Minnesota - Duluth, a top-level Division I school. I did not have a scholarship the first two-and-a-half years. I played at the junior varsity level for two years

before I was good enough for the varsity. I was
not supposed to make my college team, I made my
college team. I ended up playing professionally
seven years. How can I not think I was successful as a player?

For the most part, I've got good memories
of the seven years I played. I was captain of
two or three teams that I played on. The hockey
was a lot of fun, I enjoyed the work, I enjoyed
the camaraderie. I think when you get out of
the game you don't remember the goals you as-
sisted on or the penalties in actual games. You
miss the locker room and the people you met
along the way. I've got good memories from that
standpoint. I consider the career I had as successful. I reached the top of my profession. I
got a lot of good breaks along the way. For as
many teams as I played on, the times I was traded or demoted to the minors, they were low
points, but they turned out positive for me.

**Q. You think of yourself as a hard-working
player, will you elaborate?**

I was a defensive player, the kind you
would want to put out in key situations. I
played against some of the best lines in hockey
because I was a defensive player. I was a role
player. In most games, because I was playing
against a top offensive line, if my plus-minus
was zero, it was a successful game. As long as
I held my man on that line off the board, I was
doing my job.

It was tough being a fourth-line player at
the National League level. My first year in New
York (1976-77), I stayed with the big team for
60 games but only played for 19 or 20. I would
skate the warm-ups and when I would come off the
ice, Frank Pace, the Rangers trainer, would look
at me, put his finger in his mouth and pull it.
That meant I got the hook. We normally played
in the Garden on Sunday night. If I did not
play I would have to work hard on Monday, an

off-day for most of the players. Staying in shape and being sharp is real hard when you don't play much. Then when you do play, you play against their best. It was tough.

I perceived myself as a leader besides being a good team player. I was a great social director. I think I've got the ability to get along with most people. Peoples' personalities never really bothered me all that much. I've got good people skills, most team players generally have good people skills. I know that I've always made an extra effort to try to get along with everybody, good or bad. I remember one time during a pre-game warm-up in New York, I was skating around talking to a few guys on the other team and Phil Esposito skated up to me and said, "How the hell do you know everyone? You never played in the league." I said, "Well, I played with or against a lot of the guys somewhere along the line." He was surprised at how many players I knew. I made it a point every place I played to get to know my teammates well.

Q. What did you achieve in your career?

Playing seven years professionally is an achievement. Making it to the National Hockey League was an achievement. Any time you reach the top of your profession, it's an achievement. I played on two national teams for the United States. We won the Calder Cup Championship my first year as a pro with the Springfield Indians (AHL). I was the captain of that team. That was a real achievement. It was an unforgettable experience for me. I can still close my eyes and think about carrying the Cup around the rink, 8,000 fans screaming and cheering. I think I achieved a lot in my playing career.

Q. What about high points and low points?

There were several high points. The one real high point was winning the Calder Cup. It was a difficult year and we ended up fourth in the standings. We beat Providence, Rochester and New Haven to do it. Another high point was getting my second pro contract with the New York Rangers. I had originally signed with the L.A. Kings. I spent three years in their organization, playing on their minor league teams. Ron Stewart, who coached me in Springfield, was working for the Rangers and got me a tryout in September, 1976. I went to their rookie camp in Pointe-Claire, Quebec. John Ferguson was the new general manager and he was moving a lot of older players out, making room for younger players. I earned a contract and spent the first 60 games in New York. The second year with New York, I spent most of the year in New Haven. They brought me up in February. I played on a line with Danny Newman and Phil Esposito. Danny and I were hard workers and Phil's production went up. The team made the playoffs and I felt I made a real contribution. That was another high point.

There were a lot of low points for me personally. The first year in New York, when I was sent down to New Haven, was one. Ending every season, leaving the team and my teammates, was always a low point. Winning only one championship in seven years was a low point. As a professional athlete, you are always aspiring to win. When you don't, it's a disappointment. My final year with the Winnipeg Jets was a low point. It was an expansion team, when I was sent down to Tulsa. It was a real low point. But by that time I was in the midst of real personal problems with chemical dependency. I think towards the end of my career, when chemical abuse started to take its toll on me, I stopped improving as a player. That was a bit discouraging, but at that point in time I really didn't know what was going on in my life. Looking back, the end of my playing career was a low point but I didn't know it at the time.

My memories are mostly good. I don't remember a whole lot of the bad stuff. I enjoyed
being a hockey player. I don't hold any animos-
ity or grudges as to how my career went. You
remember how management can be insensitive, or
how you think they can be insensitive, cold,
shuffling you around and seeming to be uncaring.
But I don't hold any animosities. I do regret
that I didn't take advantage of my free time as
a player. Professional hockey players have a
lot of free time, too much free time, and I
wasted a lot of my time. The everyday things
like going for lunch, sitting around a bar when
I could have been doing something a lot more
productive. Just playing hockey at the time
seemed to be good enough.

Q. Can you define your transition period?

My transition started with the end of my
playing career which was April, 1980 and lasted
until April 21, 1984. That day is significant
because it was my first day of treatment at the
Hazelden Treatment Center. I was at Hazelden
because I was suffering from an illness called
alcoholism. As I look back, I was trying the
best I could, but I was in the midst of a very
active illness.

The Winnipeg Jets bought me out of my last
year of my contract in 1980. I had been out of
a contract before, once in L.A. and once in New
York, and in my mind there was no reason why I
wouldn't get another chance to play. I ended up
carousing and drinking for another summer. Come
fall, I just didn't go back. I stayed in Duluth
and thought, "I'm going to get out of the game
because I'm burned out competitively." In
reality, I was burned out for another reason. I
thought, being a hometown boy, finding a job
would be relatively easy. I didn't try that
hard. I was pretty content with just drinking.

The jobs I got in Duluth were all
alcohol-related jobs. I got a job with a beer

distributor as a salesman and I tended bar. I
lasted at the salesman's job for maybe three or
four months. I was great at the public relations end of the job, but I was a little short
at the work end. Then I started working at a
bar. I was real content doing that, not really
working or trying to improve myself. I was
around alcohol and I was content with the situation.

Q. How did you handle the transition?

Apparently, it wasn't a whole lot of fun.
I guess it's easy for me to compare that now.
Since I went into treatment and started to take
a look at myself and what I was doing to myself,
life's been a lot better for me. It was a pretty miserable time.

I was definitely in a fog, waiting for
something to fall in my lap. I never realized,
"Hey, Mark, you got where you got when playing
hockey through hard work." I thought I was
working hard but I was treading water, waking up
with a gigantic head and trying to recover from
the night before.

I got arrested in January, 1984, for con-
spiracy to sell and distribute cocaine. I was
working at a bar and had a lot of contact with
people who used and sold drugs. I thought I was
hiding it from everyone. I was a good drunk. I
was never obnoxious. I never slurred. The cocaine and alcohol started to go hand and hand.
The cocaine used to perk me up so I could drink
more. All of a sudden I wasn't hiding it
anymore. Eventually, through plea-bargaining, I
pleaded guilty to a felony on the charge and was
sentenced to three years' probation and three
hundred hours of community service.

I always thought I was a pretty easy-going
guy, just throwing everything on the back burner. Pretty soon, I had a grease fire on my back
burner. After I was arrested there was a lot of

real human emotions, a lot of shame and self-pity. I said, "That's it, I'm not going to do it again." I quit drinking, I quit using, but within a week I was back doing it again. I couldn't figure out why. It got to a point that it was bigger than me. I couldn't control it. I have a friend, Bob Grytdahl, who is a policeman in Duluth and he had seen a segment on the Phil Esposito Foundation between periods of a North Star game. He contacted Phil and Phil got ahold of me. Phil talked about the alcohol and drug evaluations and career counseling that could be done. I can remember saying to Phil, "Phil, if I had a good job I wouldn't be having these problems." I was still trying to deny the fact that I had a problem. Fortunately, Phil was wise enough to say, "Let's get the evaluation and then we'll take a look at the career counseling."

At one time I had a criminal lawyer, a divorce lawyer and a tax lawyer. I was attorneyed out. My family supported me a lot. My dad was chief probation officer for northern Minnesota. I told my dad I would go into treatment after my court case. Well, needless to say, the court system in our country doesn't move very quickly. I was still drinking, using. My dad and my uncle talked to me. We decided to get into treatment right away and try to straighten out my life. Within five days there was a bed waiting for me at Hazelden. Finally, for the first time, I got a chance to look at Mark Heaslip. Denial in this disease is the first and biggest block to overcome. Through the Phil Esposito Foundation, having a family that cares, the denial finally got broken down. I began to realize that I needed help, that I couldn't handle this anymore by myself. That was probably the lowest part of my life because I was defeated. I knew there was something I couldn't handle by myself and that was real discouraging.

Q. If your transition ended when you entered Hazelden, your life after hockey began then. What was Hazelden like?

It was painfully rewarding. I spent 28 days in the Hazelden Treatment Center taking a hard look at my own abuse of chemicals. I was able to take a look at a lot of feelings that I hadn't examined before. I was always a pretty happy-go-lucky guy. I never really talked about how I felt, never took a look at my defects of character. I found out through the counseling I was sensitive, over-sensitive. I had a lot of anger built up. When I was playing hockey, I think I was able to release much of it. After I didn't have hockey, I didn't have an outlet for it. I began to realize I'm impatient. I want things yesterday. I began to realize that I needed to work on my humility. I'm not the most humble guy.

At the time I went in, I thought maybe the treatment would teach me how to be a normal drinker. I would be able to sit down and have one or two drinks. That wasn't the case. I was beyond that point. Abstinence is really the only way of leading a normal productive life for me. I came to realize that while I was there. I was able to take a look at my abuse problems that I had had since a young person. Alcoholism is real prevalent in my family. I feel real strongly that there's hereditary factors involved. I started drinking when I was 13. I was never drinking for the taste, I was drinking for the effect. My knowledge of the disease was enhanced during my treatment. I began to accept that I was an alcoholic. It was worthwhile.

I was in a room with three roommates, one from Texas, one from New York City and one from Minneapolis. We were together most of the time. There are 24 people to a unit. Ninety percent of the treatment is the interaction within the unit, 10 percent with counselors. Let's face it, it's pretty hard to fool 23 other people who know all the excuses, lines and stories.

Q. What is a typical day like at Hazelden?

You get up at 6:30 in the morning and do basic personal health things like brushing your teeth, making the bed, taking a shower, things that you weren't doing before. You have a basic job. My job was to mop the kitchen floor. I did such a good job that they never gave me another one. We would have a little meditation time and then go for breakfast. After breakfast there was usually a lecture followed by group sessions. After lunch there would be more group sessions with some free time. Dinner was followed by group sessions and free time as well. During the course of the day we would be encouraged to read, write and reflect on the reasons we were there.

It's funny, in a unit there would be 24 different stories. But, in the end, they were surprisingly similar. After two weeks or so, you were put on the "hot seat." You had to give your story. I practiced mine and it took 30 minutes. When I gave it, it actually took 45 minutes. I kept breaking down. Each member of the unit would critique your story, tell you what he thought of you and how you should try to work to help your problems. After three weeks, my counselor wanted me to join the family program. I was beginning to feel good about myself. In the family program, the family members actually go through a five-day program to help them understand what you are going through. This program forced me to face another form of reality. I realized the problems I had caused my family members.

After the family program I was close to being released. When the 28 days are up, they recommend half-way houses, extended - or after-care programs among a variety of other post-care programs. Twenty-eight days does not undo decades of alcohol and drug abuse.

Q. When you left Hazelden, what did you do about a job?

Leaving Hazelden was a strange experience because it was like leaving the womb. I was safe in there. All of a sudden I had to go out in the world again. I went through some career counseling in the Twin Cities. They helped me with career evaluating, gave me some direction, taught me how to write a resume. The fact that I didn't graduate from college came back to haunt me. The doors would open because I was Mark Heaslip, because I had played hockey and I was a personable guy. But, it's funny how they look for a degree. It's important. I got some odd jobs. I was on general assistance which is a form of welfare. I was working on the docks loading and unloading ships. I remember real well lifting the 100-pound sacks of pinto beans.

I lived with my father on a lake about 20 miles outside of Duluth. That helped me to get away from Duluth for a while. I went to AA meetings in the evenings and read a lot. It made me reflect on my future. A man named Art Cranes brought me to New York. He worked at Bear Stearns and showed me Wall Street. I was offered a job. Emotionally, that was real important because it made me realize I could do something worthwhile. It rejuvenated my self-confidence. I turned it down for two reasons. First, I have a daughter in Duluth and I didn't want to move away from her. Second, I didn't think I was ready for New York.

In February (1985), I got a break. I was hired to sell advertising for a local cable TV network. Shortly after that, George Couture, the sales manager for WDIO, the local ABC affiliate, approached me and said there would be an opening soon in his department. I worked with WDIO until August, 1986. During this time, I was also selling clothes under the brand name of 'No Sweat.' I would go to New York to make sales calls at some of the major wholesale houses. I'm still selling the clothes part-time.

Q. Quitting your job at WDIO was a little drastic, would you agree?

I was doing some speaking engagements on chemical abuse and awareness. The people with WDIO had been real good about letting me leave to do this. Late August (1986), Phil Esposito, who had been recently hired as general manager of the New York Rangers, asked me to come to New York and do some chemical abuse and awareness things with the Rangers. At the same time I was talking with some of the people at the National Hockey League about doing some things with the different teams. I knew I would be gone from my job for more than a few days. It was a decision I had to make at the time. As it turned out, I went to the Ranger camp, but not to any other teams. Looking back, I don't think it was drastic; I'd do it again.

It was funny, ever since I got out of treatment, it was in the back of my mind that I wanted to get a tryout. Just go back and skate. I was in great shape. I worked out every day, played hockey two, three times a week. Because I had gotten out of the game on a sour note, I wanted to do it for myself. I didn't care if I made the team, I just wanted to go and try out. So, when Phil contacted me about the chemical stuff, I talked him into giving me a tryout. I went to their rookie camp. I thought it would be a good angle for me to get to know the rookies. I thought I could do the chemical awareness thing by being on the players' side. I'd be one of them, rather than from management's side. I think that did help.

Q. How did the tryout go?

I surprised myself. I was in great shape, but I'd been out of the game for six years and was rusty. I had trouble doing little things like picking the puck off the boards and staying close to my check. I did fairly well. Some of the Ranger staff suggested I keep at it and see how far I could go. I was game. I ended up at their farm team's camp in New Haven. I was one of the last guys cut. I don't know if the experience was good or bad because I was starting to get the competitive itch again.

One thing is worth mentioning here. All during my career, during the National Anthem I would think about things that were important to me. How lucky I was to be a pro, how good my family had been to me, what it was like to play with some of the great players of all time. Well, we had an exhibition game in Springfield against the Indians. I realized during the National Anthem that this would probably be my last game. I had played my first pro game with Springfield in the same building. I knew the circle had been completed. I had tears in my eyes as I thought about everything that had happened to me during this period (1973-1986).

Q. In this second life after hockey, can you give a personal evaluation?

Life's been pretty good to me. I've been to the top and I've been to the bottom and lived through it. Through it all, I've got a deep appreciation of life. I'm walking around a grateful guy, for what I've done, for what I'm doing and for what the future holds. That is, if I stay sober. It's gotten to the point that sobriety is the number one priority in my life. If I stay sober, there isn't a whole lot that I can't do.

I work at Hazelden as a consultant. I do some workshops and seminars. I have a couple of projects that I'm working on. Last summer I was able to put on a charity game in Duluth to raise funds for a local chemical awareness program. The game was between all the Duluth All-Americans and the Duluth pros, and we raised $25,000. We are going to have a similar game this summer (1987) to raise funds for the chemical abuse programs in Duluth.

MIKE ERUZIONE

Mike Eruzione was born on October 25, 1954, in Winthrop, Massachusetts. He grew up and attended school in Winthrop. After graduating from high school in 1972, he attended Berwick Academy (Maine) for one year. Boston University became his college and he graduated in June, 1977. The next two hockey seasons, 1977-78 and 1978-79, he played for the Toledo Goaldiggers of the International Hockey League. The first year he was part of the New York Rangers organization while the second he was there on his own. A member and captain of the 1980 U.S. Olympic hockey team, Mike retired from hockey following the Gold Medal championship in Lake Placid. The one thing that is consistent throughout Mike Eruzione's career is championship teams. Conference champs in 1972 at Winthrop, ECAC championships all four years at Boston University, the Turner Cup in 1978 with Toledo and the Gold Medal in 1980, Mike played on seven championship teams his last nine years in the game.

A lifelong resident of Winthrop, he remains a staunch supporter of Winthrop as a community to live in and raise a family. Mike has worked in the public relations field and as a sports announcer since quitting the game. Mike, his wife, Donna, and two children, Leigh Ann, and Mike, live in Winthrop.

* * * * * *

Bob Murray, one of Mike's coaches at Boston University and currently his legal advisor:

"He is the type of competitor with the kind of personality that wants to be successful at whatever he does. He showed this through sports in his early years. He accomplished a lot both as a player and as a team person. He has played on a lot of winning teams and remains the third all-time leading scorer at BU. The fact he was captain of the Olympic team showed the amount of respect teammates had for him."

"The Olympics enabled Mike to get his foot in the door with the business world. The things he is now doing are a result of what he did once inside the door. He has a great ability to relate to people. He is comfortable with the executives of the business world and the people who are the workers in the same world. People see him as an average guy who has achieved good things through work."

Bob Defelice, Mike's high school football coach:

"Having seen Mike since junior high school, through BU and the Olympics in 1980, I think he never forgot where he came from. The fame and prestige never affected him one bit. He's the same person today. He's always trying to give something back and can always find time for charities and kids. A classic overachiever, he probably had less talent in hockey than baseball and football. Also, he was not a gifted student, he worked for everything he got. This is probably why he appreciates everything he has received."

* * * * * *

I met Mike when he came to the New York Rangers' training camp in the fall of 1977. The following year I arranged a tryout for him with the Colorado Rockies believing he was good enough to earn a spot in that organization. Our paths crossed from time to time in the years after this. We did the interview at the Sheraton Towers - Boston while I was on a scouting trip at "Hockey Night In Boston." We spent a few minutes catching up on the news of each other and quickly got on to the interview. The interview went quite well and I commented after it, "It went well, but you probably have answered these questions a number of times before." He replied, "No, not really, matter of fact, I've been waiting for someone to ask me. I'm glad I got the chance to answer them."

One of the important aspects of Mike's story is how he always had a second possible avenue available when he did things. He never lost sight of what he intended to do with his life. When other opportunities arose, he eagerly tried them. In his mind he knew that if something did not work out, he could always teach and coach. This philosophy permitted him to play much longer than most people expected. He still adheres to the same philosophy in his present career. He knows he can always teach and coach and be happy doing it.

* * * * * *

Q. How do you view your playing career?

My career is probably very different than a guy who might have played in the NHL. The perception of my career, how I view it, was outstanding. From an 8-year-old who just learned to skate, to a guy who played on an Olympic team, I enjoyed every aspect of hockey. I can remember being a 12-year-old and winning a championship pee-wee game in Melrose. I remember my first year in high school and making the varsity, playing at Berwick Academy and then playing at Boston University. They were all positive experiences because I enjoyed playing the game, enjoyed playing the sport. I was successful at the levels I played at, which obviously made it more enjoyable when you're winning and part of a winning program. It's a lot easier to go to the rink and to practices.

Just playing and being around the other players, that's the most fun I had. Just the friendships that I got as a hockey player were the most special things to me. Enjoying the game, going to and playing the games, playing against another team, the competition, the thrill of scoring a goal, whether as a 10-year-old or a 24-year-old, the thrill of winning. To know that you were doing something you wanted to do was a great thrill, plus the idea that my parents and family gave me the opportunity to play. My father worked three jobs and one of the main reasons was so I could play hockey. So I was sort of giving them part of the rewards and they were getting the excitement and thrill knowing that I was enjoying what I was doing.

To this day, I believe I was a good player. That is one thing that will bother me the rest of my life, that some people thought that maybe I couldn't play in the National Hockey League. I really think I could have if given the right opportunity. After the Olympics I had decided not to play any more, and the statement, "Well, he wouldn't have made it" is one I will argue a lot. I think if John Ferguson had never been fired (1978) from the New York Rangers, I would have signed a contract. It might have been a small contract but I think it would have worked out somewhere along the line. Besides, a lot of my college and Olympic teammates went on to play pro and do very well.

Q. You did play two years with Toledo in The International League, how was it?

I liked Toledo because of the people who were there. The fans were outstanding. You were somebody. You're a member of the Toledo Goaldiggers. To the people in Toledo, you were like a Montreal Canadien and you were treated very well and you kind of liked the special treatment, like when you walked to a shopping mall and somebody would walk by with a t-shirt

on with your picture on it. It was exciting.
But there was also the physical part, fighting,
bench-clearing brawls. I fought and did what I
had to do but I thought it was kind of ridicu-
lous. It made me wonder, "I'm a college graduate, I have some intelligence, why am I doing
this?" The reason was that I loved playing
hockey. It wasn't like I was playing for the
money -- I made something like $8,500. It was a
dream to play in the NHL. It was an opportunity
to show people I could play at that level, handle the bump and grind.

**Q. In 1978, you attended the Colorado Rockies
camp, what was that like?**

I went to the Rockies camp because I
thought I had a good opportunity to make Colorado. To me, that training camp was probably the
biggest joke of any year I spent in hockey. It
was a total waste of time. I saw it as nobody
knew what was going on. My view was I was an
outsider with no shot of even getting an opportunity to play. I played one game against the
Minnesota North Stars down in Oklahoma City and
thought I did pretty well. Never got another
chance to play. It's funny because I talk about
it all the time. Mike Gillis was the big rookie, the first-round draft pick. I hit him with
a hip check and he tore his knee ligaments and
was out for the whole year. The next day I hit
Paul Gardner in the head with a slap shot and
soon after I got assigned to Philly.

To me, that was probably the lowest point
in my career because now the game wasn't any fun
anymore, because I didn't think the people were
being honest with me. One thing, when I went to
the Rangers camp, I felt they were being honest
with me. I went to Philadelphia with the
Firebirds (AHL). That was a total disaster because there was no coach. We didn't have a
coach! They offered me a contract to play in
Philly for about $10,000. I would have been a

pro. At the time, the team was 0-9 or 0-10. At the same time, Herb Brooks, who was going to coach the '80 Olympic team, contacted me and told me I had a chance to play on the Olympic team. I didn't know I was still eligible for the Olympics. I said, "Why not? This is a total joke here, I'm not going to gain anything by playing in Philadelphia. I'll go back to Toledo where I'm going to have some fun, go back to the guys I played with the year before."

Q. It sounds as if the Colorado experience helped you keep your amateur standing, which later turned out to be your good fortune?

I was always told to be honest with people, don't bullshit people, and I found in this particular situation I was not being treated fairly or honestly. I figured that I didn't need it. I felt I had a good thing to fall back on with a college degree. It was one thing my father had always told me, "Get your degree and take it from there." With that college degree, I knew that I could always get a job as a teacher and a coach. So, it was a low point, the Philly-Colorado experience.

Money was never an objective in my life. It was always to be happy and to be able to say that I'm doing what I want to do. I went back to Toledo with open arms. I had something to shoot for, I was going to play in the Olympics or at least try out for the Olympic team. I had no guarantee, but I had a lot of confidence in my own ability and thought I could make the team. I tried to use the Colorado thing as a stepping stone, a learning experience of what not to be and not let it happen again. I was smart enough to know I would be treated fairly and honestly at the Olympic camp.

Q. How did the Olympic camp go?

I knew that if I didn't make the Olympic team, I would probably go back to BU and take an assistant coaching job. I geared my whole summer to getting in shape, running, skating. There were a lot of great players there and I was concerned. I thought that, "Well, a Minnesota coach and a lot of Minnesota players, I didn't have a legitimate shot." But it turned out that I knew I had to play well and I did. It was one of the few times in my life that I realized that I had to go do something. Myself, I had a great camp, I had five goals and three assists. My team won the gold medal, I was captain of my team, elected by players whom I had never met before. I was very pleased with my personal accomplishment. That was something rare for me because I usually just enjoy playing on a team. I looked at the camp as time to do something on my own, step a little out of character, do something on an individual basis. Before, it was always a team concept, and that the team was the most important thing, and it should be. But I think at that point in my career I had to do something for myself.

Then I was one of 26 players, but still not guaranteed a spot. I remember we went to Europe to train in Finland, and Herb Brooks called me into his office and said he wanted me to be captain of the team. He said he wasn't going to tell me how to be captain or to lead me as captain. He felt that from my experiences in the minors, my age and the way I got along with the players, that I would be a good captain. He wanted me to be sure the players stayed in line. That was pretty easy because they were not partyers. Great people with great work habits. I'll never play on another team like that, individuals who just loved to play the game and just had great skills -- a lot better skills than a lot of people thought.

Q. The 1980 Olympic team won the Gold Medal but wouldn't you agree that the teams you played on usually won?

It's the pride of knowing you accomplished something that you set out to accomplish. My last seven years of hockey, four at BU, one of the years at Toledo and the Olympics, I won six championships. I don't care what level you're talking about, it's important to win. The thrill is still the same. Maybe the feeling of winning the Olympics was bigger because of the scope and the size of the event. But, still, sitting in the locker room and taking my skates off after winning the gold medal, emotionally I felt the same way after winning the ECACs my freshman year at BU. I don't know if you can feel better.

Q. Can you give us any insights into the '80 Olympic team?

We were just kids who loved to play. I think being the oldest one, I was very much like them at just an older level. I still loved going to the rink, playing the game of hockey, I loved practicing. I had a lot of fun. And to be with those players. This was family all along and I mean before winning the gold medal. The thrill of being around all those players -- Mark Pavelich, Kenny Morrow, Mark Wells -- and being involved with them was the greatest thing for me, win or lose.

The things that we believed in as a team were things that my father and teachers always told me. That if you believed in something and you were willing to work at something, it can happen. And if it doesn't happen, you learn the value of work. And if you learn the value of work, you'll be successful. I think that's what we as a team tried to display. To work hard, and if you work hard, good things will follow. And, if they don't at first, they will come eventually, they have to. I was fortunate to play on teams in college that were like the Olympic team. My teammates' parents probably taught them the same way as mine. I was lucky to play with goal-oriented, talented and successful players. Lots of talented players never win, never played on successful championship teams. It shows it's more important the people you surround yourself with and not yourself, the individual.

Q. Did your preparation for the Olympics give you an idea what was ahead for you?

I thought the Colorado experience was pretty much it. When I made the decision that I was going to play in the Olympics and if I didn't make it, well, two things were going through my mind. One, if I didn't make the Olympic team I was going to just go to BU where I had an opportunity to coach. And, the second thing was that if I did make the Olympic team, then maybe after the Olympics I would try pro hockey again. You know, give it another shot, see what happens.

I've always pretty much had an idea of what I wanted to do with my life. If we don't win a gold medal, I'm coaching and teaching which is fine because that is why I went to college. I wanted to be a teacher and a coach and if I could play hockey, fine. I always wanted that one thing to fall back on. When I'd made that decision to try the Olympics and if that didn't work, then to coach was just another step in my life as a person. I knew as I got older I had to make decisions on my life.

When it came time for me to stop playing, when I did not want to play hockey anymore, I looked at it as two things, play or move on with life. If I play hockey, how long would I play for, two, three years? Maybe get a three-year contract and spend the three years in the minor leagues? Well, I had experience with the minor

leagues and didn't like it. After winning a
gold medal, I didn't think I would go through
that part of my life again. I had done it, I'd
spent the time back there. I knew what it was
like, it was fun but it was a step backwards.
And I didn't want to take any steps backward.
The bottom line to me was I had opportunities to
do things after the Olympics and I think if I
had waited, kept playing, the opportunities
would not have been there. It was time to move
on and do something else with my life.

**Q. Did you have second thoughts when you
decided to quit?**

I always believed that there was more to
life than athletics. You play a sport, it is a
game, something you do for enjoyment. It's not
a career. I never thought my athletic abilities
would be a career for me. So as I was playing,
I was thinking what I would do when it was over.
I always had that in the back of my mind, even
through college -- the fact that I'm not going
to play this game forever and that when it ends,
it's going to end.

**Q. Your transition appears to have been smooth,
was that the case?**

It was a well-thought-out transition. It
was smooth because I sort of knew what was happening, it just didn't happen abruptly. It
probably really started when I was in Philadelphia and ended after the Olympics when I decided
to get on with life, do other things and not
play anymore. I said, "Okay, this is Phase Two
of life. Let's get on with it."

Having my college degree was the security,
it was knowing that when it ended, I had something to fall back on. I could always go home.
My family was there, my friends were there.
That was the way I was brought up, nobody ever
said this is what you've got to do. I looked

around my house and saw my father working, saw my brother and sisters working. I saw my friends' parents working. I was fortunate in my life to understand that at a young age, that when you want something, you have to go out and get it. I think having known that at a young age made sports, life during sports and after sports, easy for me to understand. Because to me the bottom line was that I was just playing a game and the Good Lord gave me ability to play it. While I had that ability I was going to use it, and then when I decide to move on, I'll have enough things that I've learned from my life that will make that adjustment easier.

They were my decisions which made the transition smooth. I want to be able to say when it's all said and done, I did what I wanted to do, and if I did it wrong, at least I made the decisions. Nobody said, "Why don't you do this?" and you said, "Okay" and you do it and then you say, "Gee, why did I listen to him?" I'm in control of my destiny.

Q. What do you do now?

I do a variety of public-related activities with different corporations. These include endorsements, public appearances and free-lance TV sports commentating. I also do a lot of Olympic related promotional activities.

Q. How do you enjoy it?

It's funny because in some ways, I'm still playing. If I have a speaking engagement in front of 400 people, I'm showing my life. I may be talking about the Olympics. I'm going to speak and tell them what it was like and they're getting excited. There still is applause, people come up and ask for my autograph. I'm still well enough known where I don't have a problem with saying it's ended, they forgot about me. People still remember the Olympic team, and

people still remember things that I did as an
athlete. So, it's nice to know that people remember you.

I've come down, no question, because now my
success depends on the job I do. I don't have a
contract that says that I'm going to be paid.
The success I have is the job I do. If I do a
good job speaking, I'm going to get hired by
somebody else. It's like I'm on a day-to-day
thing. Somebody calls me and says, "Look, we
have a speaking engagement in Florilda." If I go
and do a good job, then word spreads, you know,
"Gee, we had Eruzione and he did a good job. I
think you might want to use him." Now, my life
and employment really depend on the type of job
I do. The door was open for me after we won the
Olympics and it's my job to keep it open.

I'm still very close to the Olympics. I
work for companies that are involved with different Olympic sports. It's fun, I get a lot of
enjoyment out of doing this work because I'm
still involved with sports. I'm involved with
people who are excited about meeting me because
I represent something that very few people in
their lives get a chance to do, be an Olympic
and win a gold medal. So I have a lot of fun
going to different business conventions and people saying, "Yeah, that's him, Mike Eruzione,
Captain of the U.S. Olympic team and they won a
Gold Medal." And I'm involved with what I think
is a special group of people, Olympic committee
members and people who support the Olympics,
spending a lot of money supporting the Olympics.
Why I am in this situation now is because of
the success I had as an Olympian.

Q. Has anything not worked out?

Probably hockey commentating. I really enjoyed doing the commentating when I worked in
New York. That's another low point in my life,
I wasn't rehired by Madison Square Garden. One
of the reasons was I didn't want to move to New

Jersey and continue to do the Devils games.
See, I was commuting, back and forth, which was
easy for me. Hop on the shuttle, and I wasn't
about to move. Nobody said anything, it was
like if I didn't move to New York, they didn't
want me back. It was disappointing, but, hey,
life goes on. I'll do something else. That's
the thing, I don't plan on leaving Winthrop and
I may lose a lot of job opportunities because of
it but that's the way life is. If we never won
the gold medal, I'd still be living in Winthrop
and I intend to maintain that philosophy.

I would like to do color in hockey. I did
a pretty good job at it. I was hoping to hook
on here in Boston (Bruins) and I had an opportunity but the money they were offering wasn't
worth even taking. What they wanted to give me
was absurd. I would still like to do that. I
would love to do the Bruins games as a color
commentator. That was probably the only disappointment I had.

Q. Any adjustments you had to make?

The biggest thing is the locker room, just
being with the guys, having no responsibility
whatsoever, just go and play hockey and have
fun. You've got no responsibilities other than
to yourself and your teammates. You don't have
a care in the world because you're playing a
game and you're having fun doing it. That was
the biggest adjustment.

I'm married now with two kids. I can't
tell my wife I'm going to the rink for four
hours and then go hang with guys at the bar or
go shoot pool for a couple of hours and come
home when I want to come home. So, once you get
out of the game you have to face the facts,
there are responsibilities that you have outside
of the rink and the locker room.

Q. Has hockey been a force in your life?

There's no question hockey has been a major
force in my life. Now, I think it is definitely
not. If I became a color commentator in hockey,
then it would be back to being a force in my
life. But now, I'm outside looking in. I play
rarely. I enjoy skating. I enjoy the game.
The game is fun now. I would like to be a little more involved in hockey, but that's not my
decision. It's the decision of other people
around the National Hockey League or whoever
runs hockey in general. I go to high school
games in Winthrop, and I go to games at BU.
That's the way things are. Hockey used to be a
force for me and an important part of my life.
But because of the way hockey things are, I have
little to do with hockey now. That's like I
said earlier, "That's fine, if that's the way
things are, that's the way things are."

**Q. How do you view yourself, your life at this
      period of time?**

I can't be happier, more pleased. For a
lot of reasons, I have two beautiful children,
I'm married to the girl I went to high school
with, I live two houses from my mother and father, I live five houses from my mother-in-law.
I'm hanging around now with the friends I grew
up with. I have a sense of security living in
my hometown. My kids' friends will be children
of friends I grew up with. I think that is important.

Financially, things are going well. I have
a home, I own a house. When I grew up, I lived
in an apartment with my parents, my four sisters, one brother and my grandmother. How can I
not be enjoying life?

But, to be honest, if I didn't win a Gold
Medal I'd be teaching, coaching. I'd be married
to the same girl. I'd probably still have two
kids. I'd be living in and maybe renting a

house or an apartment. Financially, things would be different. But, personally and emotionally, they'd all be the same.

When I look back on my life, I played hockey, enjoyed it, it was fun. It was my decision to stop playing. I was given an opportunity to play in the Olympics. Because of the success I had as a hockey player, I had the opportunity to develop the career I now have. Because of the upbringing, the values I have, it made the career I had as a player fun and enjoyable and made me aware of and prepared for the fact that when the game ends, I had to handle it. But, I believe in the things I was taught and that made my life as a hockey player and as a businessman easy. It's still, "Life goes on and life's going to be fun."

TOM WILLIAMS

Tom Williams was born on April 17, 1940, in Duluth, Minnesota. He grew up and attended school in Duluth. He spent one year at the University of Minnesota. A member of the Gold Medal-winning U.S. Olympic team in 1960 at Squaw Valley, California, he joined the Boston Bruins organization the same year. His first year and a half were spent in Kitchener, Ontario, and he joined the Bruins in the middle of the 1961-62 season. He remained with them through the 1968-69 season. The next three seasons, 1969-70, 70-71 and 71-72 were with the Minnesota North Stars, the California Golden Seals and the Boston Braves of the American Hockey League. Two years, 1972-73 and 1973-74, were with the New England Whalers of the WHA. He then returned to the NHL with the Washington Capitals for the 1974-75 and 1975-76 season. Twenty games were played with New Haven of the American Hockey League the last year. He retired in 1976.

Upon his retirement, he quickly learned that the job he had been promised would not materialize. It took a while before he eventually landed a sales job in the concrete construction pipe business. He continues to work in that field today. He is the father of six children, Tommy, Robin, Bobby, Alex, Christopher and Marc. Tom, his wife, Connie, and family make their home in Hudson, Massachusetts.

* * * * * *

Mike Grilli, a fellow worker in the concrete pipe business:

"I find him the most sincere person I know. He is very transparent, he wears his feelings on his sleeve. You know what he's thinking. He is honest and doesn't understand people who are not honest with him. A diligent person, what he lacks in experience he makes up with work and perseverance. He has become a great success in this business and has earned the respect of those in it."

Bobby Orr, a teammate with the Boston Bruins:

"Tom has had some real tough times but has come through them and you have to admire him for it. As a player he always was a happy-go-lucky guy, not too serious, and this probably added to his problems. You have to give him a lot of credit for facing up to things and working his way out. He started right at the bottom in his business and has risen to the top through nothing but hard work. He is extremely well-respected in the business world because of it today. Tom has always been well-liked by everyone, exceptionally honest. You always knew where he stood. He has a new son, worked hard for his family and it's good to see him doing well."

* * * * * *

I met Tom Williams for the first time when we did the interview at the Boston Sheraton Towers Hotel. I had always heard he was an affable guy who could talk. We spent an hour or so talking and then got down to the interview. As soon as the tape recorder was turned on, he quit talking. After a couple of awkward moments, we got the interview rolling. He believed he had learned a lot from his life after hockey and hoped his experiences would help others. The interview moved right along and we only had to talk a couple of times later on the phone to clarify a few names an dates.

I found Tom to be quite frank and candid. He told his story with a great deal of honesty.

This is a sad story with a good ending that shows his life has moved in the right direction. A lot can be learned from his playing years. It is a trap many professional athletes fall into. His intelligence and ability to deal with his responsibilities come through strong and clear. You soon realize that he changed as a person after his playing career was finished. It took time, but he eventually made the change.

* * * * * *

Q. How do you view your career?

I think generally I had a good time playing hockey, most of the times were good. The times that were the best points were when we had the good teams in Boston. The bad times, the worst time in hockey for me, was when I lost my wife in 1970. I have no problems talking about this, I found my wife dead in the car in 1970, and I don't know what happened. I've always thought that it's impossible that she might have committed suicide, but we don't know that, only God knows. It doesn't matter how she died, it's the fact that I lost her, that's the low point for me. It's my worst enemy, but maybe I developed some inner strength out of it and maybe I'm a better person.

I really enjoyed my career. It was important for me that the players liked me and sometimes you'd even compromise being a better player just to be a good guy. There are times when people say, "Gee, are you glad you played hockey?" and I say, "You know, I'm not so sure that I should have been a hockey player." I guess you do what you do at the time, and you do the best you can and hope that it works out. I think it worked out exceptionally well for me at this point in my life. I'm happy it's over, but I'm happy I did it.

Q. You were one of the few Americans in the
   game during the sixties. Any thoughts on
   that?

   It was maybe like being a black. I was the
only American for six, seven years. I didn't
have any response because I had nothing to compare it with. I was from Northern Minnesota and
here I am going into a team that I didn't think
I was good enough to play on, and I never
thought I was good enough to play pro hockey.

   All of a sudden I'm there and I'm being offered a contract -- what the hell's going on?
The next thing I know I'm in their minor league
system and then I'm thrust onto an NHL team and
playing. And before I even had a chance to
grasp the impact of it all, I'm out there, and
hey, I got two goals my first game! I said,
"Holy Christ, this is more than I can stand!"
It all worked out pretty nice. There are players who resent you maybe a little, but I might
have been resented more or as much if I was a
Canadian, who knows?

Q. What kind of player were you?

   I would say that I was, abilitywise, a good
skater, an outstanding skater. I was a good
playmaker, a pretty good stickhandler and a good
passer, a terrible shot and terrible defensively. I had a little difficult time with the
body-checking because with the American rules
years ago, you only could check in your own defensive zone. And I had a real hard time keeping my head up at certain times and I got
whacked around a couple of times. But that's
okay, I survived it.

Q. You were a member of the Gold Medal Team in
   the 1960 Olympics. What do you recall about
   that experience?

   To me it was a bigger miracle than '80. We
were picked for last place so none of us

expected to win any gold medals, but on the other hand we were going to give it our best shot. We didn't know what to expect, we were just going to go out and play. The greatest memories? There are three things I remember about Squaw Valley. The first thing was, I remember two hookers coming to practice and wanting us to spend the night with them in Reno, before a big game! Well, we turned that down, we didn't think that was a good idea because we were scared that it might jeopardize our chance of winning the game. The second thing was that we would sit out in the brilliant sunshine with our shirts off, it would get to about 60 degrees in the afternoon, and then it would go down to 0 degrees at night. And the third thing I remember was the game against the Russians, when we were winning in the third period and I would out there and skate as hard as I could and not even know what the hell I was doing. Then go back to the bench and pray the whole time I was sitting there that they wouldn't score again. And you know, it paid off.

We had tremendous goaltending, Jack McCartan was the reason we won. He deserves all the credit, in my opinion. There wasn't the media attention in those days, and that's okay. Hey, everything is relative. I guess some of the guys had a little bit of hard feelings about the way things happened in 1980, the attention the guys got. Hey, you've got no right to expect anything really. It was good, it was great fun and the Gold Medal was more than we ever hoped for. And hell, the first of anything -- whether it's great, indifferent or horseshit -- it's still the first.

Q. Were you surprised you were the only player on that team to play in the NHL?

The Christian brothers had a tryout with Seattle, it didn't work out. Billy was real small. Very gifted playmaker, but not very big.

Roger was a bull, but he wasn't very smart.
They worked well together and I happened to be
on their line. They tried it and it didn't
work, so they went into their business and fell
flat on their faces and became millionaires, or
whatever, selling hockey sticks. And that's
great, I'm happy for them. Jack McCartan went
to the Rangers. They might have used him a little bit; even in those days people could use
people. The Rangers were drawing 8,000 fans per
game and they throw him in for five games and he
packed the place. They still made a lot of money; they gave him something like $5,000 a game.
It was a good investment for them, but I think
they exploited him somewhat. He ended up having
a long career in the Western League. I think in
my case the Bruins did the right thing with me.
They sent me to Canada and let me start in the
minor leagues and work my way to the National
Hockey League and get my feet wet in the pro-
style playing system, and I appreciated that.
The only other guy that tried pro hockey was Rod
Pavola, a youngster from Houghton, Michigan. He
played a year or two in Providence in the
American League and then he kind of got out of
it and went into business for himself. That was
it.

Q. What about high and low points?

The high point of my career was obviously
the Olympics. They mean more to me now than
they did during my career. During my career, it
was more important to play in the National Hockey League because it was the best league in the
world, the six-team league. But, the Olympics
today mean more to me because I think I understand the significance of the victory. We were
a horseshit team and ended up first because of
hard work and total dedication. Also, playing
as long as I did in the National Hockey League.
And, at that time, I was happy because I scored
more goals than any other American. That's relatively important when you're playing. You

might as well have some goals. I wanted to be the best player in the world, but I came up short. One of the other things was having a chance to play with Bobby Orr. That was one of the greatest thrills of my life. He's such a great player, but a greater person. That meant a lot to me.

The low point was obviously losing my wife in 1970. I was 30 years old, I had five children, and it was devastating. Then, as it happened, it was almost a comedy of errors. I ended up getting suspended from the North Stars, with pay. I guess my wife died in November, and in January I got suspended. I had a personality conflict with Jack Gordon. I'm not saying it was my fault or Jack Gordon's fault, I just think it was a real tough time. I was scoring goals and I was playing pretty well, sensationally well under the circumstances, but it was hard for me to live with what I had just gone through. And I'll tell you something, I used to drink just to forget it. I was never the world's greatest drinker, but I'd get shit-faced and end up some place and hey, it wasn't healthy. It's ironic because the year before was one of my higher points playing with Bill Goldworthy and J.P. Parise. We ended second in scoring as a line in the league and that was a great achievement. I felt very good about it. But it's interesting, you can have your greatest and worst moments so close and in the same place.

Q. Will you talk about your transition period?

I think that maybe my last year in Washington I had a feeling. We had a terrible team, and I had a feeling that I had one year left on my contract. I probably wasn't going to sign another contract. I was just kind of like a big wave rolling along having a great time and enjoying it and not really thinking about paying attention to what's going on around me. I don't think it was the real Tom Williams, but it was just the way it happened. I think the game of hockey bred that into me. I think now I'm a little more conscientious and I pay more attention to details, but, in reality the whole thing can be summed up by saying I never grew up until I was 40. And that's too bad. But I would say, getting back to the question, I became aware of the inevitability of ending my career in Washington in 1975. And the time it took me to get over it all, the whole period of time took me until 1980. In 1980 I stopped drinking. I didn't stop and say I never would touch another drink again, I still have a glass of wine every six months or so. I just don't drink anymore and it made me a much more productive and happier guy. I have great memories of those days, but they're gone, it's over.

I was promised a job at Wilson Sporting Goods up here in Boston, where I wanted to stay, in New England, because I loved my days in Boston, had friends, and just wanted to stay here. I remember getting all dressed up in this suit and went down to get this job and it was no longer available. Crush city! A new guy had taken over. The other guy -- I had done him a couple of favors and he promised me a job -- was no longer in that high-ranking position. The new guy wanted someone with a college degree and I didn't have one. So I was pretty upset but not totally devastated. I didn't know what was ahead for me. It was a tough time. I went and coached in the New England Junior Hockey League. The team was called the Tri-Valley Squires and I only coached them seven games because I was a widower with five children and they needed my attention. I wasn't working and I couldn't afford to be out there. I was getting paid by Washington, so I had an income until September. It wasn't like I was out of money, but I was getting desperate, I was getting close. My top salary was $50,000 a year, so I never made big money. I made $300,000 in sixteen years,

$18,725 a year. But money wasn't my main deal then and it isn't now. I knew I had to stop coaching, get a job. Nothing was available. I didn't know what I was going to do. I literally panicked. I said to myself, "What in the hell am I going to do? I've got five kids, I've got a big overhead on my house, a beautiful house that I bought with the Whalers' playoff money the year we won the championship. Now I'm in danger of losing it." So I called my folks in Duluth to ask for their advice, and they said, "Why don't you come back here and go to work out here? We'll start a business or something. Sell your house and come back." So that was my plan.

Three days before I was going to leave, I had everything packed, a guy called me up and asked me what I was doing and offered me a job in the construction business, selling plastic pipe. I said, "Keep talking because I'm listening." And I took the job. I went up to interview in Binghamton, N.Y. at a company called Robintek and they hired me that day. Elliot Putnam called me because a golfing buddy of mine told him if they needed a salesman, he thought I would be good at it. It was an act of God. I don't know how else to explain it. It was the greatest thing -- the single greatest thing -- that ever happened to me in my life. It gave me the opportunity to prove to myself what I could do outside of hockey. And I've been much more successful outside of hockey than I was in hockey.

I would describe it as rough. I probably picked 1980 as being the end of the transition because that was the time I made all the adjustments in my life. I got remarried in 1979. I married a girl from San Francisco. We had our rough moments. Part of it was she didn't like some of my drinking habits and she didn't like some of the problems we had with the kids. One of my sons had a drug problem. So, she had a difficult time and she went back to San

Francisco. I just said at that point, "Hey, what's important to you?" I decided she was pretty important. I stopped drinking, I tried to set some good examples. My oldest boy had a drug problem. I wanted to set an example for him so I stopped drinking on his birthday and I thought maybe that would help. To make a long story short, she came back. I took a good, long look at myself, but she was right. And I'll tell you something, it helped us both. It was good for her and it was good for me. It made it better all around. That's why I say 1980 was the end of something and it was the beginning of our life and it has worked out really well.

Q. Sounds like your transition period was an experience?

I'll tell you something, when you're dealing with athletes... we think we're more important than we are. Who gives a shit? I went to work outside of hockey, made $15,000 a year. The year before I paid more in taxes. The $15,000 wasn't enough to pay my bills. But I'll tell you what, I made up my mind that day that if it didn't work, it wasn't going to be my fault. And that was what I did. Went out and worked, busted my ass, built up a reputation for credibility, and today I'm better than I ever thought I was! Hey, I'm making six figures, and money isn't the end-all, but we relate success with money and I guess that's important sometimes. I'll tell you when money is important, I'll tell you right from experience: When you don't have enough money to pay your bills. I had that in 1977 and 1978. I was in such dire straits at the time. I damn near lost my house. My house was eight days from being auctioned off. My sales in the pipe business were tremendous, but I wasn't making enough money. I was working as a bartender two nights a week at the Elks Club to make ends meet. Well, I had a motor home, sold the motor home for $4,000 and that took me off the hook with the second mortgage on the house. I still have the house, thank God. I think I can honestly say I did everything in my power to keep it. That's why I still have it, partly.

The other part is that there is a greater spirit out there, a greater being that probably helped me. I was in such dire straits, I didn't know if I could get out of it. I really didn't. But I know one thing, I was not bullshitting myself, and I was doing whatever I could to take care of it. It made me a better person. Made me think, made me find out a lot about myself. And when the chips were down, I worked at my best and never quit.

Q. What companies have you worked for?

I've worked with three different companies, all in the construction pipe business. They are Robintech, Inc. of Binghamton, N.Y., Certainteed Corp. of New England, and National Pipe Company of Binghamton, N.Y. I'm currently regional sales manager for National Pipe. I am also a manufacturing rep. for two companies, Insituform and Flo-Control, Inc. I've enjoyed it and I'm still in a growth period. It's great. It's gone tremendously well since I started.

Q. How is your family doing?

At the family level, it's better than it's ever been before. I definitely would say the death of my first wife, the period when the grandparents were taking care of the kids, had an adverse effect on the kids. And it was rough for me. You sit down at a gin mill and drink. It's not as bad as when you drink when you're playing because you're working out. But when you stop working out, that's when it creates a problem. I finally quit drinking completely. You got to pay attention, it's so easy to fall into the syndrome. I made up my mind, if I got a chance, I didn't care if it was selling buffalo shit, whatever it was, I was going to make it work. And I did. It relates to playing hockey. Success is work. I wasn't Bobby Orr, but on the other hand, I wasn't one of the guys back in Duluth who couldn't push a puck from here to the window. It's relative and I'm happy with what I did.

My family, the oldest one, Tommy, Jr., is 25 years old, and I'm telling you he still has a drug problem. He hasn't been able to get out of it. Just today, I brought him to a rehab place, and they interviewed him and he agreed (he never agreed before) to go into rehabilitation. I put him, when he was a youngster, at a place in New Hampshire. I thought it would work out but it didn't. He's working on construction, making good money, but he decided that it's time to get going. He owes it to himself and his family to get straightened out. And I hope he does. We're trying to give him as much support as possible. The guy we saw today told me, "Your support is critical." I didn't realize it. You hear people say it, but to tell you, "God, that's good." I'm glad because sometimes we don't understand drugs. Some people have a hard time stopping.

Tommy has worked himself up to foreman with the construction company he works for. He seems to be making progress. Our oldest daughter, Robin, is 24 and is a student at the University of Minnesota-Duluth. She's working on an arts degree and is doing well. Bobby is 23 and is playing professional hockey for the Bruins. He graduated from Salem State and played last year in the Atlantic Coast and earned a contract with the Bruins at their training camp. Alex is 20. Well, he's trying to get his stuff together. He's having a tough time. We can only give him our support and hope he works it out. Christopher is 17 and is a senior in high school, plays on the varsity team and does well at school. Seems to be a real popular kid. The new one,

Marc, is just 1. Hey, he's a horse, weighs 30 pounds. He's a delight.

I guess my kids have been great. It hasn't been easy for them. They each are different, have their own personality. We're trying to do as much as we can for them, but, you know, parents can only do so much, then it's up to them. They are growing up in a different time than I did. The '50's were pretty stable years for us. We didn't have the peer pressure the kids have today.

Q. Are you satisfied with your current status?

If I died tomorrow, I would say that I've been the luckiest guy in the world. I'm happy because I really worked at what I had to do and I did it and I would describe myself as really successful. I've been fortunate. We're really in good shape financially, and that's just part of it. More importantly, to be respected as a quality person in your industry. I got the Associated Member of the Year Award for the New England Use of Utility Contractors Association. This was really important to me. I mean really. Here was something I didn't know diddley-shit about, I was in it for five years and they gave me this award. I cherish it because you accomplish something, you break into an area where people are very tough on you, they really work you over before they allow you into the group.

So, I would say, evaluating myself, I would say I'm in a real strong growth period. And most importantly, I want to continue the thing with my family. I had my dark days and they made me a better person. My wife made me take a good look at myself.

We have normal everyday problems of life but, hey, if you can handle them, no problem. I have a much better ability to handle the problems of life that come along than I did before. You get benched back when we were playing, I mean you'd move heaven and earth just to get a chance to get on the ice if you could, and it was devastating. Today, those things aren't important, you do what you have to do to control what you can, and forget the rest. Too many people think they control more than they do. How much control do we have over our lives? My dad's a Christian Scientist. He doesn't believe any of this stuff, he thinks it's all thought. And I admire him and respect him because he's been reading the Bible every day since I can remember, the last 40 years. So how can you not admire somebody who lives that type of life? My folks have been a real good influence on me too. My dad has never drank and they were tickled pink when I made the decision to cut the shit and stop drinking. They were really happy about that.

I'll tell you a funny little story. When I was a kid, I told my parents when I grow up, I'm going to buy them a brand new Cadillac. I got my own kids, I have a family to support and I'm not making that kind of money, but anyway, in the fall of 1983, I drove them out a new Cadillac. And my dad, to this day, he won't drive it during the wintertime. He keeps it in the garage during the winter, and if I'd known it was going to mean so much to him, I wouldn't even have had second thoughts. I thought, "Gee, maybe I shouldn't because this is kind of corny." To this day, he's thrilled to death. But they did a lot for me.

* * * * * *

Four weeks before this book was to go to print, June 1, 1987, Robert Williams, 23, died unexpectedly from an asthma attack. He was working at his off-season job.

ROGER BOURBONNAIS

Roger Bourbonnais was born on October 26, 1942, in Edmonton, Alberta. He grew up in farm country 20 miles northwest of Edmonton and attended school there. He played junior hockey with the Edmonton Oil Kings. He attended the University of Alberta while playing for the Oil Kings. The Oil Kings were considered by most hockey people to have the best team in Western Canada and were always competitive for the Memorial Cup. The Oil Kings won the Memorial Cup in 1963 with Roger the captain. Following his junior career, Roger attended law school at the University of British Columbia and played for the Canadian Olympic team at the '64 Olympics. He moved to Winnipeg for the '64-65 season to play with the Canadian National Team. He attended law school at the University of Manitoba, receiving his law degree in 1967. He moved back to Edmonton to do his articling in the fall of 1967 and played with and was captain of the Canadian Olympic team in Grenoble, France, in February, 1968. Following the 1969 World Championship, Roger quit playing hockey.

Roger's law career began in Edmonton. He practiced law there for several years. In 1980, Roger left Edmonton and spent the year traveling in Europe with his family. He moved to Vancouver and currently practices law with a local firm, Alexander, Holburn, Beaudin and Lang. Roger, his wife, Jeannette, and three children, Roger, Jr., Nicole and Danielle, live in Vancouver.

* * * * * *

Don Baizley, a Winnipeg lawyer and law school classmate:

"As long as I've known Roger -- we were in law school together -- he was a natural leader. The kind of guy who would

be part of a group but with the ability
to defer to others   while still being at
the center of the group. He had broad
interests for someone so preoccupied with
hockey. I would be surprised at how
he could study while playing at World
Tournaments and the Olympics. You knew
he wanted to do other things besides his
law course and hockey.   Roger sees things
in the long term, he always has been
looking at things 10-12 years down the
road."

Morris Mott, a teammate with the Canadian
National team:

"As a player he was a good skater, a solid
checker, well-balanced on his feet. He
had a poor shot. His skating stride was
as good as I ever saw. He was the demon-
strator for a skating instructional film
made back then. He was a low-key person
and a good, solid player. A very direct
type of person, he had certain things he
wanted to accomplish, he wanted to be a
lawyer.   More than the rest of us on the
National team, he was career oriented. He
knew he was going to do something besides
be a hockey player. He was more negative
toward the pro game than most of us; he
thought salaries were extremely low for
veteran pro players. He lived in an
apartment across the river from the leg-
islative buildings where the law school
was. I remember that to get to law
school during the winter he would just
walk across the frozen river."

* * * * * *

I met Roger the first time when we did the
interview. It was at the Hotel Vancouver prior
to an exhibition game between the Canucks and
the Jets. I explained to him that he was going
to be part of a separate group, those who could

have played pro but decided not to and went on to pursue their careers. We talked briefly about the earlier interviews of former players that had been completed. Roger suggested he tell his story historically. He was direct, right to the point.

This is the story of someone who took advantage of the opportunities that have become available for many young players today. He combined education with hockey and then turned away from the pro game to pursue his law career. He took advantage of a junior program and the National team program of the '60's that encouraged education. Because he had an education, Roger came to a crossroads and had a choice between a law career and a pro hockey career. He chose the law career. This is a story that illustrates how a person can elect not to play the pro game and live easily with that decision.

* * * * * *

Q. Your hockey career had a different focus than most in the 60's. Can you talk about it?

When I finished my high school, which would have been in 1959, I made a decision to go to a university. I was accepted at the University of Alberta and I went into the pre-law program. I tried out for the junior team in Edmonton, the Edmonton Oil Kings, the same year. I was fortunate, I made the team that year.

We were a very successful team the three years of juniors. We were in the Memorial Cup three years running. The last year, I was captain of the Oil Kings, we won the Memorial Cup, and I graduated with my BA.

Q. Why did you pursue the educational avenue?

My parents were very supportive of the educational route. I was raised on the farm. My

parents were prepared to pay whatever the costs
for school. I was fortunate to always have
scholarships that paid the tuition. My parents
were very supportive of combining education and
hockey. Later, when pro hockey became an option, they never really expressed an opinion either way. They left the decision to me. I really think the greatest influence around at that
time was a man named Leo LeClerc. He was the
team manager of the Oil Kings. He made sure
that my marks were up to snuff, checked with the
professors.

I can remember games that we played down
east in the playoffs. We would have a private
plane take the University students, maybe three
or four of us, home the next morning so we
wouldn't miss classes. In a couple of instanc-
es, I wrote my final exams in Brandon during the
playoffs and Hamilton during the Memorial Cup.
The arrangements for this were made by the team
management who encouraged all the players to go
to school.

**Q. How do you think this might have been dif-
ferent from other junior programs?**

Most of the players were going to high
school or to trade school while three or four of
us were in the university. We weren't playing
in a major junior hockey league. We weren't
leaving for two or three weeks at a time to play
through Saskatchewan or Manitoba. We played in
the Central Alberta Hockey League. We were
playing Drumheller, Calgary, Red Deer and
Lacombe and were bused home after the games
which allowed us to go to school. I would go to
school during the day, study during the day.
Our practices were late in the afternoons. I
would practice and go right back to the university with the other university students right
after practice. We never really had any social
life with the rest of the team.

It was very unusual for a junior program in

Canada. We only played about 40 games in our league. I had friends in Saskatchewan who were playing 60-70 games and traveling. The Edmonton Oil Kings were financed by the Edmonton Exhibition Association. The Edmonton Exhibition Association was an agricultural association which owned the fairgrounds and rink. They decided to support the junior hockey program. They were successful financially because they had a powerful team that was supported very well by the fans. They were able to attract players from across Canada. Pat Quinn was an example. He was from Hamilton, came to the Oil Kings and also attended university.

Q. What happened next?

Father David Bauer initiated a program in the fall of 1963 for the 1964 Olympic games in Innsbruck. I attended a camp in Edmonton and was asked to join the team. I also enrolled in law school at the University of British Columbia. I was asked, after I guess about two months, to come into the dean's office. He indicated to me that he was just made aware of the fact that I would be missing six to eight weeks of school (for the Olympics). He said that would not be acceptable to the law school. I dropped out of law school, took a few courses on a Masters of Economics. I wasn't real happy with the courses so I basically dropped out of school for the year.

Q. How did the 1964 Olympic team do?

We lost the last game at Innsbruck to the Russians 1-0. If we had won that game, we would have won the gold medal. By losing the game and with the goals for and against, we ended up fourth behind the Russians, Swedes and Czechs. We had a very young team that was basically a university team. We had a very good year, very successful year.

Q. Was this the period of time the Canadian National Team was formed on Winnipeg?

Yes, I went to Winnipeg and played for the Canadian National Team. The first year (1964), about half the players were in school and the other half were basically from the Winnipeg Maroons senior team and they were working. Again for me it was strictly hockey and school. I took my three years of law at the University of Manitoba Law School and played in three world championships (Stockholm, Vienna and Tampere). The National Team practiced during the week while most of the games were played on the weekends. There were times, for instance, during the World Championships, that I would miss two or three weeks of school. During these periods of absence, a classmate would carbon the class notes and fly them to where we were playing. This way I was able to continue with my schoolwork while on road trips, even at the World Championships.

After the three years in Winnipeg, I got my law degree (1967). I came back to Edmonton and started my articling. I was asked to join the 1968 Olympic team which was based in Winnipeg. I was given permission to break my articles which normally take one year. It was the first time an articling student was permitted to break his articles in Alberta. I took about four or five months off, joined the team in Winnipeg and participated in the '68 Olympics at Grenoble. We ended up with a bronze medal doing very well as a team. We were very competitive.

It was at this time the National Program came to an end. I can't remember all the details now, but I think it was in 1969 that the World Championships were supposed to be in Canada. Hockey Canada was going to replace the National Team. There was a dispute between Hockey Canada and Bunny Ahern of the International Ice Hockey Federation over whether ex-pros could play for Canada. Hockey Canada felt the European

teams were basically professional and, in a
sense, I think they were. Again, the details
are unclear but the National Program was dis-
banded. I was very disappointed and I think
most of the players were very disappointed.
That particular year we felt that we would have
the support of the Canadian people, we would
have been playing in our own backyard. The end
of my playing career was 1969. I was 27. I
simply continued on in the legal field.

**Q. Did you have any chances to play profession-
ally during the time period of 1963 to 1969?**

I was tempted several times. There were
only the six teams at that time. I belonged to
Detroit. I was on their protected list. I was
asked every year to go to camp. I would get
phone calls from their scouts asking me to sign
a "C" form. They were prepared to offer me a
contract to go to Detroit. When I look back
now, if they would have given me what I asked
for, I guess I was asking a lot, I might have
turned professional.

When I had one year left in law school,
that would have been the fall of 1966, they offered me a two-way contract. Springfield was
their farm team so the contract was for Detroit,
Springfield and another team in the Central Pro
league. I said I was not prepared to go and
take that chance with a two-way contract. If
they would offer me a one-way contract, if I
could be on the big team, then I would go.
Their comment was, "Who in the hell do you think
you are, Gordie Howe?" So that was basically
the end of my option as far as pro hockey was
concerned.

Q. Did you ever regret not having tried it?

There was a feeling of regret for a time
not playing for Detroit on a two-way contract.
I had played with a lot of players who turned
pro, who were doing very well at the pro level,
who were making big dollars. I was practicing

law during this time period of NHL expansion but I wasn't making anything near the dollars some of the players I had played with were making. That was sort of burning a little hole in my stomach. I was out of hockey, that option was gone. But I felt a twinge that maybe I should have tried it. I didn't know how well I would have done in the big league. There was always that feeling. Marshall Johnston, a good friend from Winnipeg, was playing in Oakland. I remember visiting Marshall in Oakland. He was playing, traveling all over the place. I just had a little twinge, maybe I should have tried it, taken a couple of years out of my legal career to try it. To see how far I could have gone. It was a tremendous attraction -- pretty compelling. I don't have that twinge feeling anymore.

Q. Now when you look back, how do you view your decision to combine education with hockey?

I consider myself very fortunate that I was involved with hockey organizations from the point of view that the people who were managing them were very conscious of having the players get as much education as possible. The schedules were conducive for the players to continue on in school, the schedules were tailored to make sure we had no long trips and that we were home nearly every night. The players were accommodated during the playoffs by being flown in and out. I really think if I had been playing in other centers, if I had played my junior hockey in Saskatchewan or in Manitoba where there was a tremendous amount of traveling, I don't think I would have been able to complete my education as quickly as I did. I was never faced with the dilemma of making that decision between continuing on in junior hockey or continuing on in the university. It was not just with the Oil Kings but also with the National Team. Again with Father Bauer coaching and with Bob Hindmarch the manager, they were all very oriented toward the education route. They made sure we got our education, that it was important to have an alternative to hockey. The hockey option was always there, but we had a lot of influence in the education direction. I was very fortunate. I was always in a program that I could do both.

Q. Your hockey career was over in 1969. What about your law career?

I went back to Edmonton. I finished my articling and stayed on with that law firm for four or five years. We started to raise a family. I formed a law firm with three other lawyers in 1974. I was very fortunate. I had good contacts through hockey. I had tremendous friends and a lot of acquaintances who opened up a lot of doors. It was the boom years in Alberta. I was reasonably successful in law. I was in the solicitor's side which was mostly in real estate. I decided to leave the practice in Edmonton in 1980.

Q. What led you to this decision?

I was burned out, working long hours, spending too much time away from my family and home. I didn't have time to do much besides work. It was time to reassess my priorities. I was with a small firm and it was the boom years for my practice. I had been at it for six or seven years. I decided to spend more time with my family. I left the law firm in Edmonton.

We took a year off, a kind of sabbatical. We spent a year traveling with the children. We went through most of Western Europe. We spent time in Spain, Italy, France, Switzerland, England, Scotland and Holland. I found out during this year that my priorities were a little out of whack in Edmonton with the law practice. The year traveling was a very good year for the whole family. We then decided to move to Vancouver. My wife and I had always talked about retiring in the Vancouver area. Our children were getting to the secondary school age. We felt it was a good time to move to Vancouver. We wanted to stay in the west, loved the Vancouver area and wanted our children to get acclimated to the area.

Q. Have you been satisfied with the law career?

The law practice allows our family to live in a relatively good fashion. There is a sense of security in having a profession that provides a certain comfort level.

When we came to Vancouver, I was not sure I would practice law. I looked at some businesses. The interest rate was 22% and the solidarity movement in BC was real. The business world seemed in a depressed mood. I was lucky enough to find a law firm that allowed me to stay at the same level. I was permitted to combine my interests in business affairs with my law training. I became a partner fairly quickly.

The practice allows me more time to do things that I enjoy. I am able to play golf, do things around the house, spend time with the family. I did not have the time for this in Edmonton. In a sense, I think there is better balance to my life in Vancouver than in Edmonton.

Q. Do you see your life as different from your hockey contemporaries who went the hockey routes?

I have very good friends that I played junior hockey with that didn't go on to the university, didn't get on with their schooling and are having a very difficult time right now. Even at this late time, they have no career, they are going from job to job. I see them now playing old-timers hockey. They haven't had that much success getting a job or keeping a job. They don't have the training, the background and I think it is the discipline as well.

I was fortunate when I was going to school that I could turn off my hockey and get on with my schoolwork, and vice-versa. Some players found it difficult during the playoffs, when the hockey was intense, to turn it off and to continue with their schoolwork. It was very important that I could turn it off, get back to the books and be very intense. I think that's been so through to the legal career. I have been able to discipline myself throughout right up to now.

I have never had a period of time where I have had to adjust. When I finished hockey, I went right to working full time, the practice was very busy. I was getting my ego fed with clients, bringing in clients, it was an on-going thing. I never had to sort of sit back and say, "Well, I'm no longer part of society." I know that some of my friends, the hockey players, have had the transition problem. The real shocker for them is to realize that all of a sudden there's nobody calling, there's nobody saying, "Come on over to dinner." Hockey friends are moving on, to another team or to a different city. They find themselves very lonely.

I had no transition period because of my education and training. I always had that option. I had two options. If I went the hockey route, I could fall back on my education. The other way, I could continue on with life. I never played pro, but talking to a lot of the pros, well there are certain things I suppose you miss with the pro side, but it is very short term. It doesn't have any lasting effect.

ULF NILSSON

Ulf Nilsson was born on May 11, 1950, in
the town of Nynashamn, Sweden. He grew up and
went to school in Nynashamn. At the age of 17,
he moved to Stockholm to attend the University
of Stockholm and to play soccer in the sports
club AIK. A knee injury the first year that required surgery forced him to concentrate on
hockey. Ulf played for AIK in the Swedish Elite
League from 1967 to 1974. At the same time, he
was a member of the Swedish Junior National Team
(1967-1970) and the Swedish National Team (1970-
1974). In 1974 he came to North America to play
for the Winnipeg Jets and remained with them
until the conclusion of the 1977-78 season.
These years were the glory years for the Winnipeg Jets in the World Hockey Association. It
was during this time that Ulf was a member of
the famous line of Bobby Hull-Ulf Nilsson-Anders
Hedberg. He moved to the New York Rangers along
with Anders Hedberg in June, 1978 and remained
with the Rangers until his retirement in the
spring of 1983.

Scarsdale, N.Y. remained home for Ulf and
his family while playing in New York. It has
remained home as he has stayed in the New York
area. He was initially employed with a Swedish
beverage company. He is currently the U.S.
sales representative with Classic Hus, a Swedish
house company that manufactures and exports
pre-fabricated homes. Ulf and his wife, Barbro,
have three children, Anna, Mikael, and Daniel.

* * * * * *

Anders Hedberg, a former teammate and
linemate:

"Ulf has an ability for the perfect set-
up while teasing people in a pleasant
and nice way. He can needle people in a
way that the person likes and enjoys.

68

But, you must keep in mind, he doesn't
like to be needled himself. I spent
many years with Ulf. I really enjoy his
company, he's fun to be with."

"He is a 'go get 'em' type of individual
who grasps things quickly and is willing
to try new and different things. A
strength of his is he is open for new
ideas, he is very open-minded in that
sense. His basic values are conservative yet he is willing to reach out and
try new things."

Don Baizley, Ulf's lawyer while playing in
Winnipeg and New York:

"At a personal level, he is a sensitive
and considerate person. He is extremely
competitive and always wants to be on
the winning team, even at neighborhood
informal games. He cares about people.
You could see this when he was playing.
During warm-ups he would acknowledge
handicapped fans with a wink or a wave
of his stick. He functions with a lot
of integrity and loyalty. He definitely
believes his word is his bond. He has
the ability to look to others for advice, listen to them and decide how the
advice can help him."

* * * * * *

I met Ulf when Mario Marois introduced him
to me in front of McNichols Arena in Denver in
1979. He was playing with the Rangers while I
was a coach with the Colorado Rockies. I would
occasionally see him when his family would be
visiting the Wayne Thomas family on Cape Cod
during the summers. When I contacted him about
the interview, he was enthusiastic. We met at
his house in Scarsdale on a day when the Jets
were playing the New York Islanders. Ulf was

prepared. He spoke with ease, yet was deliberate, giving me the impression that he wanted to
be sure about what he said and what he meant.
There was no question in my mind that he had
made a commitment to talk about his after-hockey
career problems and would stick it out. We met
a second time to clarify a few points.

My reaction to Ulf's story was how he was,
initially, naive about the real world. How a
bright and articulate person could be so unreal-
listic of what life after hockey was going to
be, surprised me. At the same time, I could see
the growth and maturity of someone who was willing to face his disappointments. He is in the
process of getting his after-hockey career going
and is remarkably honest with himself about why
it has not been as successful as his playing
career.

* * * * * *

Q. How do you view your career?

I guess it changes from day to day but,
overall, I feel pretty good about what I
achieved playing hockey. It was not planned to
end the way it did because it's not a good feeling at all when you know you're getting paid really well and you cannot fulfill the expectations of the people who are paying you well.
But, at the same time, for me to be able to survive, that is to say I gave it all that I had.

I am satisfied with the hockey career because it gave me a really good start at life.
Hockey has been really good to me because I grew
up with fairly tough situations. My father
passed away when I was 13 and we didn't have
very much money. Hockey and sports helped me
get through high school and a year and a half at
the University of Stockholm, and then getting me
the start that I have now on a new life in the
United States. And I have to thank hockey for
that.

Q. Then, you have experienced things through hockey that the average Swedish person does not?

Definitely. I think one of the most exciting things for me was that I had a chance to go to Russia many times. How many people have that chance? It was such a good experience to see that part of the world. I had a chance to go to Japan. I would never have had the chance if I hadn't played hockey. But I think the positive things outweigh the negative of the pain from bad knees and things like that.

Q. What kind of player were you?

I feel that I was probably one of the toughest players per pound. We were never really taught to fight in hockey in Sweden. But when we played in Winnipeg, the treatment we got there was unbelievable. The game was different in Canada, it was more physical. I passed the puck well. I had a lousy shot. But afterwards, I was probably stuck with playing with Bobby Hull and Anders Hedberg. Those two guys were so good that I got a little lazy and felt that they were sort of carrying me. It was an interesting experience playing with those two guys because I felt if I passed the puck to Bobby, I got shit from Anders and if I passed to Anders, I got shit from Bobby and if I shot myself, I got shit from both of them. So, that was kind of a difficult situation.

But, overall, I didn't think I was a very good skater but a good puck-handler and a good passer. And, I played every night, definitely.

Q. What did you achieve as a player?

Well, that's a hard one. I was maybe too tough on myself afterwards. A friend of mine in Sweden told me that he thought my father must have been hard on me. My father was a good soccer player. When I would come home from a game and say, "Dad, I had a good game and scored two goals," he would answer, "Ah, that was nothing, you probably could have gotten three or four." I think that happened to me a lot. If I was voted the first star of the game, I was thrilled and excited. Afterwards, I would look back and think, "Gee, I missed that chance and I missed that chance." But, you almost kill yourself in the long run if you think that way.

The good things that happened to me? We won two championships in Winnipeg and when we won in '77-'78, the last game I played in Winnipeg, that's when I had the chance to skate around with the Avco Cup. A lot of heights the first year in New York (1978-79) when we went to the Stanley Cup finals and I was voted the players' player the same year. We had a lot of injuries against Montreal in '78-'79 and we just couldn't beat them. The great experiences that came after the '78-'79 season have kept us in the New York City area. We like the energy and excitement of the city. We want to make our home here. We have good friends here. We like what the city has to offer our family. This is a positive result of having played in New York.

Q. Can you pick out high and low points?

Well, high points are definitely the championships in Winnipeg and when we won in '77-'78, the last game I played in Winnipeg and that's when I had the chance to skate around with the Avco Cup. A lot of heights the first year in New York. It was unbelievable some of the receptions we got from the fans in Madison Square Garden. And beating the Islanders in the semi-finals and to be able to play in the Stanley Cup finals.

Q. Would your low points be linked with your injuries?

Definitely, the injuries. I can sympathize a little bit with Barry Beck and the recent article about him in the New York Times. I had some injuries like all athletes. I cracked a vertabrae while I played in Sweden. There were several operations on both my knees. I had some broken bones -- wrist, arm, ankle. The right side of my body bothers me at times. The hip, knee and shoulder are probably arthritic. I'm glad I'm left-handed so I'm not restricted. I can still play catch with my kids. These lasting pains are part of being a professional athlete. I realize they go with playing the game.

It is so hard to be around a team when you are injured for a long time. Because it's a tough, very tough atmosphere in the dressing room. And when you sort of can't be part of it, you can't play the game but you have to be there, work out with the guys and you can't play. I would wonder, "Is it really my head or am I going crazy?"

It's true when you're injured you're not really part of the team. And it was hard for me because I couldn't get over that I didn't have the same feeling for the team when I wasn't playing. And that bothered me, that I didn't care as much when I didn't play. I hated to lose when I played, it was different when I didn't play. I could see sitting in the stands that people were really excited, the fans were really excited but I couldn't get that excited when I didn't play. I really didn't feel part of it.

Q. Will you talk about your transition period?

Well, the way I looked at my career was that I wanted to get better all the time. I remember, maybe around '78-'79, I was 29 years old and I said, "Gee, this is my peak now and with the injuries I'm starting to go downhill." I said to myself that I was going to try to get something to do after hockey that I will really enjoy and take the same approach that I was successful with in the hockey career.

I felt I had done what I wanted to do in hockey by '83. The Rangers asked me to sign a new contract for the '83-'84 season but I didn't play any in '82-'83. So I didn't even want to ask what they were going to offer me. I felt I was finished with hockey because I could hardly stand up on skates. I realized it was time to stop playing and that my good years as a player in New York were over.

I got a good opportunity to work for a Swedish beverage company. It had a lot of interesting and challenging things with it. I got to meet a lot of interesting people. But, there wasn't any substance to the job and that was very frustrating to me. It was also frustrating because the success that I'd had from playing hockey was that I surrounded myself with very good people, had good people to look up to, to learn from. Suddenly I felt lost being with my new job because those people weren't around. I felt that they were doing business backwards or they didn't do business the way I saw it. I didn't feel I had a lot of self-confidence when I was playing hockey, but now I had even less self-confidence, because I didn't have the people that I had in confidence in around me.

It took a long time for me to be able to get out of that job situation and now I feel very good about the choice that I've made going to work with and representing a Swedish architect and marketing guy. I think they have an absolutely fascinating market idea of how to sell Swedish pre-constructed homes in the United States.

Q. Is it fair to say that your transition started during your last contract with the Rangers and ended when you left the Swedish business concern, lasting a 4-5 year period?

Yes, I wanted to finish the contract with the Rangers in '83, but it was definitely clear that I wasn't going to play anymore. And I didn't feel comfortable with the people running the Rangers at the time because they asked me if I wanted to stay in hockey. I'd been playing with the idea if I wanted to stay in hockey or not, but I think it's very important that if you want to go into something that you feel confident about the people that you are going to be with because I'm a firm believer in teamwork. I was frustrated in my Swedish job because the company was not making money and by not making money I felt we were losing. I hate losing with a passion, and I felt I had stayed a little too long in a losing situation.

Q. Did anyone help you with your transition?

I have had a lot of help from Paul Henry, a former Ranger scout and psychologist. He's been helping me and my wife with a lot of stuff. You get stuck, you don't see, you don't have any choices and to work with someone who knows a little bit about how people work, it gives you the opportunity to maybe see the same situation from a different angle and it's been very helpful. I was able to make a decision with my initial job that I was not going to be able to stay with it and I had to move on to something else. And I feel really good about it.

I took some seminars. I would call them self-discovery seminars, and started to realize it was me and myself that didn't prepare myself during my playing career for life after hockey. I came to realize that I was placing the blame for my frustration with my job on the company and that it was really my lack of career preparation that was making me unhappy. I am learning now that it's what you do for yourself that is important. It's different from being a player, knowing this is making me a different person.

Q. Do you feel your playing status helped you?

Definitely. Maybe I didn't look at that so much at the time when I took the job just after retiring, but I see that it is an advantage to have done what I've done as a player and it opens a lot of doors. But you cannot rely on your past career to help you make money today. I realize that the success I have is determined by the job I do now and not what I did as a player.

Q. Would you describe your transition as rough?

Rough, yes. I think because I started working with a losing proposition. And with the intensity that I have and the pride that I feel I'm taking, and the hate I have for losing, it made it rough. I probably didn't have to look at it that way because it has probably been a great learning experience for me. Now, I see it not as two or three wasted years but see it as two or three really well-invested years of learning that maybe this is not the way to do things.

Q. What would you do differently if you went through the transition again?

I wouldn't take the same job. I was thinking about doing the Swedish pre-constructed homes at that time. I had a chance to go and work for SAS. But I chose, I guess, security. With the job I took, I was to get a salary. Now I'm working with no salary. I have to be creative. I like to depend on my instincts, my abilities to do a good job and it's up to me to make my job a success. I want to be in a position that it is what I do that helps the people I work with. That's the sort of the challenge that I had when I was playing and that's what makes me feel good.

Q. Is there any one thing about your transition period that stands out now when you look back?

Well, one thing that maybe you're missing from the playing career is that you play so many games and you get instant rewards or results. You score a goal or have a successful pass, you can see it. It's either success or failure where in the business world it's hard to see immediate results. Maybe it comes with experience, the people that you surround yourself with that can help you see these things. I think you have to feel it yourself if you've done a good job or not today and not have to rely on being told, not have to rely on other people telling you that you did a good job or not.

Q. In your life after hockey, can you talk about your new job, why you're excited about it, why you think you made a good move to change jobs?

The way I look at the trend in society is that people are starting to look more for quality and value in things versus trying to make something as cheap as possible. Society is getting away from the buy, use and throw away trend. It's like the car industry where people are starting to buy more imported cars. Why do people buy a Mercedes? Well, it's status, but it's also good quality and it holds the value a lot better.

I've been interested in the real estate market here. Prices have gone up and I see they charge so much for houses and the new construction over here is terrible, just terrible. They have a superior technique of building a custom

home in a manufacturing plant in Sweden. They
have a capacity to export and they've gone in
the opposite direction than most manufacturers
in Sweden. They go to the high end, they really
go for the Mercedes/Rolls-Royce type of market
instead of trying to cut costs in order to make
it as cheap as possible and really being on the
border line of making it on the down side. We
want to make the thickest exterior walls, for
example, and sell it to people who really know
what quality is all about, what value is about.
When people over here say, What's the difference?, I say the difference is like when you
close the door in a Mercedes or you close the
door in a Chevrolet. That's the difference when
closing a door or a window in a Swedish home and
one here.

A lot of people that I have spoken to see
the tremendous advantages right away. They ask,
though, about how expensive it is to ship it
from Sweden. It depends on the real estate market area you're building in because I'm looking
at the shipping cost as a percentage of the total price. If you're building in areas like
Greenwich (Connecticut) and Scarsdale (New York)
and Bedford (New York) or the more affluent areas in Long Island or New Jersey, the freight
cost is maybe 2 to 5 percent of the total cost.
You can justify it. But, if you're going into
areas where the house prices are not that high
and you're talking about a 10 percent freight
cost, then you can't justify it. So that's why
I feel so excited about this thing and I have
some good projects starting.

Q. **What adjustments have you made?**

Even when I played and I was successful I
felt I was dependent on my teammates and I really didn't give myself the credit that I deserved. That same kind of thinking followed me
into the business world. Now I had that good
feeling that I know what I can do and the things

that I can't do. I know the importance of sur-
rounding myself with people who are honest about
what they can do and what they can help you
with, and not being able to be afraid to pay
someone who gives you good advice.

**Q. You and your wife have a Swedish glass
gallery in New York. Has that been a good
experience?**

Definitely. My wife opened a glass shop or
glass gallery a little over two years ago in
Soho in New York. It's been a tough battle but
because my wife loves the work and the product,
we've kept at it. It's been hard because the
sales really haven't come as fast as we were
hoping. But we've been sticking with it and see
the trend changing for the better. If the trend
continues the way it's been going the last two
years, we feel it's going to be great. Everybody who sees the product loves it. We feel
very comfortable about it because the business
has been improving.

**Q. Are you comfortable with your level of per-
sonal satisfaction?**

Well, I think, as I spoke before, you feel
when you're 22-23 you are getting better every
year as a hockey player. I probably stopped improving at 28 or 29 when I had so many injuries.
I was at my peak and I realized it. Now with
the business world I have to go down a step and
then try to gradually get better and better and
better. In my first job situation, I felt I was
just getting further and further down but now I
feel I'm on my way up again. I feel my life is
moving at the speed I want and in the direction
that I'd like it to move.

I enjoy what I am doing because of the intense periods of work, planning and negotiations. I am also able to take an afternoon and
do what I enjoy without it affecting my job.

There's a balance to it that I like. There's an excitement that I get from working with both the manufacturing in Sweden and the home developers here. There's a challenge for me to make the two connect. It is this challenge for me that makes me look optimistically at my work.

MORRIS MOTT

Morris Mott was born on May 25, 1946, in Creelman, Saskatchewan. He grew up and attended school in Creelman. He played his junior hockey in the Saskatchewan Junior League with Weyburn. In the fall of 1965 he moved to Winnipeg and played with the Canadian National Team until 1970. While in Winnipeg he attended the University of Manitoba, receiving a bachelor's and master's degree. He attended Queens University in Kingston, Ontario from 1970 to 1972 working on a Ph.D. in history. He played university hockey during this period. The next three years, 1972-75 he played professionally with the California Golden Seals. The 1975-76 season was spent with Vastra Frolunda in Goteborg, Sweden. After that season, Morris retired professionally to complete his doctorate. The 1976-77 season was spent with the St. Boniface Mohawks in the Central Amateur Hockey League while working toward his degree.

After teaching several years at the University of Manitoba, Mott became a professor of Canadian history at Brandon University. He and his wife, Raymonde, and their children, Shelley and Kenneth, live in Brandon.

* * * * * *

Roger Bourbonnais, a teammate on the Canadian National Team:

"He was a Saskatchewan farm boy who moved in the direction of academics and sports. Morris was a relaxed, comfortable sort of person, naive as we all were when he showed up in Winnipeg. Dependable, calm, stable and reliable, he never got flustered in crisis situations. I'm not surprised he became a professor. He never had an enemy. I doubt if fame and success changed Morris, he is still the same down-to-earth person."

Bill Lesuk, a boyhood friend who played juniors with him:

"Growing up, we all had a chance for school, but it was Morris who always made sure he made it to school. Always the studious sort, he'd be reading Shakespeare and start laughing. He'd explain to me why he was laughing. You could tell he was into school. Morris always tried to excel at whatever he did. He was determined, always thought he could beat me in a footrace. It would only cost him an ice cream bar. He never did."

"I was impressed that he was so competitive yet he stayed within the rules. It told me a lot about what kind of person he was. He was serious yet he wanted to have fun, too. A great sense of humor, he was always singing, liked to dance. He could really dance with a door knob as a partner. We're good friends today and I still enjoy his company."

* * * * *

I met Morris while he was teaching at the University of Manitoba and I was coaching in Winnipeg. Our paths never crossed after the first meeting until we met to do the interview in his office on the campus of Brandon University. The office, strewn with books, papers and maps, provided a comfortable place for a professor to look back and reflect on his career and decisions that led to where he is now. When I mailed a copy of the interview to him, he sent it back with the grammar corrected. My thoughts were, "This guy is a true teacher." During the interview, he would clarify the questions as he understood them and then proceed to answer them in a calm, well-thought-out manner that is indicative of his teaching methods.

I came away from Morris' interview thinking how much a coach would enjoy having him as a player. His goal as a player was to play at the highest possible level. This forced him to be a team player. He was quite comfortable with the status of being an average player. As he approached his 30's, he recognized his diminishing worth to hockey management. Since he was never seduced by the lifestyle or money of a pro career, he was able to make a smooth transition to the academic field. In fact, the only difficulty he encountered was trying to get himself to adjust to the lack of a need to train physically. This was solved quite logically.

* * * * * *

Q. How do you view your career?

As far as defining my career or how do I now view my career, I think back on a lot of good things about it and a few bad things. To some extent I wish I would have played longer, but on the other hand I am aware now that I paid a price for playing even as long as I did. I wish I had played serious hockey longer because really the one major regret that I have is about the way I quit. I knew in my mind that I was a better player at 30 than I was at 25 or 20, but I was no longer in demand. The age factor catches up to you, so that even though you can do things better than what you once could do, people just won't give you credit for it. People are coming in from junior every year. They are 20 years old and have great potential. Management and coaches tend to see the good things in those people whereas they start to concentrate more on your shortcomings the older you get. I don't blame anybody for that, that's just the way life is and I am sure it's like that in any sport. It's probably that way among ballet dancers. The only thing I can say is that I wish I had played serious hockey longer.

On the other hand, I know that by getting out of it when I did, it was of some benefit to me.

I am happy now looking back on it, that I got a chance to play pro hockey. In effect, maybe I could say in retrospect that I had two different playing careers. I played junior and then played with the Canadian National Team in the '60's. Then, I went to Queen's University for two years and got a chance to get into pro hockey. By that time, I was a better player than I had been before, but I was fortunate to get the chance for pro. I was by that time in my mid-20's. Most guys nowadays are being let go in their mid-20's. At the time I started, there was a demand for players in their mid-20's. I got a chance to play pro hockey and I am glad that I got that chance. It was a second chance to play serious hockey, you might say.

Q. What kind of player were you?

As I try to analyze my own type of play, what type of player was I, I think I would have to say that I was a different player at different levels and to some extent this resulted from simply the different levels of competition. There are certain things that I could do at certain levels that I couldn't do at others. When I was in junior hockey, for example, we played under the old sponsorship system in the Saskatchewan Junior Hockey League. We had, in the Saskatchewan Junior Hockey League, the best league in western Canada. The Edmonton Oil Kings were almost always the best team, but we had the best league in western Canada. At this level, I was sort of a playmaking centerman type of player. I had a lot of skills making plays, passing the puck and so forth. And I got to do a lot of playing in junior hockey because I was good offensively.

As I moved up, when I came to the National Team I still did reasonably well offensively,

although I went to the wing and as a result
scored more goals than I had normally scored.
But then when I moved into pro hockey, I discovered my offensive skills were not really the
strong part of my game and I became more of a
checker than an offensive player.

I think the one regret that I have, although I don't know what I could have done about
it really, was that I didn't really have one exceptional quality. I wasn't exceptionally fast.
For a small player like I was, I think it helps
to be an exceptional player in some category of
the game. You have to have an exceptional shot,
or you have to be exceptionally fast. Yvan
Cournoyer comes to mind. Or you've got to be an
exceptionally tough player. Garry Howatt comes
to mind. But you have to have some aspect of
your game that really stands out. I was reasonably solid, I think, in different phases of the
game but I didn't have that one exceptional
quality that would have made it easier to be a
star player.

Q. What did you achieve as a player?

What did I achieve as a player? Well, I
think the one thing that I am proud of is that I
always played at the highest level I was capable
of. I think I really tried to do that. You
know, it was tough for me to make some teams.
When I first came to the National Team, it was
tough for me to make that club. When I went to
pro hockey, it was tough for me. I was on the
edge of being a top player in the minors or a
low player in the NHL. I managed to hang on to
play in the NHL and I will always look on that
as kind of an accomplishment on my part. I
wasn't satisfied to be a top player at a lower
caliber. I was never a superstar in any league
I played in, not even a star. In fact, in the
NHL I was just a fringe player. But part of
what I am proud of is that I always tried to
play at a level that was kind of above me. I
reached my level.

Q. What were your high and low points in your career?

As far as the high points are concerned, I think one of them would be playing at the levels I played at. I think there are various games that come to mind, but no outstanding achievements. I wasn't on a Stanley Cup winner. I wasn't on a world championship winner. I would like to have been. I think playing in the 1968 Olympics in Grenoble was a high point as I look back on in. When I was with the Salt Lake City team, we won the Central Hockey League championship. Sure, I am proud of those things. But I wouldn't say that there was anything outstanding like a Stanley Cup victory that I could point to and say, "This was the highlight of my career and I wouldn't be happy if I hadn't achieved it."

As far as low points are concerned, I think that the last year with the National Team was a whole frustrating type of year. Hockey Canada had been formed. I didn't have anything against Hockey Canada but the whole arrangement with that team had changed and we didn't have a very good team. We weren't doing very well, at least I wasn't. Actually, the problem started in 1969 and carried on into 1970. I wasn't happy in that situation but at the time there wasn't a better alternative for me. I wasn't in much demand in pro hockey so I felt I was better off to stay with the National Team and go to school. But the last year or maybe even two years with the National Team, I'm just not thrilled about it.

Q. Do you have good and bad memories from your career?

As far as good and bad memories are concerned, I think the good memories that you retain are always the people who you played with. Some people who played pro hockey might say now, "Well, the money was important." I really don't think that professional hockey players and serious amateur players are much different from each other when they actually hit the ice. I know I wasn't any different as a pro than I was as an amateur. The main concern I had was for our team to do as well as possible. The good memories that I have have nothing to do with whether I was playing pro or amateur. They just have to do with the people who were on the clubs.

A lot of the guys I was fondest of, and who I thought were most dedicated to hockey, were the guys who I played with on the California Seals. The Seals are now defunct and became kind of a joke after a while, but a lot of the guys who played there were really good. The best hockey player who I ever played with was Gilles Meloche. He didn't care about anything, all he wanted to do was stop the puck. He never blamed anybody. He was a better player than most of us were, but if the puck went into the net, it was his fault. I got along real well with Barry McKenzie and Terry O'Malley on the National Team. They were guys who really worked hard at the game, tried as hard as they could. Billy Lesuk was another guy in Weyburn. We played on a good team there. I remember we had a lot of good players. Don Caley, who later played for Phoenix in the Western League, was in goal and Jimmy Cardiff and Dwight Carruthers also played there.

The good memories I have are mostly memories of specific people who I met through the game and the people I remained attached to over the course of several years.

I wouldn't say that I have any particular bad memories. I don't think I have any regrets about my involvement with hockey. It was a serious involvement. I moved into the junior hockey network at the age of 15 and I spent the

next 15 years in the wintertime playing serious
hockey. I can't say I have any bad memories associated with it really. One thing I can say
about playing hockey is that I never enjoyed the
traveling. That's one thing I hated about it.
One of the attractive things about playing in
Sweden was you played two games a week, one at
home and one on the road. There was a very organized routine and I liked that and my wife
liked that a lot. A better situation for domes-
tic bliss, if you want to call it that, than in
pro hockey where you might spend a two-week period on the road. Both of us really liked the
Swedish experience for that reason. I was playing serious hockey which was great with me and
yet I wasn't gone all that much. Part of the
reason I got out of pro hockey was that I had
the chance to go to Sweden. I hated the traveling part of pro hockey.

If I was to elaborate on my approach to
hockey and the different approaches between amateur and pro hockey, I would say that there was
always a consciousness when you were playing amateur hockey that you were also doing something
else. You were either going to school or working. At the levels I am talking about, junior,
the National team and senior, when you actually
went out on the ice, the approach was professional. People were trying as hard as they
could. You knew all your energy was concentrated on the endeavor. I think the big difference
in pro hockey would be that your whole day was
focused on what took place on the ice. But as
far as what you might call a striving for excellence, once you got on the ice, that was what it
was all about in both amateur and pro hockey.

Q. **This may be a good point to move to your
transition period, can you define it?**

I had a pretty good idea, even when I was
playing hockey, what I was going to do once this
was all over. I was a serious academic by the

time I was playing pro hockey so I knew pretty
well what I was going to do. It was just a matter of time of when I was going to do it.

When I quit playing, I think one of the
things that I have often mentioned to people is
that I was lucky to have a senior hockey league
handy, the Central Amateur Hockey League (Manitoba), to play in, because I wouldn't have been
able to quit, cold turkey, playing serious hockey. I liked being in shape. I liked going out
on the ice and taking it seriously. The guys
who played in the Senior Hockey League were serious enough about the game that I still felt I
wasn't just rotting away.

I played serious hockey that year in
1976-77 and then I coached serious hockey for,
well, two years, three years after that. To be
honest with myself, a part of the reason I wanted to coach was because I was still playing, you
know, in my mind. One year I remember I coached
a midget team of 16-year-olds. I would quite
often do the drills, partly demonstrating the
drills, partly because it was still a challenge
to me. I know now that it's common among former
players to do that and it was certainly the case
with me. I think it was probably three or four
years after I quit playing that I would come to
the rink and actually prepare myself as a coach
rather than as a player.

As far as the physical part of the game was
concerned, it took me a long time to get rid of
the desire to be in top shape and to really exercise hard. I can honestly say that I don't
have the motivation to do that now. Here is
what happened that is interesting to me. Over
the years, I ran into some people at old-timers
games where I either played with or against people who were still pretty close to their prime.
I discovered that I was so far out of shape compared to what they were, and they were so much
better than me, that it became less and less fun
as the years went by. I can honestly say now

that it never occurs to me now to try to challenge myself against people who are still really
active in hockey. That side of it took quite a
while for me to adjust to.

**Q. Did you have any doubts about the teaching
profession at this time?**

I was always enthusiastic about what I am
doing now, I always had that to look forward to.
I liked that part of my life. I knew that path
was in front of me, although I let it slide for
about four years while playing pro hockey. It
wasn't planned that way, but that's the way it
worked out. I knew I had that challenge still
to come.

Q. Any regrets during the transition?

I have wished for several years now that I
would have managed to accumulate more money out
of hockey, but at the time I was playing, money
was no problem at all. Since then I have had a
couple of kids. I look back and say, "Gee whiz,
I wish I could have saved up another $50,000."
But, at the time, no. It was the playing itself
I liked and had to get out of my system. I
think that if I had been involved in a sport
like baseball, where the academic and athletic
seasons are different, it would have been an
easier transition coming down off that physical
high. A lot of problems that people have had
retiring, with psychological problems and alcohol and things like this -- this is off the top
of my head, but I know research could back this
up -- the problems people have, come because
they have no challenging second career. That
was never my difficulty.

**Q. How do you view your transition, smooth or
rough?**

By and large, compared to the other people
that I know, the transition was reasonably

smooth. I think that my wife was surprisingly supportive of what was going on. I remember in 1976, I decided, "Well I've got to go back to work on this thesis", and we decided I was going to take a year off, no job, no nothing, just work on this thesis because we had some money saved up. I remember saying to her, "Gee, this hockey, I just can't get it off my mind. I've got to be playing some kind of hockey. If we stay in Winnipeg, there is a senior league I can play in and you know, I think I would like to do that rather than take the teaching job available in Saskatchewan." She understood what I was talking about. It made perfect sense to her. I often look back at that and I'm kind of surprised. My feelings were something that I wasn't fully aware of myself at the time. But, they seemed to make perfect sense to her and I have always thought that this was kind of neat, that she had that kind of perception of what was going on in my head.

Q. Once through the transition, what adjustments did you make for your new career?

I think as far as making the change from being a player to a non-player, one of the things you find if you are not a star, and I wasn't, is that you don't have the same problems dealing with the lack of recognition after retirement. In a way, hockey has opened many doors for me. It did, because a lot of people recognized my name. But I wasn't involved in any endorsements or anything like that. That wasn't part of my league at all. I wasn't a big enough name, so as far as becoming just another face in the crowd after retirement, that side did not bother me very much.

If you are part of the National team or pro hockey, you walk into a restaurant and you get a certain amount of recognition. Gradually, less and less people recognize you after you quit. I especially noticed this working hockey schools.

Every year that went by, fewer and fewer kids had ever heard of me, and now, it's rare for me to find a kid who's even heard of the California Seals or the Canadian National team, which were the two main teams that I played for when I was in my prime. Of course, I enjoyed it when people recognized me. "Aren't you the guy that used to play hockey?" But, I had always been kind of anonymous as a player so it really wasn't a big comedown for me.

I think that in my life after hockey, I think I have mentioned to people that in being honest with myself, I picked up on my second career, really got serious about it, at the age of 30 or 31. Certainly, the years I spent in hockey put me behind other people the same age in my academic career. All the time I had been studying while playing, although I wasn't as aware as I should have been that I had huge gaps in my knowledge that would result from being away and traveling with a hockey team. I had huge gaps in my historical knowledge from missed classes. I just never managed to pick up any knowledge, for example, of the French Revolution. I still don't know anything about the French Revolution because it was covered while I was away. All I'm saying is that my second career was damaged by my involvement in hockey. You know whatever you commit yourself to, there are going to be positive and negative consequences and that's one of the negative ones. In my second career, I found that I was behind other people my age and I was competing for jobs with people 10 years younger than myself. But, on balance, I wouldn't change this.

What other adjustments have I made? I'm not nearly as active now physically. A lot of my day when I was playing hockey, I would say four hours a day, 12 months a year was taken up with something to do with training. It took me a long time to come off of that. And the other adjustment I think would be, well, when I first quit playing it kind of bothered me every now

and then, I knew that I was a better player at
32 than when I was 29. I'd think maybe I got
out of it too early. This was something that
used to eat at me. I would periodically go
through a couple of days where I would think I
should still be playing. But, now it never occurs to me.

**Q. Would it be fair to say that hockey was a
powerful force in your life?**

To what extent has hockey been a force in
my life? I think I would rephrase that to say
sport has been a very important part of my life.
I think I was always, ever since I was a kid,
aware that I would have a chance to play hockey
at higher levels unless there were guys who were
a lot better than I thought they were. I think
I have always taken sports seriously, not only
hockey but also baseball and other sports as
well.

Even today, a lot of what I do in the university setting is kind of study sports from the
academic perspective. I spend a lot of time on
the history of sport. So, I would say that
sports has been something that has been my whole
existence in a sense. Sport still tells me a
lot of what's good and bad and indifferent, what
I admire and don't admire in people. I don't
find that cause for celebration or self-criti-
cism. I just say that's the way I have been.
Maybe I am lucky that I have always had some way
that I could keep body and soul together while
following my interest in sports.

Q. Are you satisfied with your second career?

I consider myself pretty well adjusted. I
look forward to coming to work every day. I
think I am lucky in that respect. A lot of people aren't as enthusiastic about their jobs as I
am. I teach primarily Canadian and Western Canadian history at Brandon University, although

I've also taught some North American and even a little World History. I love the intellectual challenge involved in making sense of the past. I find it fulfilling to publish, and in doing so to create new knowledge about historical developments. I like helping students understand how people lived in previous decades or centuries, and how institutions or ideas originated and evolved. You see, in my view, historical information is just about the only useful information. I enjoy acquiring it, then sharing it. The only frustration for me has been that it's taken me a long while to establish myself, a long time in terms of age. I am 40 years of age. You should be well established in your career by that age. I am still on the ground level. On balance, I am glad I went the hockey route. It may be a blessing in disguise, because by the time I am out of the academic business, let's say at the age of 65, I might be tired of it anyhow. But right now -- sitting here 40 years of age -- one of the prices I have paid is that I am a little behind.

The one thing that I can say about hockey players when they retire is that they tend to downplay their own strengths. They don't realize the kind of assets they can bring to any new career. If they have played hockey with any degree of success, they have the capacity to focus their energy. They tend to think of themselves, especially if they haven't established themselves in the NHL for 10 years, as failures. A lot of people have businesses and go bankrupt, or don't get into law school or they don't get into medical school. They've got to start over. All I am saying is that hockey players tend to feel sorry for themselves, they think they're the only ones who have to start over. There are lots of people who start over.

As I've said, there are certain negative consequences when you have to start over at a later age. But there are certain advantages that you bring out of the hockey experience as

well. The reason I am bringing this up at this
point, is that a lot of the guys who are married
with kids are very anxious when they retire to
latch on to the first thing that is available to
them. They have to support a family and they
tend to get into jobs that are not satisfying.
They are not willing to stand back a little. I
think that hockey players don't realize that
starting over is something a lot of people have
to do in life and hockey players are better
equipped to do it than most people.

JEAN PRONOVOST

Jean Pronovost was born on December 18, 1945 in Shawinigan Falls, Quebec. He lived there until he was 8 when his family moved to Beaufarnois, Quebec. He joined the Niagara Falls Flyers in the Ontario Hockey Association for two years of Junior A, and the team won a Memorial Cup. His professional career started with the Boston Bruins' farm team in Oklahoma City where he spent the 1966-67 and 1967-68 seasons. Jean's NHL career began with the Pittsburgh Penguins in 1968, and he stayed with them for 10 seasons. Traded to the Atlanta Flames in 1978, he spent two seasons with them. He was traded to the Washington Capitals in 1980 and spent the last two years of his career with them. The last season before his retirement, 1981-82, was divided between Washington and their farm team, the Hershey Bears. Jean played for Team Canada in 1977 and 1978.

While with the Atlanta Flames, Jean became a Christian. Following his retirement he eventually moved to the Montreal area with his wife, Diane, and four children, Eric, Marty, Sara, and Amy. He currently works for the Hockey Ministries International in Montreal.

* * * * * *

Ryan Walter, a player with the Montreal Canadiens:

"Jean and his family are best friends with my family. Jean has amazing boldness, strength and character and this is reflected in his kids. These exceptional qualities, with his faith, enable him to handle different and difficult situations. I think his adjustment has been a learning time. He spent his first year away from the game studying the Scriptures, seeking God's direction in his

98

adjustment to life after hockey. He believes he is in the right place now. His
wife, Diane, was a big help. She quickly
was able to perceive the changes that
were taking place, in lifestyle, income,
and profile, and they were able to settle
into the new life as a family together."

Don Liesemer, a minister with Hockey Ministries International:

"One of the things that amazes me is his
attitude toward money. The fact that he
holds no bitterness toward the things
that happened to him, in terms of people
abusing him financially, simply amazes
me. His idea of dedication and commitment to Christianity is remarkable. We
work closely together and he is really a
committed Christian individual. Jean is
held in high regard across Canada by the
Christian community. He is a real family man. His children are just beautiful
kids. I think they are a reflection of
Jean's love for his kids and family. He
spends a lot of time with them and is a
good example of a fine Christian father."

* * * * * *

I met Jean Pronovost for the first time
when we did the interview at the Manoir Lemoyne
in Montreal. We had talked on the phone to set
up the time. He showed up around 10 a.m. after
an hour of hockey with a group he skates with
every week. He had bumped into his brother,
Marcel, on the elevator. Marcel, who had a
great career with the Detroit Redwings, was in
town for the same reason I was, scouting the
Quebec Hockey League. Jean and I talked awhile
about hockey and life in general and got to the
interview. He said he had given the questions a
lot of thought and was looking forward to doing
it.

When Jean had left following the interview, I thought about how his career had ended. He played in the NHL for 14 years, had a solid career with some glorious accomplishments, scored 52 goals one year, played for Team Canada, played in All-Star games and was considered a good, honest and dependable player. A year after it was over, he drove a rented truck with his family and belongings to Montreal with no job to go to. Jean got through it because of his Christianity and faith in God. He had the intelligence and family support to use his faith. Good for him that he got through it. But, there is a lesson here in terms of lack of preparation for life after hockey. It was not a glorious way to end a glorious hockey career.

* * * * * *

Q. How do you view your career?

I look back on it as a very positive thing in my life because it gave me an opportunity to find out about myself. I was able to develop confidence in my talent and abilities to play hockey. The other thing it did was it enabled me to learn about people and to meet some nice people, and travel a lot. In a way, the hockey career has given me a better understanding of what life is all about.

Hockey, basically, was my God. Ever since I was a youngster, I was influenced by my brother, Marcel. I wanted to be a hockey player. Most players are looking for respect from their peers. I was no different. I wanted to establish myself as a good two-way hockey player. I would like to think that I was able to show to my peers over the length of my career that I was a good two-way hockey player. The only regret that I have, as far as my hockey career is concerned, is that I did not go to college to play hockey. In my day the quickest way was junior hockey. I now miss the education although I

understand that today the juniors have a good
education program.

Q. What kind of player were you?

I wasn't a goal scorer, although I did
score 52 goals in 1975-76. My biggest asset was
that I was determined that I was going to make
it, able and willing to pay the price. I didn't
care what it cost me, I was going to play hockey. I was very dedicated to what I wanted because I knew that there was a lot of work involved. During the summer I spent a lot of time
keeping in shape. I figured if I would be ahead
of the other players at training camp that I
would be better for it.

I guess to rate myself I would say I fit
in. I was no superstar but I could play both
ways, offensively and defensively. I was
brought up in the old school when the game was
not as wide open as it is today. When I would
be in a slump, I would not think to go offense,
I would think defense, to protect my own defensive zone. That's the way I played. Like I
said, I think I fit in and I'm glad that I was
able to play all those years.

Q. What did you achieve as a player?

My peak as a junior was my first year in
Niagara Falls. We won the Memorial Cup beating
the Edmonton Oil Kings. We played until mid-
May. Ironically, my first year as a pro was
with Oklahoma City in the Central League and we
won the championship, too. We won the Adams Cup.
I figured that maybe I would be on a Stanley Cup
winner right away, but it was not to be so.

There are some personal things. The year I
scored 52 goals and had 104 points is one. The
year I was voted the players' player meant a lot
to me. I think that says a lot about you, how
you come across to other people and what they
realize you do for the team. That is an
achievement which I think is a good one.

In Pittsburgh we had some good years and we had some off years. We never were very close to winning the Stanley Cup. When I went to Atlanta, we had the team but not the desire. As a team we were not willing to pay the price. In Washington, we had the desire but not the quality players. I was never able to play on a Stanley Cup team, which would have been a real achievement.

Q. Do you see the fact that you never played on a Stanley Cup championship team as a low point in your career?

No, not really. What I could not understand was the fact that I would look at guys that were on Cup winners and say, "Those guys are lucky, they are with the right team." I could see being with Pittsburgh was not going to work out. I would have loved to win a Stanley Cup, to be a winner, to see how it felt.

I didn't have any low points as far as not producing. I was always consistent. You have to be realistic about your team -- if you don't have the horses, you can't win. I think a good hockey team starts from the top down. We had five different coaches and three general managers in the 10 years I spent in Pittsburgh. That shows instability.

Q. Do you have any good or bad memories?

There are a couple of good memories. The year I scored 52 goals, I scored the 50th against the Bruins, my old team. They had sold me to Pittsburgh. The other memory is that I played for Team Canada twice in the World Tournament. I enjoyed international competition. We played in Vienna and Prague in 1977 and 1978 and they were real learning times.

I have one bad memory that stands out. It was during a game and I was struggling as far as putting the puck in the net. I made a remark to the referee, and he retorted back. I lost control, really blew it, and he threw me out of the game. I was so mad and out of control, I wanted to just give it to him. Then, it dawned on me that what I was doing was dumb. I realized, "This is stupid." I was just acting like a spoiled brat. I had lost it completely, did not have control of myself and that's one bad memory. I did apologize to the referee after the game.

Q. Can you describe your transition?

For me, I never thought the end would come. Or, I never wanted to think about it, let's put it that way. When I was traded from Pittsburgh to Atlanta, I was an older player, 32, on a young team. The average age was 23. I was a veteran and I began to think this might be where I was going to retire. But, as a player you don't really want to think about it or to pay a lot of attention to it. I really didn't get prepared for the time I would be done playing. I thought I could play more and more.

One thing did happen when I was in Atlanta that helped me to cope with the transition. I became a committed believer in Jesus Christ. I knew that the Bible told me that God had a plan for my life. I figured, "Well, let's see the plan after." I knew what the plan was then, it was to play hockey. I said, "Let's see what the plan is when I retire."

When I was traded from Atlanta to Washington, I was in Israel. In the fall, I went to Washington and figured I had a couple of more years before the end would come. I really enjoyed Washington and the area. Really loved it. As a matter of fact, I started to think that maybe I would get to live there, settle down in the area. We missed the playoffs the first year by one point. We had high aspirations for the next year. But when the second year came around, I was left behind when the team left for

Europe during training camp. I could read between the lines that something was happening,
there was something that was different. When
the season started, I was on the fourth line and
was used sparingly. I hardly played the first
11 or 12 games. Then there was a coaching
change and I was sent to Hershey in the American
League. I spent the rest of the year in
Hershey. As it turns out, I finished my career
in Hershey.

During the off-season, I was a free agent
without compensation, but I was 36 years old. I
still had the drive, the desire to play. All I
wanted was a chance to prove it. There were no
phone calls, nothing over the summer. I got a
phone call from Jack Button, the director of
player personnel in Washington, in early September. He said, "We're not interested in your
services, you're free to go wherever you want to
go." I knew then that nobody expressed an interest in me because my phone did not exactly
ring off the hook during that time. It was then
that I realized that this is it. It was the
end.

What do I do now? I did not know exactly
what I wanted to do. I might have liked to stay
in hockey in some capacities, but my mistake is
that I never really inquired around the league
and offered myself to the NHL teams. Being a
committed believer, I thought I might like to be
involved with a Christian Ministry, maybe join
Campus Crusades with my friends in Atlanta. I
had talked to Don Liesemer, the president of
Hockey Ministries. I didn't really know what I
was going to do. I waited for directions.

We decided to sell our house. It took 10
months to sell it. I waited around from September to June until it was sold. I worked on construction for a month or two to help with the
expenses. Not much was happening as far as a
hockey opportunity was concerned. I was waiting
for the Lord to show me. Eventually, we sold

the house in June, packed up in a rented truck and moved back to the Montreal area. We rented a small townhouse for a year or so and I started to work for Hockey Ministries International. I was sure then that this was where the Lord was calling me to work, to remain within hockey, and be a witness to other players, and others that I would come in contact with. This is what I have been doing for the last four years.

Q. How would you characterize the transition, rough or smooth?

Smooth, because I knew that God is a personal god and that he had a plan for my life. I realized that it was a personal relationship between him and me.

Because as an athlete with no education, just grade 12, and no formal training in Christian work or any other form of training, where did I fit in? There always seems to be a waiting period that God puts you through. I believe now that it was for testing my faith in Christ. For a period of 10 months, there was no news, no one knocking at the door saying, "Come on, I want to hire you." I found myself saying, "Are you sure you do have a plan for me?" I think during the waiting period he dealt with my pride and many different aspects of my character.

My wife, Diane, has been a big help throughout my career because she always stuck by me. It was hard on her while I was a player, with no real identification for herself, and now all of a sudden her husband is no longer a hockey player. I was doing a lot of hanging around the house. She was very understanding and helpful. I remember when I hung up the phone after talking to Jack Button, I said, "It really happened, this is it." I was down and she said, "Jean, God has closed this door but he will open others, just wait." That perked me up. You have a tendency to look at your circumstances, and I did feel a bit rejected. I wasn't ready to retire. But, I realized that there is life after hockey, so, these simple words that she said really helped me. She stuck by me and still does.

I characterize my transition as smooth, but not without doubts. Well, certainly my perspective is different than other people. The faith I have in the Lord God really helped me to understand what this life is all about. The transition period offered me an opportunity to know a bit more about trusting God. There are times when you start questioning but you know there is a purpose. You just have to wait and find out what the purpose is. That is why I think the transition was bearable because of my faith in Jesus Christ.

Q. Your transition ended when you left Washington in June 1983. What have you been doing since then?

I have been working for Hockey Ministries International. Our approach is threefold with camps for youngsters (age 10-17). I'm also involved in the pro division with chapels and team meetings and pro conferences and counseling and discipleship, and so forth. We encourage the pros in their walk with the Lord and sometime will provide materials to them that will help their Christian growth. I also do speaking engagements. As a former professional hockey player, people seem to enjoy listening to what I have to say and I definitely use my status as an ex-hockey player to share about my relationship with the Lord Jesus. I want them to see the reality of Christ in my life. We also have a communication which is a 16mm film called "Breakaway" and also a book with the same title. Basically, the film and book are testimonies of some of the Christian pros in the NHL.

Our goal at the ministry is to present the Gospel to the hockey world. I am able to go places where pastors or preachers could not go.

I'm not an ordained minister but considered a lay person. I have not gone to a seminary but have taken a number of Bible courses. My work is considered that of a lay person, not a minister. We are an evangelical ministry within the world of hockey. We consider our organization international because hockey is played in more than 30 countries. We are ministers, which means servants. So, we're servants to the hockey world.

I find the work very rewarding, but demanding because of the spiritual aspect of it. I enjoy dealing with people at the personal level. I like to be able to help people in their personal life, and lead them to a personal faith in Christ. That's the part of the ministry I enjoy doing the most, because it is the most fulfilling.

Q. What adjustments have you made?

We have an eight-and-a-half hour day. The biggest adjustment has been the time. As a hockey player, I spent about two hours at the rink and then it was free time. And in the summer, you had four or five months off, just basically spending time with your family, relaxing, keeping in shape. It was fun, but it was not structured like my life is now. The time factor of working every day has been a big adjustment. The administration work is something I am not gifted for. I'm not too crazy about it, but I realize that I have to do it because it's part of my work as a servant. I prefer to be with people, talking and helping people rather than sitting at a desk.

When I was playing, I didn't have a business mind and, because of that, put my money affairs in the hands of others. Doing that allowed me to concentrate on the game. As other players found out, it was not the right thing to do. If I were to do it again, I would manage my own money and be personally involved in my contract negotiations. The person handling my money made several bad investments and is no longer in the business. I trusted him, but I'm not bitter. The blame can't be placed only on him. I'm partially responsible for the losses. I did learn from it though.

Q. How do you view yourself today, personally and professionally?

I do enjoy what I'm doing because my faith in Jesus is the thing that I wanted to share with people. I realize that God has allowed me to be a hockey player so someday he could use my talents to teach the youngsters - but he also expects me to share about the most important decision in a person's life, which is to receive Christ as your personal saviour and lord. We do not present the Gospel in a forceful way, but we want to make sure that the person or persons are left with that very important decision. Our desire is to see that pros or youngsters make this decision and understand God's grace.

Q. To what extent has hockey been a force in your life?

Hockey was all that I had, and I dedicated my life to it at one point. But today, hockey is a vehicle for my work. I have heard people talk as if hockey is their god and for me it was my god for many years. At least, until I was introduced to the real God. Some people may make money or material possessions or sex their god. But all these things will not fill that god-shaped vacuum. It is important to keep a good perspective on who is the true God.

Hockey has been very good, but I realize now that it is temporary and that there is more to life than being a pro hockey player.

HENRI RICHARD

Henri Richard was born on February 29, 1936 in Montreal. He grew up and attended school in Montreal. He played one year of junior hockey with Montreal National Junior A and three years with the Montreal Junior Canadiens. He joined the Canadiens directly from junior hockey and spent 20 seasons with them from 1955 to 1975. His entire career was spent with Montreal. He was inducted into the National Hockey League Hall of Fame in 1979. Considered to be one of the hardest working and most honest players to play the game, Henri played on 11 Stanley Cup championship teams.

After his retirement, Henri continued to operate the tavern that he had owned as a player. He sold the tavern in 1986. A member of the Montreal Canadiens Old-Timers, he continues to play 40 or so games a year. The father of five children, Michelle, Gilles, Dennis, Marie-France, and Natalie, Henri and his wife, Liese, live in the Montreal area.

* * * * * *

Sam Pollock, former Montreal Canadiens general manager:

"Henri Richard started playing Junior A hockey at age 15. He was a very inspirational player and the brother of Maurice Richard. He centered a line with his brother and Dickie Moore, a great line. An 11-time Stanley Cup winner who scored goals to win the Stanley Cup against Detroit in 1965 and Chicago in 1971. Both of these goals were scored away from home. He was a very dedicated player who never took a backward step to anyone despite his size. He was a great all-around athlete and an intense competitor. He is a Montreal hockey legend."

Dickie Moore, a former teammate with the Montreal Canadiens:

"Henri broke a real barrier following in his brother's footsteps. Maurice was one of the greatest to have played and for Henri to have followed in his footsteps and to have achieved what he did speaks well for him. With his size, it showed the speed and determination that he had as a player. Being a former teammate of his, I know that Henri was really dedicated to his teammates and the team. He hated to lose, did he ever."

* * * * * *

Gary Smith suggested Henri Richard as a possible interview. They were playing together with the Montreal Canadiens Old-Timers. Gary said, "He's pretty quiet, can still play the game, is in great shape and would do it because he's a good guy." I called Henri and we spoke briefly about the project. I said I would be in Montreal in five weeks on a Thursday and he suggested 11 a.m. Five weeks later I showed up in his office in Laval, Quebec, and we did the interview. As he spoke I looked around his office at the pictures hanging. There was a picture of Henri and Maurice, another one of Jean Belliveau, a couple of action shots, a team picture, one with Arnold Palmer and his Hall of Fame induction program framed and autographed by the other inductees. He spoke so softly I wondered if the typist could pick up everything he said. He was direct and to the point.

As I drove away from his office, I thought of a college professor I had. He would always say before a test, "Just answer the questions and if you can say it in 100 words, it would be better if you said it in 25." Henri would have gotten straight A's from this guy. He answered the questions, expressed an opinion where he felt appropriate, and the interview was quickly

over. He was brief but said a lot. He had accomplished a lot as a player and he was proud of
it. This was a proud person. But, there was a
humbleness there, his success was not flaunted.
The impression I got was of a hard-working and
honest person who knew what he wanted and did
it. When he felt it was time to quit, he quit
and went on to do other things without any
hesitation or remorse.

* * * * * *

Q. Looking back, how do you view your career?

If I had to do it again, I'd do exactly the
same. I worked at it all my life. As a matter
of fact I never worked, but I played quite a
bit. I don't call playing hockey work.

I spent 20 years with the Montreal
Canadiens, from 1955 to 1975. Never went to the
minors. We won 11 Stanley Cups. I guess it was
being at the right place at the right time.
There was the initial expansion around 1967 and
then there was another expansion around 1971.
That helped me play the 20 years. When I first
started in 1955 I said I'd be happy if I played
10 years, but I was fortunate enough to play 20.
I played until I was 39. Today, players are old
men at that age. They don't play much past 33.

I wanted all my life to play with the Canadiens. It's different today, but back then if
you were from Montreal or Quebec, you wanted to
play in Montreal. If you were from Ontario, you
wanted to play with the Toronto Maple Leafs. It
was great for me. We had good players all the
years I played. Like I said, it was luck to be
on 11 Stanley Cup teams. I was fortunate to be
able to play with my brother Maurice, Doug
Harvey, Jean Beliveau, Geofferion, Lemaire,
Lafleur, Steve Shutt and Larry Robinson, to name
a few.

Q. What kind of player were you?

I was a hard-worker type. As a junior I thought I was a pretty good scorer, at least I got quite a few goals. But then I had to change my style when I started to play in the NHL. Of course, I played with my brother and I was looking for him all the time to pass the puck and tried to get him in on the goal. I thought I wanted to be like him, but I soon found out I couldn't be like him. I just couldn't put the puck in the net. So, I had to change my style. I worked hard every game. I had my own style. I only weighed about 150-160 pounds, wasn't big. That's why I had to skate, to get away from the big guy.

Today, at that size, hockey people won't look at the player. But take a guy like Mats Naslund, he's doing pretty well in Montreal. He's about my size, even shorter. There's so much hooking and holding today. That's one of the reasons the small guys have a hard time playing. But that's not hockey. The pros do a lot of hooking and holding and the refs let everything go in that department. High-sticking, holding, crosschecking, that's all you see today. And it starts even before juniors.

Q. What achievements do you remember from your career?

I guess winning the Stanley Cup is an achievement. It's a team effort, of course. Being able to play with the Montreal Canadiens and stay that long I think is quite an achievement. And if I may say it again, I was quite lucky to play with all the all-stars and good hockey players.

In 1971, and I'll remember it all my life, we beat Chicago 3-2 (seventh game) and I had two assists and the winning goal to win the Stanley Cup. I think that's one of my highlights. I was quite fortunate because I could have been a bum. I criticized the coach. I said he was the worst coach that I ever played with. It wasn't exactly the right thing to do, but it was true. I felt that way because I was mad at him because he didn't play me one game. I did play again and it was a highlight. We beat Boston that year when no one thought we would and then beat Chicago for the Stanley Cup.

Q. Do you have any low points?

I had a few. I guess the year Jacques Lamaire came was one. I was always afraid of losing my job, it's only natural. I wanted to play hockey and wanted to be a regular and that's what I was scared of at the time. It was my job and everybody thought a young guy, Lemaire, was pushing me. I stayed on the bench maybe two games and didn't appreciate it. I didn't like it. It was nobody's fault, it was just that Lemaire was coming up. It's the same today, the kids, 18-19 years old, are pushing the older guys. It was the same when I came up. I was only 19 and I wasn't supposed to make the team, but I did.

It would have been a low point to be traded. I didn't want to sit on the bench and be paid to do it. I could have stayed on with the Montreal Canadiens two more years, just sit there and not play much. That wasn't my style. I could have made quite a bit of money, but it wasn't my style. I just wanted to play hockey, so I decided to quit.

Q. What good memories do you have?

Being able to play with my brother Maurice is a good memory. I was only 6 years old when he started to play with Montreal in 1941. He got married and left. He was more like an uncle to me. And then being able to play with him for five years and we won five Stanley Cups those first five years. I liked that.

Q. Can you define your transition period?

It might be a little different than the others. My transition only lasted one day. Once I was finished playing hockey that was it. When I'm finished doing something, it's in the past, it's gone, it's yesterday. I played 20 years with the Montreal Canadiens, I quit and it was time for a new life. Of course, I already had a business. So, when I retired I knew what I was going to do. I bought the tavern in 1960. I was there every day when I played with Montreal. It wasn't much of a transition. It was quick. I said, "This is it, it's finished, forget about it." The day after I retired, it was another thing. I did think about retiring for two, maybe three years. A lot of people said things like I should retire. When I did, it was behind me. I have no regrets about it. I think I did the right thing and if I had to do it again, I'd do exactly the same thing.

Q. Why did you buy your tavern when you were playing?

When I was growing up, there were two things I wanted to do, play hockey and own a tavern. I knew I wouldn't be going far in school because of the hockey. I thought I could combine running the tavern with playing hockey and I would have it when I was done playing. I also knew I could run it while I was playing.

Q. Did your playing status help your tavern business?

Sure. A lot of people who came to town for the Canadiens games used to come down before the game or the day before the game. We had a lot of regular customers also. I think it continued after I was done playing.

Q. What have you done in the employment area since you finished playing?

I haven't done much. I had my tavern. I had that for 26 years and 6 months. I just recently sold it. I'm still working for Carling-O'Keefe. I've been working there for four years now. I do promotion, special events type of work. That's about all. I like to enjoy myself. I play a lot of tennis, a lot of golf. Still play a lot of hockey, maybe 40 games a year with the Canadiens Old-Timers.

Q. Do you enjoy the Old-Timers hockey?

I've been retired from the Montreal Canadiens for 12 years now. The last 10 years I have been saying, "I don't want to play anymore, next year I'll quit." I'm saying that again, "Next year, I don't want to play anymore." We'll see what happens. I enjoy playing. Now that I have sold my tavern, I have more time. Even when I had the tavern, I had a lot of help. My son was there quite a bit. So I had a lot of time. I enjoyed the trips across Canada, going from Vancouver to Newfoundland. This year we went to Europe. That was a good trip.

Q. How do you view yourself today?

My playing career is in the past. I had a lot of success playing hockey. I was very successful with my tavern, now I am semi-retired. I do a little work with Carling-O'Keefe and, like I said, I play a lot of golf. I didn't think I worked hard as a player, but I must have worked hard. It wasn't work to me, everything I did I enjoyed. When something is work, it's something I don't like to do. I think I am very honest in everything I accomplished in sports.

Q. Has hockey been a force in your life?

It's quite simple, it's been my life, always been my life. Playing hockey was what I wanted to do since I was 6 years old. I wanted to play with Montreal. Hockey has been my life. Without hockey, I don't know what I would have done.

JERRY KRUK

Jerry Kruk was born in Winnipeg, Manitoba,
on April 3, 1940. He grew up and went to school
in Winnipeg. He played his junior hockey with
the St. Boniface Canadiens from 1956 to 1960.
The Winnipeg Braves added him to their roster in
1957 for the Memorial Cup playoffs, which they
won. His professional career was spent in the
International League with the Minneapolis Mill-
ers and the St. Paul Saints for two seasons
through 1962. In 1962, he was traded to Indianapolis which quickly traded him to Toledo. He
retired after the trade to Toledo at the age of
22.

Winnipeg has been Jerry's home for his entire life. While playing junior hockey with St.
Boniface he attended the University of Manitoba.
He received a degree in mechanical engineering
in 1960. Greater Winnipeg Gas Company has been
his employer since 1962. While working for
Greater Winnipeg Gas Company he received his MBA
in Finance in 1976 from the University of Manitoba. He is currently vice-president of operations. Jerry, his wife, Ruth, and his two
daughters, Mary Ann, and Carolyn, reside in Winnipeg.

* * * * * *

Ted Green, a teammate in juniors and now a
coach with the Edmonton Oilers:

"Jerry was a very energetic, intelligent
player. He was one of the better players at the time. I remember when we
were in the Western finals one year in
Regina, he had missed leaving with the
team because of school. He showed up in
the locker room with a sheet of equa-
tions and said, 'If I can handle these,
I'll have no problem.'"

Austin Rathke, president of Greater Winnipeg Gas Company:

"What made Jerry a good hockey player was a) he was a competitor, and, b) he was a team player. He is the same in the business community. He is active, aggressive, a self-starter. He works well with others. He keeps others well informed and they do the same for him, which creates good teamwork."

"He is active in the community as a board member of a hospital, a health-care unit, and Winnipeg Enterprises, which is involved with the Winnipeg Arena and the Winnipeg Jets. He takes a great deal of pride in his community. The sort of individual who wanted more education and went out and got his MBA. He did it the hard way, at night, and it took four or five years to do it. It shows his determination, how he sets a goal, keeps it in sight and gets it."

* * * * * *

I met Jerry for a few minutes the day we did the interview. We talked for a few minutes about the project and what I had in mind. He wanted to know a little bit about how some of the earlier interviews had gone to be sure he understood the parameters for his. We met the next day in the Winnipeg Jets' board room prior to a Jets-St. Louis Blues game. His story was given historically, stating the reasons for his decisions. His initial interview was almost complete. We spoke over the phone once afterwards to clarify a few factual things.

Jerry's interview is a good contrast to what most would expect from a player of that era. He had worked hard to get his education while playing hockey. It quickly became clear in the interview that the education was more important than the hockey. He tried pro hockey, got it out of his system, and went on with his engineering career. As part of the alternative group, Jerry's story is a good example of some- one who played pro hockey but turned away from it very quickly to pursue what he had always seen as his real career. And with no regret.

* * * * * *

Q. Would you talk about combining hockey and education while you were growing up in Winnipeg?

My parents are both of Ukranian descent, meager beginnings, my father being a shoemaker and my mother cleaning houses for people in or- der to make ends meet. The consequence of that was that both my brother and myself were put in a position that we had to look after ourselves as we went along. Primarily, the issue of get- ting ahead and doing well came from within as opposed to having everything handed to you. One of the things I got involved with early was sports and playing hockey. I played with the St. Boniface Canadiens throughout my junior ca- reer. At that time (late 1950's) there were four junior hockey clubs in Manitoba with three of them based in Winnipeg and one in Brandon. The total schedule for us was something like 35 to 40 games.

One of the fortunate things that happened to me was that I had gotten ahead of my age group in school by a couple of years. It turned out that while I was playing junior hockey I was at the University of Manitoba, taking engineer- ing. I was able to finish and graduate with an engineering degree the same year I finished playing junior hockey. I graduated at the age of 20. Our schedule was such that most of our games were played locally. Actually, hockey was an off-shoot of school. The hockey was a good outlet for me and allowed me to get completely away from the schoolwork at night. We would play one or two games a week and practice the other nights. It was always a two-fold thing in the sense that I had an opportunity to play and go to school at the same time, but the primary focus was the degree. I was able to graduate in 1960 and to go from there.

Don't misunderstand, once I got my engineering degree, to me I was the All-Canadian kid who wanted to play in the National Hockey League. But in terms of the focus, it was going to school and getting a degree. The impetus for education came from my family and our background. My parents couldn't afford to send me to school so one of the ways of getting to school was to play junior hockey. The St. Boniface Canadiens and the Winnipeg Braves were owned by the Winnipeg Warriors and the owner helped with my tuition fees.

Q. Was this a different path than most of your teammates were taking?

As I mentioned, I was a couple of years ahead of myself in school. While I was attending the university, most of my teammates were going to high school. Our outlooks were totally different. The hockey provided almost an opportunity to relax from the schoolwork. It allowed me to concentrate on school during the days and the same for hockey at night, and because I was so occupied with both it taught me not to waste any free time. I was still hoping, at the same time, that I had a hockey career ahead of me. At that point in time, once I finished my engineering degree, I was going to play in the National Hockey League.

Q. Did you find the people running your junior team open to your attending the university?

I think because three of the teams in the Manitoba Junior League were in Winnipeg and the fourth in Brandon, unlike today's junior leagues, the travel was minimal except during the playoffs. When we got to the playoffs, I ran into some problems. One year, when we were playing in Regina, they actually flew me in and out of Regina to play. They were supportive, if for no other reason than I was unique. There weren't many of us going to the university while I was playing.

Q. When you finished your education, what came next?

From the hockey view, I still wanted to play. Hockey was not easy, but, at least in terms of performance, I was one of the better players on the team. An example of this is that during the Memorial Cup Playoffs in 1957, the Winnipeg Braves had the opportunity to pick up players like Cliff Pennington, Vic Meisner and Red Berenson. They chose not to, but instead picked up players like Teddy Green and myself. This led me to think that the opportunity would be there for me to play hockey for a living.

There were six teams in the National Hockey League. The St. Boniface Canadiens belonged to the Montreal Canadiens. This meant my pro rights belonged to Montreal. Now, when I look back, my chances of playing for Montreal were slim. Nevertheless, I thought I had a real good chance to play. After I graduated, I decided that I would try it for a couple of years and see exactly where it would take me.

With that in mind, I went to the training camp of the Winnipeg Warriors and ended up being sent to Minneapolis. From Minneapolis, I ended up playing in St. Paul for Fred Shero. I was there for about a year and a half and it went reasonably well. But, from my perspective, I was able to see that all I ever would be was a journeyman hockey player as opposed to one of the three or four stars on any team. I realized where I would find myself in the hockey spectrum. The turning point came when I was traded to Indianapolis. What this meant was that I was getting traded from a first place hockey team to a last place hockey team which was in total disarray at that time. I decided to report, but my heart wasn't in it. I literally stopped there for a couple of days and decided I was going home.

Q. When you look back, how do you remember the time in the minors?

I loved the year-and-a-half of pro hockey. As a single kid, working towards a pro career was heaven. Somebody was paying me for something that I loved, namely playing pro hockey. But the bloom comes off the rose very quickly in terms of the travel. After a year-and-a-half I just had to make an assessment from my perspective whether or not I felt I was going to get ahead and get to the National Hockey League. And I concluded that if I did -- I didn't say that I was going to get there -- but if I did, I might be someone who might be there one day and then sent down the next day. I knew I would not be one of the key four or five players but would be one of the other 12 or 15 players. I decided, hey, did I really want that for the rest of my life?

Q. When you left Indianapolis, did you know what you would do next?

The International League, at that time, was made up of players who were finishing their careers and were, in my words, hanging on to make their last couple of bucks, and young fellows like myself, who were coming out of junior hockey. When I looked around the room, particularly at those toward the end of their careers making their last earnings in the game, I became very aware of the fact that I did have an option because of my education. I knew that I did not have to find myself in their situation some day. The result of this when I was traded to Indianapolis was that I took a good look at myself. When I did that, I said to hell with it. It's that time. I tried it for a couple of years. I decided it was time to put my engineering degree to work.

I came back to Winnipeg. The interesting thing is that, coming from playing hockey where the hours are not the 9-5 routine, there was a period of adjustment. What I mean is that when you played in the evenings, you didn't get settled until 2, 3 or 4 o'clock in the morning. You'd sleep to 11, the practices were around noon. When I came home, of course, none of that was reality and it took awhile to get in the situation where I would be up by 8 a.m. I left my name with the Association of Professional Engineers, which was kind of a storing house for what might be happening around town. One morning when I was sleeping at 11 in the morning, the phone kept ringing. My mother was away working. It was the Greater Winnipeg Gas Company looking for an engineer. Somebody had recognized my name from junior hockey and was calling. I went down to the office, went through all the various interviews and so on. I joined them in January, 1962, and have been with them ever since.

Q. What was your job at Greater Winnipeg Gas Company?

I began as an engineer in the construction and maintenance department. I learned a little bit about the business. After six months they moved me over to the sales department. I stayed there until 1966, got to know a little more about the business, and by 1966 I had moved into a supervisory capacity. Around that time the company had been taken over by Northern Ontario Natural Gas to form Northern and Central Gas. I was moved to Toronto in a sales supervisory capacity. I moved back to Winnipeg in 1968 and in 1970 I became the general sales manager. Then, in 1978, I was made vice-president of operations and I've been that ever since.

One of the things that is interesting to me when you say how did hockey affect this kind of thing, well, when I was playing hockey you did things on your own in terms of your individual style, effort, whatever, but always in concert with the team. It's interesting that that's the same kind of style you run into when you get involved with business. There are something like 250 people who report directly or indirectly to me. There are six to eight people who report directly to me. Even though each of them does his thing individually, it's to be part and parcel of the whole operation. It's important to be a team. Some of the things that you learn in terms of teamwork when you're playing hockey do, in fact, apply to business. Some of the individual things you do, whether it be stickhandling, shooting, or whatever, are the same kind of individual characteristics that you take forth in terms of your leadership in whatever you do.

Q. You have stayed with the same company since 1962. When did you realize you had a real future there?

I assumed the company has been happy with me. I've certainly been happy at it. I think, as one might say, the clicking has been there. It's interesting that I have spent so long with one company. There's no question that today young people are not likely to spend as long with one company.

I really don't know how long or when I realized I had a real future there. Let me answer that question this way: I enjoyed everything I ever did with the company and, as you learn playing sports, you want to do whatever you're doing to the best of your ability. So anything I was ever given to do by the organization, I did it in that context and I always felt, and still feel, that whatever I'm doing, if I do it to the best of my ability, somebody will notice. Whether it was three or four years before I noticed that I had a long-term future with the company, I really can't answer that.

Q. You completed an MBA in 1976. Why did you think this should be obtained?

I had spent some time as an engineer. My background was a technical one. I had spent 15 years in marketing and sales. I felt what I was missing was in the finance area. The best way of obtaining this was getting an MBA in finance. What I then saw myself as was someone who had training in all the areas that you use on a day-to-day basis. The time I spent combining school with work reminded me of my junior hockey days when I combined school with hockey. There is little time for anything else. This time period was difficult for my family.

Q. Looking back, how important do you think the decision to leave Indianapolis was?

Obviously, to me now it's made all my life since then. When I left I had tears in my eyes. Looking back now, I think it's the best thing that ever happened to me.

The times I spent playing hockey are prized in my life. However, for whatever reason back then, I felt that if I left my engineering degree sitting on the shelf for more than a couple of years, with things changing so quickly in the technology field, that maybe my degree would become dated. It was just a gut feeling. That's why I gave myself two years to try it. But, I wouldn't have missed it. I think that any time somebody has an opportunity to try pro hockey they should take it. Remember, I'm talking as an individual who had a degree by the time I tried it.

Q. How would you evaluate yourself today?

I'm pretty satisfied with myself as an individual. I have a wife and two children. My family life is ideal from my perspective. I've very pleased with the way the children have grown, very pleased with the kinds of things that they're doing and attempting to do. In terms of my role as a business person, I think I've enjoyed what I've done. I think I have the respect of the people who associate with me. I've enjoyed the community work that I have gotten into on a voluntary basis. I have been heavily involved as a volunteer with the health community in the city, spent a lot of time on it and enjoy it immensely. So, in terms of how do I feel or how would I evaluate myself, I think I've contributed to the community and I think that as long as one is satisfied with their family life first, and that they've added something to the community, hell, what more can you ask for?

Q. Has hockey been a major force in your life?

I don't think there's any question that hockey was a major force in my life. When I look back, hockey allowed me to get my education, directly and indirectly. Directly in the sense that some of my tuition fees were picked up by the owner of the hockey club. Indirectly in the sense that hockey allowed me to totally free up my mind from whatever it was that I was doing during the day. Hockey has taught me to be an individual, but also to be a team player. That was of major importance. And lastly, you can't live in the community of Winnipeg today without having hockey affect you. Whether you like it or not, it's a big part of the city.

How the team (Jets) does is important to how
people are feeling. I think in some ways this
community lives or dies with its hockey club. I
still play a little. I think you described it
well when you said, "For some, it's an addic-
tion."

**Q. If hockey has been important, then the edu-
cation you received has been as well. Did
the initiative to go to school come from
your parents?**

I was the first in my family who had an opportunity to go to school. My brother didn't
because of our financial inability. It was important to my parents that I receive an education. There are two points in my life that I
remember my father most vividly. The first was
the day I graduated and we had our convocation
at the University of Manitoba. To me it was,
I'm exaggerating, literally another day. But to
my father, it was the be-all and end-all and he
had a smile pasted on him from ear to ear that
one could never wipe off. To him, I guess, it
was the culmination of something that he could
see of his life. The second was that he attended only one hockey game of mine while he was
alive. It was the first Russian hockey team
that had come to Canada and they played a team
of junior all-stars in Winnipeg. I was fortunate to get picked to that team and he kept
hearing my name as he sat around in the section
he was sitting in. And that's the second time,
I'm told, in my life that he had a smile on him
from ear to ear. That was 1958 or '59.

I remember that game. The Winnipeg Arena
had 10,000 seats. They packed in something like
12,000 that day. It was the first time the arena ever had that many people in it. We lost 8-1
or 8-2. That was the first time I played
against the Russians. When you hit 'em, they
fell over. Two years later, they came back and
played the Winnipeg Maroons and I was playing

for the Maroons at that time. You hit 'em, they
didn't fall over. The following year, they came
back, you hit 'em, they hit you back. It was
upward and downward from there.

DON SALESKI

Don Saleski was born on November 10, 1949, in Regina, Saskatchewan. He grew up and attended school in Regina. His junior hockey was played with the Regina Pats of the Western Junior League. He joined the Philadelphia Flyers organization in 1969. His first two pro years were spent with the Quebec Aces of the American Hockey League. He played for the Richmond Robins of the AHL, another Flyers' farm team, during the 1971-72 season. He joined the Flyers in 1972 and played with them until being traded to the Colorado Rockies in 1978. While with the Flyers, Don won two Stanley Cups. He played with the Rockies until 1980, when he retired.

After his retirement, Don and his family returned to the Philadelphia area. His initial job was a sales position with ARA Services. He remained with them until 1986 when he moved to Spectacor Management. Recently, Don returned to ARA Services. Don, his wife, Mary Ann, and two children, Erika and Adam, live in Media, Pennsylvania.

* * * * * *

Bob Clarke, a Philly teammate who later became general manager of the Philadelphia Flyers:

"Don's a strong person, he always had an idea where he was heading and wanted to play in the NHL. The success he had was due to his willingness to work, to put an effort toward what he wanted and to just about do anything to achieve it. He's a bright person, a smart man which helped him in every way."

Ed Snider, owner of the Philadelphia Flyers and Spectacor Management:

"Don is an outstanding gentleman and a great family man. He made the transition

from hockey and moved to the business
world as well as any athlete I have known.
At ARA, he survived many major personnel
changes and prospered. He is now one of
their top executives. He has a bright
intellectual mind. His development has
been a wonderful thing to watch."

"His wife, Mary Ann, successfully operates the Seniors Golf Tournament, being
the only full-time employee. Together
they have made the adjustment exceptionally well. He still is involved in hockey and coaches a pee-wee team. This is a
well-rounded person."

* * * * * *

I met Don when he was traded to the Colorado Rockies during the 1978-79 season. He struck
me almost immediately as a bright, articulate
person with a mind of his own. He certainly did
not fit the image of the "Broad Street Bully,"
as he was often portrayed. We met to do the
interview at the Philadelphia Stadium Hilton the
afternoon of a Jets-Flyers game. He mentioned
just before we started that he did not like to
talk about his playing days. When I replied
that we could forget the interview, he replied,
"No, I want to do this, it's just that I want to
be known for what I am and not what I was, an
ex-Philadelphia Flyer." The interview went
well. Twice we stopped. The first time he
called his wife and asked her to take Adam to
practice. The second time, he called his assistant coach to tell him he would be a little late
for practice. The interview took longer than he
had anticipated. We talked on the phone a couple of times. He rewrote some parts of the interview to clarify parts he was uncomfortable
about.

The one thing that stands out for me with
Don's interview is his relationship with

reality. He appears to always do what he wants to and is cognizant of who he is, where he is and where he wants to go. This is reflected in his role on a winning hockey team, his decision to leave the game and his post-hockey choices and success.

* * * * * *

Q. How do you view your career?

Looking back at hockey, I have to say I was very fortunate to have the type of career that I had mainly because I played on a great team. We may have been closer as a team than any other in sports. The camaraderie on the Flyers was unparalleled. Our team spirit and the way we played and lived together was a great experience. So, I feel fortunate to be part of that. The Flyers were a great organization to be associated with. They treated each player well and we responded by winning two Stanley Cups. A lot of great players played in the NHL, had super careers, but never won the Cup. Reflecting back on your career, winning the Stanley Cup is something that you achieved which can never be taken away from you. As far as being a hockey player, obviously we obtained the ultimate.

Q. What kind of player were you?

I was a role-player who never achieved greatness as a goal-scorer or a playmaker, although I had three 20-goal seasons. My career had its ups and downs in Philadelphia. One year, the fans just about booed me out of the building. That year, I thought bulking up would help my play. I went from 208 to 228 with off-season weight training and thought it was going to make me a better hockey player. On the contrary, it slowed me down so much I couldn't keep up with anybody. So, I had a tough start that season and the fans got on me. It got to the point where Freddie Shero didn't even play

me in Philadelphia, he would only play me on the
road. That helped me work my way out of it.
After that, I enjoyed two more seasons with the
Flyers and most of the fans forgot about my
tough times.

Having a close team association was always
important to me. I don't believe that is much
different from what most of the guys believed
who played on the Flyers. Looking back, we had
some very good players but we didn't have a lot
of great players. There were a lot of guys similar to me, steady players not superstars, like
Dave Schultz, Bob Kelly, Orest Kindrachuk, Billy
Clement and Simon Nolet, Joe Watson, Jimmy Watson and Barry Ashbee and Ed Van Impe. The only
way we were going to win, and the way that we
won the Cups, was by playing together and being
a close-knit team.

Q. **When you speak of these players, one thinks
about the Flyers of the '70's. What about
the Flyers?**

The word "respect" comes to mind. We respected each other's roles and each other's
abilities. There was a real good feeling for
each other's shortcomings, strengths and weaknesses. That enabled us to play off each other.
Freddie had an uncanny ability to read individuals and he molded the team very well, playing to
everybody's strengths by putting individuals in
roles where they could benefit the team. He
never defined your role as a checker, penalty
killer, or as a protector. When the going got
tough, you were there. He never told Moose
Dupont or any other player he had to play tough,
it was understood.

There was a perception that we called the
"Goon Squad" or the "Broad Street Bullies." But
I never viewed myself as that. We were a
close-knit team that when there were problems on
the ice, we'd stick together, and if you fought
one Flyer, you fought everybody. People viewed

us as being bullies or goons for intimidating
and picking on other teams, but we never viewed
ourselves as such. I pictured myself as a
checker. Freddie used my line against big scoring lines of the other team. When you're playing against guys like Yvan Cournoyer and Jacques
Lemaire who are a lot faster than you are, had
more skills and were more talented, you had to
use whatever strengths you had to be able to
play against them. We were bigger, stronger,
and we had to hold, clutch and play physical to
stop them.

One of the problems I experienced in Colorado was similar to the problem that other guys
with the Flyers experienced when they were traded to other teams. People associated with other
teams viewed us differently. I was skilled at
my role and other Flyers also gave a specific
strength to the team. But, other people didn't
view us as role players. There was a perception
that we were more complete players than we really were, thereby expecting more out of us. They
expected us to be complete leaders for their
teams and looked for a greater contribution than
we really could provide. In Colorado, I felt
they were expecting more than what they got.
People looked at former Flyers and said, "Gee,
he did all this for Philadelphia." But, when
they took the Flyer out of Philadelphia, he
wasn't the same player.

**Q. Was the trade to Colorado your career low
point?**

Everybody says, "Was going to Colorado a
low point?" It was frustrating as hell, only
winning 15 games a year. It was tough playing
with guys who weren't used to winning and
weren't motivated the same way we were in
Philly. Everything was more individual. Players were only playing for themselves and a lot
of that was due to the lack of the team. There
really was very little team spirit. It was more

individual and everybody was worried about surviving the year.

However, at that point my my career, I was ready to be out of Philadelphia because I wasn't playing anymore. Pat Quinn had taken over the team as coach and was changing the team's style. With the new league rules, everything was moving away from the checking and the hitting and the fighting toward a faster style of play. Speed was a factor and they were just looking for a different type of team in Philadelphia. I wasn't happy, as a hockey player, not playing. To be happy, you've got to be playing. Sitting on the bench or sitting in the stands wasn't my idea of fun. So, I wanted to move. The Flyers accommodated my desire and traded me to Colorado. Colorado's a nice place to live. The team was terrible, but I enjoyed the city of Denver.

The low point in my career was not as much going to Colorado as it was playing the next year under Don Cherry. Cherry had come from Boston where he had a similar type of team as the Flyers. He had a lot of strong, tough players with good work ethics. Then he arrived in Colorado where he had a lot of misguided kids. They didn't have a lot of direction or confidence. Combining that with little talent was something Cherry couldn't handle. He didn't know how to deal with that team. He didn't know how to relate to those guys. He didn't know how to motivate them. He motivated them by intimidation. It wasn't so much the way he treated me, I felt terrible the way he treated the younger kids on the team. He'd take guys that were 20-21 and he'd throw things around the dressing room, rant and rave, call them yellow and chicken. The way he treated players was dehumanizing. Finally, in a game, I confronted him. We wound up having an argument. For my own good I should have known better than to confront a coach. I'd never said anything to a coach before, but we had an argument in front of the team between periods. I think that maybe I dressed for one or two more games after that and I would up going down to Fort Worth. In Fort Worth, at the time, we were in fourth place and all I wanted was to get that season over with and get back to Philadelphia. However, we wound up in the playoffs and went to the finals. I had another year, my option year, on my contract and being sent to Fort Worth, my decision was made. It was time to retire, option year or not.

Q. With the Fort Worth experience in mind, can you define your transition period?

Defining my transition is a little tough. When I was sent down to Fort Worth, in my mind, that was it. I wasn't going to go back and play my option year in Colorado and drag my family out from Philadelphia. I didn't want the situation of hoping we'd be in Colorado and then risk being sent down halfway through the season and be pulled back and forth between Colorado and Fort Worth. Also, I didn't want to play my last year of my career in the minors. What I viewed as a great career in the National Hockey League wasn't about to end by playing a season in Fort Worth, Texas.

Looking back at my whole career with the Flyers, I always felt that as a role-player and a fringe player, that I had to make the team every year. Each year I had to work just to stay there, and I was very fortunate to have played with the Flyers as long as I did. But also, understanding that, I knew that hockey could end at any time. Therefore, I went to Villanova in the off-season. I had a hockey school in Philadelphia. I also worked for a company called Anchor Container as a salesman. The purpose was to prepare myself for retirement. When I started playing, I hoped that I could play till I was 30. That was my goal, to make it to 30. You can never be fully prepared for leaving hockey.

But, I was conscious of it and always did something to prepare myself for the day of reckoning. The only regret I have is that I didn't finish my college degree. I sure would like to have it now.

When I was sent down to Fort Worth, I phoned my wife in Denver. I had already played a couple of games, and I said, "Mary Ann, that's it. I'm done. It's over." She said, "What, are you crazy? You've got your option year in your contract, you'd be giving up a lot of money." Later, I talked to Ed Snyder, the owner of the Flyers and a good personal friend. He said, "Don, you're crazy, why not just play another year?" I said, "Look, it's over, it's time to leave. The signals are there, I'm not going to play in the minors." After the playoffs, I came back to Philadelphia and started looking for a job that summer.

Not having any idea what I'd do, I started putting out feelers. I didn't want to sell insurance. It seemed like everybody who retires tries selling insurance at one time. It's not that I think selling insurance is a bad business, it's just something I didn't want to do. What I was looking for was an association with a major corporation so I could gain an understanding of business. I wanted to learn about management at a major corporation and develop an association with someone who would put me in sales, train me, help me prepare for my future.

There wasn't a lot of opportunity out there. However, after several meetings with ARA Services, they decided to take a shot with me. They hired me for a sales program, starting at $25,000 a year with a bonus plan. When I got my first check, I thought it was meal money for a road trip! This was the real world. You have a tendency to take your salary for granted when you're playing. It's a real shocker when you start looking for a job thinking you'll get one for $50-60,000. That's not the real world.

Once I accepted the position at $25,000 I
thought, "Holy shit, I can't even live on that!"
I realized I had to progress fairly quickly with
ARA. There wasn't enough money to live on, at
least, not enough to maintain the lifestyle I
was accustomed to as a pro athlete.

ARA put me in a training program, running a
vending route. I remember being out at Honey-
well Corporation in my first week. People
walked by, looking at me filling vending machines and saying, "Isn't that Don Saleski?" I
had to swallow a little pride, it was a very
humbling experience. I then worked in employee
cafeterias learning salad preps and stuff like
that, and finally made it into sales.

Q. How did you make out in sales?

I progressed very well in sales with ARA,
progressing from business to industry to the
health care group in my second year. My next
promotion was to the position of sales manager
responsible for selling food service contracts
for stadiums, arenas, racetracks, and convention
centers. I was back a little bit into the
sports environment dealing with people in the
entertainment field, something I enjoyed. I did
that for about a year. Our group reorganized
and added the airport group. I was promoted to
vice-president of operations with management responsibilities for ARA's airport and racetrack
division. This happened after three years with
ARA. I was on a fast track. Business associates couldn't believe how fast I was moving with
ARA. I had progressed from being a salesman in
business and industry to the number one salesman
in hospitals. The next year I sold $25 million
worth of business in leisure services and was
promoted into management, where I had been until
recently.

I believe there were three phases to the
transition. Initially, saying, "That's it, I'm
quitting," then, reflecting back, to filling

vending machines in my training program and saying, "Man, somehow I wish I could get back into hockey, be a coach, an assistant general manager or, do something in hockey because it's got to be better than this." But, finally, I established myself and became successful. The whole transition took about a year and a half.

Q. Would you describe your transition as rough or smooth?

It was not a matter of winning or losing. There was no way I was not going to succeed. Once I made the commitment, that I was retiring and going to work with ARA, my wife, Mary Ann, helped me through the tough times. I got very aggressive, applied myself and made the commitment to be successful. Once that commitment was made, it wasn't that rough.

I remember in the training program, doing the vending machine deal, I'd get up at 4 a.m. to go to the vending division. I'd be out on the road, going to the various locations. The other guys that ran the vending trucks were working toward their goal to finish by noon every day so they could go golfing in the afternoon. I'd finish by noon every day, but I was so god-damned tired, I went home and slept every afternoon. It was a tough experience.

There are always ups and downs. I look back at hockey, the report card was great, everyday after every game you could evaluate yourself, the coaches and fans let you know where you stood. In the business I'm involved in, you close possibly four or five deals a year. So, there was a long wait between report cards. It wasn't like playing 80 games a year where you can look toward a game within two days to redeem yourself.

Q. You believe yourself to be successful. What can you say about your second career?

One of the reasons I pursued a career with ARA was that with a large corporation I realized they could provide the training and support that's needed to become acclimated to the business world. I didn't anticipate being with ARA the rest of my life. I was focusing on what they could do for Don Saleski and my future more than anything. ARA did that and more through a lot of sales programs and, later, management development programs. In my last sales position, I had responsibility for the eastern half of the country to attain contracts to provide food services at federal parks, arenas, stadiums, racetracks, and other leisure type facilities. It was an enjoyable position dealing with 10-year contracts and high volume sales. The structure of the deals was very interesting, generally requiring significant capital outlays. I dealt with people who were at fairly high levels. It was an experience for me.

When the opportunity for reorganization of the airport came about, ARA decided to give me a shot as vice-president in charge of management of that group, which was a good opportunity for me. The total sales volume reporting to me was about $65 million. I was in charge of management of the food facilities at airports like Philadelphia, Houston, Boise and Fairbanks.

I had the responsibility to reorganize and divest a couple of accounts. My job was to take the group and reorganize it, get us out of a couple of bad deals and restructure the management and operations accounts.

Q. You recently decided to leave ARA. Why the change?

I've joined Spectacor as director of business development. It's a career change although the business parallels the service related

business I had been associated with at ARA.
With ARA my involvement was in managing in arenas, stages and racetracks and now I'm involved
in building management of those facilities. It
was time for Don Saleski's next move, something
new.

I evaluated my stature at ARA and I felt if
I got a promotion, my next step could get me a
15 percent raise. Other than that, I've got to
look forward to 4, 5 and 6 percent raises. I
was at a comfortable level. I could have said,
"I'm going to be content." But from a personal
standpoint, I wanted to grow and continue growing. I still want to encounter new challenges.

With that in mind, I started to look
around. Talks developed with Spectacor Management. Only 5 percent of the buildings in the
country are under management contracts. Most
buildings are managed by city or county govern-
ments. I viewed the potential for growth in the
public assembly management business as unlimit-
ed. It's an opportunity where I'll have the responsibility for the development of new business
and make a significant contribution to the development of the organization. Helping
Spectacor Management shape their future will be
very rewarding. From a personal standpoint,
what can I get out of it? I've got the sales
and management experience from the food business
and now I can expand my horizons to gain a working knowledge of building management. As far as
my future goes, when I put the food expertise
and the building management expertise together,
I all of a sudden become a very valuable commod-
ity to someone. Especially to myself.

Q. How do you evaluate your life after hockey?

I'm enjoying life after hockey. Part of it
is I've been relatively successful and I've enjoyed my careers. I have a lot of enthusiasm
and enjoy my successes. I'd never even dreamed
that there's any kind of downside or chance of

not succeeding in anything I did. Therefore, I have a lot of confidence in myself, and look forward to new opportunities. I believe that I've got a lot to accomplish in the future and I'm looking forward to it.

I view hockey now as -- it's gone, those days are behind me. It was like a stepping stone. It was part of my career. I was with ARA for six years, about the same time with the Flyers. Looking back, I have several accomplishments I'm proud of and have enjoyed. Now I'm just moving onto the next phase of my life.

The fact that I can look back at those Cups, we won them, as I stated earlier, nobody can take them away from you. In terms of self-confidence, playing at that level, being a professional athlete in any sport, is rewarding. And it is something you reflect back on with good memories. Like other former Flyers, I have all the plaques up in the family room, and I'm very proud of them. You don't go around bragging about great success, but they are something you value and are proud of.

Q. Your current satisfaction level is good. Did your off-season work experience help you?

After my third year with the Flyers, the first year we won the Cup, instead of working hockey schools, I worked for Anchor Container selling corrugated cardboard boxes. I wanted to get a taste of the business world to test what it was like out there. I enjoyed that summer. I was successful and that gave me confidence away from the hockey environment. You never know how you're going to do away from the rink. At the time I worked for Anchor, we were so successful in Philadelphia that hockey opened the door going into that business. I was well received at businesses I called on. However, I still had to pick up the phone, make those sales calls and meet with people. I had to learn the

product, tell the people about the product, what
the company had to offer and all that stuff.
Quickly, I found out that companies rarely do
business with an individual because he's a nice
guy. For me, being able to learn a business and
enjoy success at it during the summer gave me a
lot of confidence. I knew, "Hey, Don, when
hockey is over, you can do something else, even
if it is going back and selling corrugated cardboard," which was not necessarily something I
wanted to do.

**Q. Do you have any regrets on anything with
your playing and business career?**

The one thing that has always bothered me,
through my career, is that I don't have a college degree. Something I wished I had done is
played college hockey instead of playing junior
hockey. That's a regret, that I didn't play
college hockey, or when I was playing junior, go
to college. I observe guys playing now and I'd
like to help them. When you're playing, there's
time to address things for life after the sport
although most guys seem to think that the sport
will continue forever. Unfortunately, a lot of
athletes believe when it's over, their names are
going to help them get a job. That's totally
wrong. Now a lot of NHL players enter the
league at 18 and a lot of them are out of it
when they're 23. It's, "What are you going to
do with the rest of your life?" It's unfortunate that there's not more time spent by hockey
organizations working with these guys to help
prepare for the life after hockey.

(Note: Four months after Don's interview was
done, his former employer ARA approached him
with a new job position, and he returned to
ARA.)

Q. You recently returned to ARA. Would you talk about your decision?

I was happy at Spectacor and enthusiastic about my future there. However, I heard from John Dee, my former boss at ARA. He offered me the position of national vice president of sales in the business dining group. There are 65 salesmen and five vice-presidents nationally who report to me. The position was attractive. ARA is a large company with annual sales in the area of three and a half billion dollars. It had gone through a leveraged buyout a few years ago and became privately owned. They have a policy which issues stock to some of the executives. I was offered a sizable stock position. This was a major consideration. It is an opportunity that many people never receive. It was really too good an offer to refuse.

At Spectacor I was responsible for new business accounts. I realized I missed something that I had at ARA. The management of people was something I enjoyed and valued. I now have that responsibility. I enjoy working with people in the group, watching them develop and contribute. Leading the group is something I like. At a personal level, I am satisfied with the position and will be for quite a while.

GARY SMITH

Gary Smith was born on February 4, 1944, in Ottawa, Ontario. He grew up and attended school in the Ottawa area. At the age of 15, he went to St. Mike's in Toronto to play hockey and attend high school. He played with St. Mike's until 1963 when he moved over to the Toronto Marlboros. His pro career began with the Toronto Maple Leafs in 1964. Between 1964 and 1980 he played with the Maple Leafs, Oakland Seals, Chicago Blackhawks, Vancouver Canucks, Minnesota North Stars, Washington Capitals, Indianapolis Racers and Winnipeg Jets. These stops included several minor league teams in perhaps every minor league that existed during this time span. This itinerary earned him his nickname "Suitcase." The nickname his teammates called him, "Ax," referred to the way he handled his goal stick around his goal crease. As a player he was the good guys' good guy.

Following his retirement in 1980, Gary spent one year, the 1980-81 season, scouting for the Winnipeg Jets. Several jobs followed in the Phoenix area including his "dream" job, working at a racetrack. Following his divorce he moved back to the Ottawa area to live with his son, Marshall. His two daughters, Sunny and Chelsea, live in California with their mother. He works for the sheriff's office in Ottawa.

* * * * * *

Nick Beverly, a teammate with the Minnesota North Stars:

"I found Gary to be a great guy, a good team man. He was a happy-go-lucky type who at the same time, down under, really cared about what he did. In some ways, he was a typical goaltender -- a little off the wall, different. He was real good with young players. I remember he

spent a lot of time with Pete LoPresti
when he was a rookie helping him cope
with the pro game. Nothing seemed to
bother him; he seemed to enjoy life.
He definitely did it his way. I enjoyed
him and liked him as a person."

John Ferguson, Winnipeg Jets general manager:

"He was probably one of the most popular,
best-liked players by his teammates of
anyone who ever played the game that I
have been associated with. Maybe he
could have been one of the top goaltenders in hockey. His generosity toward
his teammates probably hurt him. One
year in Vancouver I believed he should
have received the Hart trophy as the
league's Most Valuable Player. He was
simply great all that year. When I picked
him up for Winnipeg in 1979 from Indianapolis I told him to get in shape. He
did and played admirably and we won the
Avco Cup. A very likable and good person, definitely a free spirit."

* * * * * *

I met Gary when I coached him in Tulsa during his last season as a player, 1979-80. I had
heard several Gary Smith stories and was to witness a few in person that year. There may be no
other player around who has as many stories told
about him as Ax. He remains a well-liked person
to everyone who has known him that I know. The
season following his retirement, 1980-81, we
worked together in the Winnipeg Jets organization. Between that time and when we did the interview, we had only run into each other once,
at a Team Canada-Soviet Union game in Ottawa.

We met at the Sheraton in Hull, Quebec, to
do the interview. It was tough getting away
from talking about the people we knew and

hockey, in general, to get down to the interview.

A quality about Ax has always been his honesty, both about himself and others. He was quite straightforward in the interview. As I expected he was honest, using a "This is the way it is" approach. The interview touches a lot of emotions. We were able to complete the interview with a phone call.

I was left with contrasting feelings after listening to his story. On the one hand, here was a person who did what he wanted to, pulled no punches, enjoyed his hockey career and lived a life that a lot of people would have wanted to. On the other hand, I found myself saying, "Come on Ax, it's time to get going." But, I knew this was a person who was realistic, who knew where he was and accepted it. There is something refreshing about him.

* * * * * *

Q. What kind of career did you have?

It seems a bit of a blur over the years. I ended up playing for 17 years in pro and it seems to me that it was almost like someone else that was playing. I really enjoyed it, especially the guys I met. On each team I would have three or four guys that I really would enjoy and get along with. During my whole career, I think that I found only three or four guys that I didn't really like. There are guys that I played with all my career that I figure are still good friends of mine who I seldom see, but I know they'd be there if I really needed them. I think and feel that any of these guys that I could help I certainly would. That's the way I view my career, as just the friends that I met.

I left home at an early age, 15 years old, and I can remember my dad taking me down to

Toronto and introducing me to a priest at St.
Mike's and the priest said, "What are you here
for?" I said, "I'm here to play hockey." And
as far as figuring it out, I wasn't there to go
to school, I was there to play hockey. I wasn't
sure why other people were there, but I certainly figured out why I was there. As far as going
to school was concerned, I didn't have much use
for it, which turns out now was unfortunate.

**Q. You got traded often and moved around a lot,
how do you feel about that?**

I thought moving around was a good part of
hockey. For some reason -- I don't know what it
was, maybe because I left home early -- I got to
enjoy moving around a lot. I think a lot of the
problems that I got into on different teams were
caused by myself because I wanted to go somewhere else. You know, they say the grass is always greener and I guess that's what I figured.
As far as being traded, I enjoyed being traded.
Usually when I was going to another place, it
was because I had enough of the place I just
came from, and I'm sure they'd had enough of me!
I enjoyed that part of hockey, I looked forward
to going somewhere else.

My first year in pro was with Toronto.
They had a lot of goalies. They had Johnny Bow-
er, Terry Sawchuck, Don Simmons, Gerry Cheevers
and Al Miller. So I had no way to break into
the lineup and I had to travel to where anybody
got hurt. I'd go there and get to see the country. Heck, for a guy from Ottawa getting to
places like San Francisco and Tulsa, I loved it.
You know, it was another way of life. It was
part of the game. It seemed to me the games
were sort of secondary compared to the lifestyle
you were living at the time. I felt I showed up
for the games, I know I did the best I could in
any of the games I played in. Although, being
the best I could was a little bit hampered by
several brutal hangovers.

Q. What kind of player were you?

Naturally, I'm going to think that I was a good player. When I got a good team in front of me, I think I played real well. I read Ken Dryden's book, <u>The Game</u>, which I really appreciated because I thought I saw a lot of the game through his eyes the same as I think I saw it. He described me as a good bad team goalie, where I could make some good saves, keep a team in a game, maybe steal the odd game that we didn't deserve to win. I never was successful on a real good team. I played in Chicago when we had a hell of a team with Tony Esposito, I played well but he certainly played better. In talking with Tony, who I really respected, I sort of got the impression that that was pretty well what I was. I could play well on a bad team. In a lot of cases, it's tough to play really well on a good team. But I think I improved a lot of teams I went to, so I think I was a good player. I probably wasn't as dedicated as I should have been, but that's me. I was having a good time while I was doing it.

Q. Were you not the goalie for the Winnipeg Jets one year when they won the Avco Cup (1979)?

That was sort of a unique situation. I came there late in the season. They gave me a shot, let me get in shape. I only played three games before the end of the season and then I played in the playoffs. It was exactly the same time Lars-Erik Sjoberg was coming back from an injury, he hadn't played all year. And we had a good team there for the WHA. I went from not being able to play in the NHL at all to being able to play in the WHA. However, it was a quick type of thing where I just played the playoffs. The next year they went to the NHL and again I found I couldn't play in the NHL. My impression of the WHA because of this was that it was an inferior league.

Q. What did you achieve as a player?

As far as hockey was concerned, we won the Vezina Trophy in Chicago. In Vancouver, we went from a last-place team to a first-place team in one year. In Winnipeg we won the Avco Cup. We won the Memorial Cup at St. Mike's, but that was a long time ago. I think I achieved not having to work for 20 years. I never considered hockey as work. I don't know if I was the all-time greatest goalie, but I helped anyone I shared goaltending with. If he wanted to play, he was very welcome. I was happy not to play. And these are just things that are part of my personality. Not that I'm not proud of them, but I wish that I had done some things a little differently. I was happy, I wish that I did have a little more ambition, even now in my life, to try to achieve better things. But I don't, and it's up to me to get her going.

Q. How about high or low points and good and bad memories?

Looking back, a high point was when I got drafted by Oakland in the original expansion draft to go to the NHL. To go to a new place that I knew nothing about was great. Then four years later, I wanted to get out of there and it was a high point for me to go to Chicago. A low point would be when my career was over. The first time was when Indianapolis folded. I had to go out and get a job. I didn't know what to do, so I went home and hung around for three or four months. I got lucky enough to come back with Winnipeg. Another low point was when I was in Washington and Max McNab sent me down to Hershey for two weeks in the minor leagues. First time I'd been in the minors in 12 years or so.

And I always regretted I never scored a goal. As a goaltender, I was never happy until the game was over so I never had the immediate

high you get scoring a goal. Being a goalie,
the game is over, you've won or you've lost.
You're happy when you won, and you're unhappy
when you lost so you go out and get hammered.
But never having scored a goal, and never having
hit a home run in baseball, never had a fence to
hit it over, are two things I missed out on.

I got one chance to score. I played forward in one game. I was in Tulsa and it was my
last year as a player (1979-80). We were short
players because of injuries but had three goalies. I dressed and played forward one shift.
It was one of the highlights of my career. I
remember talking to Larry Sacharuk after the
game. I had bumped him and the Birmingham
coach, John Brophy, had said to him, "What do
you mean letting that guy run you?" Sacharuk
replied, "What are you talking about? He played
12 years in the NHL." But, I didn't score.

The way I view my career is that I never
really got screwed, I don't think. I run every
day now with my brother Brian and he's saying
Eddie Shore did this and Wren Blair did that. I
was fortunate never to meet guys like that. I
was with guys that I think treated me fair and
whatever I deserved, I got. I did it myself.

I would say bad memories, maybe a couple of
injuries. Practices were bad memories. Guys
shooting at your head all the time. I can remember a few of the shots. One that stands out
in my memory was in Winnipeg. We were practicing the power play and the puck went back to
Barry Long who was moving in. It was coming
right at my head. If it ever nailed me, I was
dead! I can remember Yvon Cournoyer one time in
Montreal banging one off the glass that just
missed my head. So, those are bad memories. I
almost got killed. I was scared of the puck!
Of course, I think pretty well everyone is.

Q. Can you define your transition in terms of time?

I worked as a scout for the Jets for a year, my first out of hockey. I see that year as being still in hockey. I thought the scouting was great. I didn't have much to do living in Phoenix. But I enjoyed it and enjoyed seeing it from the other level. I was a little surprised at some of the things that happen. Here I was going to training camps for years, trying to make the team, and most of the years I pretty well had the team made when I was going to them. Scouting, I realized that the team was pretty well picked before camp except for maybe a couple of spots. But, back to the transition. For some reason, I always thought that I was going to get back into hockey. Now, I have no wish to get into hockey at all. I work at hockey schools during the summer so I can make some money and I just dread the time on the ice, I hate being on the ice. However, I don't mind working with the goaltenders. I think the game is simpler now that I'm not playing it anymore. I would like to think my transition period started after I was released from scouting with the Jets and I figured, "What the hell am I going to do?" You know, "I'm finished with hockey, what I am going to do?" Since then, I've had several jobs, moved from Arizona back to Ottawa and went through a divorce.

I got gassed from Winnipeg in July 1981 and I was hoping to maybe get a job in hockey for about a year. Maybe by 1984 I was happy not to be in hockey. Now I like to watch hockey as a fan. During that period, I was in Phoenix. I worked as a bartender in a hotel for awhile. Nice, classy hotel. I hated that job. You had guys telling you, "Clean up the ashtray," and I ended up getting a jerk for a boss and I quit it after awhile. I then got the greatest job I ever had, working at a racetrack in Phoenix. I was working for a newspaper out of New York

called <u>Sports Eye</u>. The only trouble was that
the job paid $400 a week and I used to lose
$600-700 a week at the track. But it was a
great job because it's where I wanted to be and
I just loved it. And I didn't get any aggrava-
tion from my wife because I was at work. So, it
was a job where I had to be at work by 1 p.m.
and I was there at 6 a.m. because I loved it so
much.

Q. Did being a former player help you at all?

It's surprising living in a place like
Phoenix, but the job I got at the track was the
result of being a hockey player. It just happened there was an ad in the paper for this job.
I was always looking at the ads in the paper for
a job. So when I saw this ad, I called up this
guy, John McGourty, who was back in Boston.
Turned out the guy was a hockey fan from Boston.
So he may have had 20 or 100 applications for
this job, I don't know how many he had, but we
just talked hockey when I called him and he
said, "Okay, you've got the job."

Q. How would you characterize your transition?

It was rough, because you've got to get a
job. For a year I had the shitty job as a bartender which I hated, so it was rough. I didn't
miss playing the game. I was glad there weren't
any more games. I still dream about playing
hockey now, all the time. My dreams are mostly
that I'm with a good team, lately with Montreal
and Chicago. I can't get my stuff, my gear, on.
I can't get up there to get on the ice, and
they're going to put another guy in the net. I
keep taking my stuff off and trying to put it
back on. I'm not sure what the dreams mean.

Q. Is there anything you might do differently a second time?

I would've seen my transition coming. Know that I was going to play a couple of more years and try to get involved in something. So if I would have done anything to make the transition I would have, maybe when I was in Winnipeg, tried to get into broadcasting, talked to someone like Ken Nicolson. Certainly, everyone should try to plan for when it (the hockey career) is over. I think the kids are smarter today and they will end up preparing for it. So that's what I would do differently, prepare for it. Because after you're finished, then you've got to get a job and I didn't realize that. There's a lot I didn't realize.

Q. What can you say about your life after hockey?

Well, I'm divorced. I think that my wife had a tougher time adjusting to being out of hockey than I did. When I was playing, we would move to a new city every three or four years. Once out of hockey, we had to settle down, and she got into the mainstream of things and she enjoyed it. She got to go to lunches and stuff like that and she ended up getting a boyfriend. I was happy in Phoenix. I didn't have any problem with alcohol or drugs or anything like that. My problem with alcohol was the same problem I always had with alcohol. I enjoyed getting hammered, but I don't think it was a real problem. So, she gassed me and the divorce came about. I was happy with my life, I loved my jobs. My kids were a couple of blocks from school and she was screwing it up. The marriage was over and I had to get out of there before I did something I would regret later. What this has to do with hockey is I think she had more trouble adjusting to not making big money -- not real big money but, you know, $70,000 or $100,000 -- than I did. She had to go out and get the things she

was used to and get a job and by that it caused
her to be unhappy with me. I figure she had
more trouble adjusting to life after hockey than
I did.

Q. What are you doing now for a job?

Now, I'm working for the sheriff's office
in Ottawa. It's hockey player's hours, a couple
of hours a day, which I enjoy. I deliver war-
rants, bailiffs, subpoenas and so forth. I go
in at 9 a.m. and I get my stuff that I have to
do. I usually make one run at the people I have
to get in the morning and, if they're there, I
give it to them and if they're not, I go back at
night. They offered me a job inside to go along
with this job where I can make another $300 a
week, but so far I've chosen not to. Mainly because I'm not sure I want to stay in Ottawa. I
think I might want to go back to the States. I
miss my daughters. I have my son, Marshall, and
my wife has my two daughters. They're with her
in California. I'd kind of like to go back to
Phoenix where I'd be able to get to see them.

I hit rock bottom after the divorce. When
the divorce went through, I went with my job up
to the track in Santa Fe, New Mexico. Great
spot. I was up there by myself and I was missing my kids too much. I could have gone back to
Phoenix, but I knew it was going to be aggrava-
tion there with my ex-wife. At that point, I
just hated anything she had to do with. So, I
said I've got to get out of there and I came
back to Ottawa.

I came back to Ottawa for a race at the
track which was named after my dad, "The Des
Smith Classic." It's the biggest race all year
in Ottawa. I was planning on going back to
Phoenix. When I was here, I talked to my brother about my situation, well, he and my mother
were wondering about it. He said, "Well, why
don't you stay here? We know you can get a job
around here." Brian got me a job at a radio

station for awhile, and that was pretty good. I
enjoyed that, but they didn't have the funds for
a second sports guy, so the work was only on and
off. Then, I had a job in printing, selling
printing, and I couldn't sell printing, I'm not
a salesman. To try to sell something that someone may or may not need, I had trouble with
that. So I got this job with the sheriff's office. He was a friend of my brother's and
they've helped me a lot that way. Plus, I'm
staying at my mother's. It doesn't cost me anything for rent, 42-year-old guy staying at home.
It's tough trying to get some girls in, you
know, but you just have to find somebody with an
apartment.

I had to declare bankruptcy when I moved
back to Ottawa. I had made a bad investment in
a film-making project back in 1972. I had taken
several deductions on my income taxes from
1972-75. But, as I found out later, the film
was never finished so I wasn't eligible for the
deductions. The government came after me in
1976 to pay the taxes on the deductions. By
that time I was back in the States. To make a
long story short, I still owed the government
money when I came back and I didn't have it. I
applied for bankruptcy and the government wiped
the slate clean and I started over. It was a
bad investment. I probably would have blown it
at the track anyways, although I would have had
a better time doing it.

Then my son came. The reason Marshall came
here was he was playing with the car of a friend
of my ex-wife. He was like 12 years old. He
turned on the car, didn't know what he was doing
and it hopped through the garage and wrecked the
car, wrecked the garage. So she called me and
said, "I can't take care of him," so he's with
me and I really enjoy him. My son has been a
big help for me getting through the transition.
That's why I was going crazy when I first left.
She had the kids. When I went through the
divorce, my lawyer said, "No matter what she's

done, it doesn't matter if she left the family, it doesn't matter if she didn't see the kids for two months, if she wants them, she'll get them." So, I miss my kids and without my son I know I'd be crazy today. But I have him and that's helped me through it.

Marshall was born with spina bifida. At birth, the back of his spine didn't close. There was about a one-inch opening. The spinal fluid leaked out. They did an operation right away to correct it. He was lucky because he is more functional than most. Most kids need a wheelchair to get around because of their problem. Marshall simply does not have good balance. So, if my wife doesn't want him around, it's okay with me. He's a big help to me.

Q. How do you evaluate your life today?

I don't know about putting up with another winter. I got spoiled when I played hockey in places like Oakland, Vancouver, Tulsa and then living in Phoenix. I remember when I was playing in Minnesota, after a game that I had a shutout in, I was trying to renegotiate for the next year and I said I was thinking about going for free agency, which I did. Didn't find too many takers. My comment in the paper was, "Why do I have to put up with 40 shots every game and 40 degrees below zero every night? I'll go somewhere different."

I could go back to the track in Phoenix. A good job, but the problem would be gambling. You know, if I lost more than I made, that would be a problem. In the long run, it's probably not a good situation to be in. But, I usually don't think about the long run. I think I'm the type of guy who thinks that maybe I'm going to win the lottery or something like that. And until I face that fact that I'm not going to win a lottery, then that will be reality.

Q. You mentioned that you now enjoy hockey as a fan. How do you feel about having played hockey professionally?

I think hockey was great. I think I was fortunate to play hockey. Most people who were interested in hockey would have given their left arm to play in the NHL. I just think that hockey has given me a good life up to this point. The travel, you meet a lot of great guys and have a lot of good times. But I never really enjoyed playing that much, it was just the life that I led. I probably should have been a jockey, then I would have really enjoyed my life. I just love the horses. I do like to bet, but I don't play cards or anything like that. I just like to bet on the horses and I know I'd be better off if I never went to a racetrack, but I enjoy doing that, and by playing hockey I got to go to a lot of racetracks in North America.

Fr. Les Costello, 1959

Gary Dornhoefer, 1972

Ron Ellis, 1987

Ted Irvine, 1976

Gerry Hart, 1982   Joe Cavanaugh, 1984

Glenn Hall, 1960   Don Saleski, 1973

Mark and Courtney Heaslip, 1987

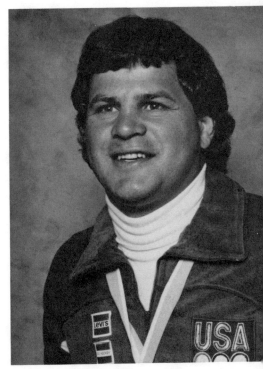

Mike Eruzione, 1980

Roger Bourbonnais, 1967

Gary Smith, 1965

 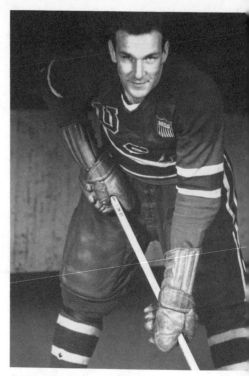

Connie Broden, 1986　　John Mayasich, 1960

Tom Williams, 1983

Cesare Maniago, 1977

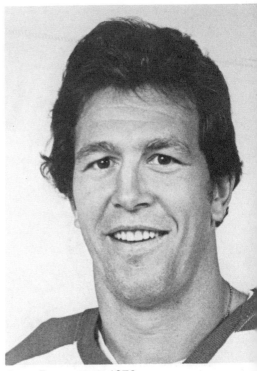

Jean Pronovost, 1978

Ulf Nilsson, 1986

Jerry Kruk, 1985

Henri Richard, 1979   Morris Mott, 1986

Dickie Moore, 1986

JOHN MAYASICH

John Mayasich was born on May 22, 1933, in Eveleth, Minnesota. He grew up and attended school in Eveleth. He attended the University of Minnesota, graduating in 1955. Following graduation, he enlisted in the United States Army for two years. During this period, he played for the 1956 U.S. Olympic team that won the Silver Medal. Upon his release from the Army, he initially took a job with KSTP radio station in the Twin Cities, thinking his hockey career was over. In November, 1959, he was approached by the Green Bay Bobcats of the United States League to play for them. He remained in Green Bay, Wisconsin, until 1974. He held several positions with the team besides being a player, such as coach, general manager, and sales manager. During his years in Green Bay, he played on several national teams, nine during his entire career, and was captain of the 1960 U.S. Olympic team that won the Gold Medal. As a player, he achieved probably every honor possible for an American, from being selected an All-American to recently being named to the United States National High School Sports Hall of Fame.

While in Green Bay, he also taught high school for a short period of time and sold encyclopedias for a year-and-a-half. In 1974, he returned to the Twin Cities to work at the KSTP-FM radio station. He is currently president of the radio division of Hubbard Communications. He and his wife, Carol, have raised three boys, Michael, Patrick and Daniel. He and his family live in Stillwater, a small town 10 miles east of the Twin cities.

* * * * * *

Dave Peterson, the 1988 U.S. Olympic hockey coach:

"He is probably the best American hockey player I have ever seen. He was one of

those players who was able to dominate
the play and set the tone of a game.
There have never been many players who
could do that. John is a hard-working
and industrious person and it is evident
in the way he conducts himself. He handles everything in a very low key business manner without a lot of hoopla."

Stan Hubbard, president of Hubbard Communications:

"We were roommates at the university and
there were four things I learned about
John quickly and they still hold true.
One, he is a very bright person; two, he
is a gentleman; three, he is a hard-working and fair-minded person in all phases
of his life; and, four, he is a winner.
He hasn't changed a bit since 1952 when
we first met. He is a straightforward
and tough competitor who always wins, but
he does it within the rules. His success
in business is the same as it was in
sports. He always finds the way to win
and be successful."

* * * * * *

I met John Mayasich once prior to our interview. It was after a Minnesota North
Stars-Soviet Union game at Met Center. I remember saying to myself while we were talking about
the game that we shared similar opinions of the
game and players. It pleased me that this great
player had a solid understanding of the funda-
mentals of the game. We met in his office at
Hubbard Communications to do the interview. We
met a second time a month later to finalize the
interview. He took time to clarify his statements.

There are a couple of things that stand out
about John's interview. It is the story of an
American player who was in his playing prime

during an era that did not include Americans in
the pro game. Yet, he had a great playing career. But because he knew when entering college
that his future was not with hockey alone, he
took a serious approach to school. Today he is
as respected in his field of communications as
he was as a player. Hopefully, players of today
and tomorrow can be so lucky. He has always
recognized the pressure: for his teams to win,
to do well himself, to get to college, to graduate, and pressure with his current job. It is a
story of living with what one perceives as pressure and succeeding.

* * * * * *

**Q. Do you have any thoughts on the role hockey
played coming out of the Iron Range?**

As far as career and occupation and how it
relates to hockey, I'd say in my era, and for a
lot of us who played hockey up on the Iron
Range, hockey opened doors to opportunity. A
hockey player with academic prowess had opportunities others didn't enjoy. And when a college
scholarship was offered to you, it was assumed
by everyone you would accept. If you said, "No,
I don't want to go to college, I want to work in
the mines and get married," you'd have been
called crazy. This environment was established
by your community, coaches, teachers, and peers.
It was never a question, "Is this what I want?"
But again, it was an opportunity I could not afford to turn down.

My first full-time summer job where I
earned decent money was on the railroad track
gang during the summer of 1951. My father
worked in the mines for 45 years. Pressures and
expectations during my college career at the
University of Minnesota from 1951 to 1955 were
extremely high. Everyone expected me to score a
couple of goals every game and do well academically. You had that pressure not only from the

student body, coaches, fellow players and fans, but also from friends and fans who followed your progress back home. The expectations grew every year. I was the type who said, "To have a good season this year, I have to do better than I did last year." I worked at it and it sort of worked out that way, too. Yes, it was fun, the practices and scrimmages, but there was still the pressure of the game and to maybe exceed the expectations others had of you. However, I had no pressure from my parents. They had never seen me play as a youth, high school, college or Olympic hockey game. My aspirations as a youth were not to play pro hockey. It was high school, college and the Olympics, in that order. It was to get married, maybe teach, and thank God for all the opportunities the sport of hockey had bestowed on me.

Q. Did you ever have an opportunity for a pro career?

A big question still today is, "Why didn't you turn pro?" Back then, it wasn't a case of pro teams coming to you and signing you. John Mariucci told me later on he got inquiries from, I think, the Red Wings and the Black Hawks and that they had an interest in me. But, John, of course, was coaching the Olympic team the next year (1956) so he didn't come to me and say, "This is an opportunity, do you want to go to their camp and try out?" That never happened. I also had a U.S. Army obligation that negatively affected any chance of trying the pros. I didn't really have a concrete written offer. When the '56 Olympics were behind me, I still had a year and a half remaining in the service. Besides, I had a degree and a family. Pro hockey wasn't foremost in my mind. Remember, there were only six National League teams in the '50's. Of course, looking back now, I still wonder if I had had an opportunity would I have made it and how might I have performed?

Q. Did you have any goals in hockey after college?

My number one priority was to play on the 1956 Olympic team which was the year following my graduation from the University of Minnesota. I again wanted to play for John Mariucci. It was to be, I thought, a once in a lifetime experience. As a member of the 1956 Silver Medal Olympic team, coming real close to the Gold, being able to travel throughout Europe and cultivate lifetime friends, it turned out great. An unforgettable experience. I think one of my high points in hockey, as far as individual accomplishments are concerned, was scoring three goals against Canada in a victory, 4-1, a great team effort. It was one of Maroosh's coaching gems, extremely satisfying to him.

My two-year stint in the Army provided me with ample time to play and improve my game of hockey. Travel opportunities throughout Europe in 1955-57 as well as playing against the world's best prepared me for a hockey-related future. During my military term, I was married and had a family. When I was through with those 21 months, I didn't say, "Well, I'll give pro hockey a try." I had a degree and it was time to start a non-hockey career. I came to Hubbard Broadcasting Radio as a sales trainee in 1957. I really felt hockey was only a memory of the past. I was a member of a hockey club at KSTP. Paulie Johnson, a 1960 Gold Medal teammate, played, and Lefty Smith, who later went to Notre Dame to coach, was playing, as well as other players from the Minnesota area. During that period, I never thought seriously about ever playing again. An opportunity in TV sales and an offer to play and coach in Green Bay interrupted the non-hockey profession.

Q. What about the 1960 Olympics?

I left St. Paul in 1958 to go to Green Bay. I knew then that I would be back in hockey. I was able, from a job prospective, to pursue sales in the broadcast business as well as coach and still play a sport I really enjoyed. What a great experience for me and my family in Green Bay. I was involved in a quality senior hockey program. I was involved in expanding the youth program. The second year I was the player-coach and general manager of the Green Bay Bobcats. I was involved in the sale of tickets and program ads plus the recruiting of players. The Packer fans were great Bobcat fans. I enjoyed the experience of selling and playing the game of hockey. I was doing something that, if hockey was dropped right then and there, I still had something to fall back on. I would still have that job training and sales background.

In 1960 I was playing with the Green Bay Bobcats and I had a heavy schedule commitment there. Jack Riley brought the 1960 team into Green Bay and we played them and beat them. I think after the game he inquired if I'd be available or if I could come after our U.S. League was completed. I joined them out at Squaw Valley probably a day before the tournament started but I had played previously with most of the players on the team. I went directly from Rochester (Minnesota) after our last league game to Squaw Valley. It was another unexpected, unbelievable experience. I look back at the 1960 Gold Medal performance, I was away from home about a week and we won it on a Sunday morning, and Sunday afternoon I returned to Green Bay like nothing happened. A great reception at the Green Bay airport made me realize that the whole U.S.A. was a part of this unprecedented achievement in hockey. Monday morning I was back on the job in TV sales. We never had a team get-together after the game. How times have changed with the pro offers and endorsement opportunities for Olympian participants of the present.

You look at the number of kids playing today, you can almost say the Gold Medal victory
in '60 really excited parents and youths. Some
of those parents' kids were to play on the '80
team, the Gold Medal winner. What happened
there just kept mushrooming and aided in the development of the American kids that are playing
today. Little did we realize the impact the
1960 Olympic games would have on the future rise
in the interest and participation of youth hockey throughout the U.S.

Q. Any low points in your hockey career?

I had a low point in Green Bay after I was
through playing. It came down to really what
did I want to do. I taught school part-time for
a year. This was in 1972. I taught four hours
a day and got part-time pay but it was a great
experience. I then went into the encyclopedia
sales business which worked out very good. However, I didn't really want to pursue that line
of work for the rest of my life. I look back
now and say it was a very valuable sales experience.

Almost every hockey player runs into this.
Once you're through playing hockey or your services are no longer in demand, it's difficult.
I knew no one was going to come along and say,
"I got a hell of a deal for you in radio sales
and we want you to coach the Toledo team." So,
I was saying to myself, "What's out there?
What's available on the basis of what I could
contribute and what are my skills for a particular job?" I think that's what every player, re-
gardless if it is in pro or semi-pro, goes
through. You're saying, "Now where do I go and
what do I do?"

Q. How did you end up back in the Twin Cities and at the same station, KSTP, that you worked at before moving to Green Bay?

Stan Hubbard, president and chief executive officer of Hubbard Communications, came to me in 1974 and said, "I have an opportunity for you in radio if you wish to come back to Minnesota." Here was a former teammate of mine at the University of Minnesota, a generous person, my former employer, contacting me for the second time with an offer. Stan is the one person responsible for what I am doing and where I am today. Hopefully, our present success at KSTP-FM and my involvement with that success is my saying, "Thanks for the opportunity, Stan."

Q. Did you ever get to a point where you had the same feeling of confidence in the radio business that you had in hockey?

No, I don't think so. In hockey, I was on the ice and it's what I did on the ice that contributed to the team's performance. Others contributed also. Teamwork was the key. In radio, I was not an on-air talent, not directly involved in on-air banter with the listener. I have to depend more on others. We have talented people on the air. They are the performers, the professionals. We have an ambitious sales department out selling. I, and the rest, are support troops. What the others contribute determines where I go and how successful I am. We have four rating periods a year. It's competitive. The Olympics happens every four years. Here in this type of job or any job, really, it's the day-to-day performance. But, I'm saying I don't have the same confidence in my total knowledge of the broadcast business industry as I might have had with hockey when I was playing. I learn every day. Winning is great in this business. Our team at KSTP is performing well. Every radio station is competing with us daily for the listening public. Promotions,

marketing, research, ideas, egos, they are all
daily concerns. There are no practice days.
Every day is like a game, the real thing.

Q. Has hockey helped you in your business career?

Definitely, job opportunities resulted directly from business contacts made through my
involvement with the sport of hockey. I would
also say my graduation from college, having that
degree, particularly affected my being considered for available employment. I would assume
my work ethics on the ice also were factored in
toward my total job qualifications. Teamwork,
the winning attitude, morale builder, empathy,
loyalty, trust, and pride, are some of the
things that were positive carry-overs to business. They are important work ingredients in my
present environment. Hopefully, these winning
elements are contributing to our present position of being number one in the Twin Cities FM
radio market and number two overall. We play to
win every day.

Q. Do you have a good feeling of satisfaction in your professional life?

The good feeling is knowing you are contributing more than the maximum toward a winning
and rewarding effort. Everyone on the team has
to be of the same mold. I grade myself daily.
Some day I hope to look back and say I, and my
fellow workers, have made this property more
valuable than it was prior to our being involved. Again, we're after the gold medal,
first place, every day. Where we are in the
market place, in the standing, is on my mind 24
hours a day. How the team as a group in totali-
ty performs greatly affects my feelings of satisfaction. You might not believe this but I
have more pride and satisfaction as part of the
Number One FM station here than I have in winning the Gold and Silver Medal in the Olympics.

Playing hockey was easy for me compared to the
daily demands of the radio business. For me,
total satisfaction someday will be presenting to
Mr. Hubbard the radio properties he has entrust-
ed me with that have increased in value tenfold.
A thank you, a pat on the back, a job well done,
an acknowledgement from Stan Hubbbard will then
be total satisfaction for me.

Q. Do you have good memories from playing?

The question most frequently asked to me
is, "What is your biggest thrill in hockey?"
And yes, I mention the Gold Medal in '60, the
Silver Medal in '56, success of the University
of Minnesota, the league championships in Green
Bay, the Minnesota High School Tournaments with
Eveleth. But, where did I really enjoy the
sport and when did I really have fun? It would
have to be from the time when I first played the
sport on the outdoor rink when we just picked
sides and had one puck with maybe 10 or 30
players. It was being able to pick up the
various skills of hockey just on the basis of
playing outdoors for two, three hours a day and
seeing you're improvement with the skating,
stickhandling, shooting and passing skills. And
looking ahead with the intent that, "Boy, I want
to be on the high school team some day and be as
good as Johnny Matchefts or a Wally Grant or a
Neal Ceilly or a Pat Finegan." This was my
dream as a youngster in hockey. I also enjoyed
playing pick up basketball in the gym as much as
playing the sport of hockey back then. Or
playing a touch football game out on the street.
This to me was as much fun as playing organized
hockey on a team like the Olympics.

**Q. Are you saying, for you, the fun was simply
playing the sport?**

I am saying that playing the sport where
you didn't have people in the stands, you didn't
have parents there, just competing with neigh-

borhood kids or kids from your hometown and doing your best and saying, boy, I'm having fun and I'll probably have a chance to make the high school football, baseball or hockey team was fun. The shared experiences, the travel, the friendships on formal teams was also fun.

Q. You coached youth hockey for over 20 years in Green Bay and the St. Croix area. With that in mind, do you have any thoughts on how much youth hockey has changed?

When I was growing up, youth hockey was playing with the neighborhood kids, all ages, no coaches, no parents pressuring their children to succeed. Winning or losing was not the important thing. Playing, having fun, emulating your high school heroes, that was youth hockey. Your priority was to make the high school team. Today, I feel parental pressures are excessive. To play the game well, score goals, stress individual performance and to win are emphasized. Coaches who never played the game are now playing the game through the kids on the team. Emphasis is on winning. There is less emphasis on improving skills, having practice at the expense of competitive game experience. If I were growing up today in a similar economic situation of the 1930's and 1940's, I could not afford to play. My parents would not be able to finance my participation. There weren't as many kids playing as today. We didn't have as many external factors that kept us from going outdoors and playing. And we didn't have the parental pressures, the coaching pressures, the winning pressures that the young kids have today. We would play a pick up game and if we lost 20-1, the game was over. And the next time if you were on the right team, you'd probably win 20-1.

There were other things that I think back on and say, "Boy, what pressure we had." Living in a community like Eveleth where it was expected if you had any ability in hockey and

scholastically you could pass the college en-
trance exams and be admitted, then you were going to go to some college or university. It was
really the pressures of the community, your family and yourself that made you feel that this
was what you had to do. The point I'm making is
that maybe I personally didn't want to do that,
but there wasn't a choice. This is what I had
to do and when I went to the university I had to
do well, not only on the ice but in the class-
room. I dreaded if I ever flunked out and had
to go home with people thinking, "Here's the one
you thought was going to do so well."

Q. Anything else you want to say here?

I sometimes sympathize with today's youth
who are involved in sports. I sympathize with
parents who placed too much priority and importance on how their child performs on the field
of sport rather than in school or church or community activities or general recreational activities. There are so many things that are much
more important, be it education or learning to
play the piano or maybe get involved in a sport
that you can do recreationally the rest of your
life. I look at the teenager today and wonder
what's going through his mind, what if he
doesn't make the high school team? Really, what
is the big deal?

The point I'm trying to make here is that
if you don't play pro hockey, so what? If your
kid doesn't play high school hockey, so what?
This is the way I perceive it. I have three
sons. The oldest, Michael, played at the University of Wisconsin - River Falls. The middle
one, Patrick, played high school hockey, but
nothing after that. Danny, the youngest, he's
25 now, probably had more talent than the other
two. He broke his leg playing soccer when he
was a junior in high school and never played serious hockey after that. He has a college degree, enjoys his profession as a TV sales rep,

plays hockey recreationally and has fun. That's important to me. I wasn't the type to say because I played hockey my kids had to play also. Getting the education is number one! I think too many youths are looking at it the other way today. Qualify for a college scholarship today and play pro hockey tomorrow. Let me add here that if someone had taken hockey away from me when I was a young teen, it would have been a loss. But I had other sports, other interests that would have filled the void.

Q. Hockey has played a big role in your life, would you agree?

Hockey, in a nutshell, provided me with enjoyment from the sport itself and great opportunity, the opportunity to grow. I have to admit, hockey was a lot easier than what I'm doing now. I'm saying mentally, the responsibility and the involvement on a day-to-day basis is demanding and pressure-packed. But, I think in the same vein, sports has really helped me in accepting and dealing with my job responsibility today. However, I still enjoy the game and watch it and still like to be a critic on the game and those playing the game. I'd say it's probably one of the better conditioning sports. A sport that anybody can play and participate in.

FATHER LES COSTELLO

Father Les Costello was born on February 16, 1928, in South Porcupine, Ontario. He grew up and attended school in South Porcupine. In 1943 he left South Porcupine for Toronto where he went to high school and played for St. Mike's. He turned professional in 1947 with the Toronto Maple Leafs, playing most of the year in Pittsburgh in the American Hockey League. That year he won the Rookie of the Year award in the AHL and was recalled for and played with the Stanley Cup winner, the Maple Leafs. He played two more seasons, 1948-49 and 1949-50, and then left the game. In 1950 he entered the seminary for the priesthood.

Fr. Costello's second career began in 1957 with his ordination. He has been a priest for the past 30 years in the Diocese of Timmins, Ontario. He has been stationed at several different locations in Northern Ontario. As one of the founding members of the Flying Fathers, a group of priests who play hockey to raise funds for charities, he has kept on playing the game. He is presently stationed at St. Alphonsus Parish in Schumacher, Ontario.

* * * * * *

Fr. David Bauer, a former teacher at St. Mike's and a former coach of Canadian National teams:

"Les came to St. Mike's from a good, solid family. He and his brothers have always been concerned with other people. He had a good Catholic upbringing. I think he really came to St. Mike's to play hockey. It's possible that while there, he had his priorities changed a bit. By playing professional hockey, he got a chance to look at the world. We at St. Mike's were surprised when he quit play-

ing hockey and attended the seminary. I
suppose the hockey people were surprised
as well."

Father Grant Neville, a teammate with the
Flying Fathers:

"He loves what he is and is what he loves.
He loves his priesthood and lives it out
as he feels it. He has tremendous humor
which enables him to come into situations
of tragedy and give them life. His humor
helps people see solutions to difficult
situations. He has real compassion and a
love of people. Playing with him on the
Flying Fathers, I am able to witness the
joy he gets from playing. The way he has
handled his own setbacks, like losing his
toes, by facing them and going on, has
been encouraging to a number of priests."

* * * * * *

I flew to Timmins to meet Fr. Costello. I
had talked to him on the phone about doing the
interview. His brother, Murray who is president
of the CAHA, had told him it was a good project.
Toni Berthier, the housekeeper, picked me up. I
suspect it was a typical day at the rectory. We
had lunch and then went to a food and clothing
sale put on by a women's group in the basement.
People were coming all day long, some to pick up
food or clothing, others just to chat. There
was never a dull moment, certainly not a quiet
moment. We did the interview, which went very
quickly. I turned on the tape machine and Fr.
Costello talked. He moved rapidly along, but
kept it to the point. The interview was completed within this session.

Late in the afternoon, Fr. Costello went
off cross-country skiing and Mrs. Berthier took
me back to the airport. My thoughts were more
on the rectory. Amidst the activity was a lot
of charity. There was a lot of serious talk.

Fr. Costello was certainly not living a hedonistic life. Nor did I get the sense that he felt he was doing much that was useless. His interview is one of a professional hockey player who made a career decision shortly after playing professionally. He would say it was a decision that led, personally, to a worthwhile career.

* * * * * *

Q. Let's start with your hockey career. To what extent was it a career?

I'll go through my career fast. I started my hockey in South Porcupine, Ontario, and I ended up with a juvenile team called the Holman Pluggers which was named after a drilling company that sponsored it. I played approximately two years with them. The second year, we played off against St. Catharines and we had a very good series. It went down to the final game and we beat them out coming from behind (5-1) and winning in the third period. I guess some of the scouts saw that game and players like myself, Billy Adamo and Roy McKay were more or less told where we could play. I was told to go to Galt and the only way out was with education. As far as education was concerned, my dad wanted me to stick with education, so naturally the only place for a good Catholic boy was St. Mike's College. As far as Galt was concerned, Billy Adamo went to Galt and Roy McKay went into the army and later came to St. Mike's.

I went to St. Michael's College in Toronto in 1943. I really got into the hockey scheme when I hit Toronto and played for St. Mike's. We had a very good team and really I was lucky. My big ability was that I could skate. As far as my shot was concerned, it wasn't much. I think I was a little lazy and didn't backcheck much. But, I liked to take the puck and go with it. They must have been impressed with my feet at training camp because I beat out guys like

Red Kelly. They said Red couldn't skate good enough to make the team so he played Junior B. I think he want on to show people later on that he could skate pretty good; he had a dynamic career.

At St. Mike's we won the Memorial Cup twice and were runners up a third time. In fact we had Winnipeg on the rails, we were leading the series 3-1. Each game we had the champagne ready. Finally, it was the seventh game, the score was tied 2-2 and some big winger came down on Ted McLean and Pat Powers on defense and gave them the old deep one and beat Pat Boehmer with a high, hard one. There were only 30 seconds to go, everybody was dejected and I can still remember McLean saying, "Well, he couldn't have went by two better guys." Winnipeg won out.

So far as St. Mike's is concerned, I met a lot of interesting people. First I met Dave Bauer and Ted McLean who both went on to become priests. I was influenced at the time by Dave Bauer. He was the guy who wanted you to read Gilson and Maritain and all the great philosophers. He said there was a lot of things to do in life besides play hockey. But at the time, I wasn't paying too much attention to him. I was thinking about what I would do in the future, wasn't real sure, so I decided to turn pro. I had finished Grade 13, so I was ready for the university but the pros wanted me, so I went down to Pittsburgh.

So far as Pittsburgh is concerned, I played in the old American League with the Pittsburgh Hornets. We had the Frozen Five, we had a small arena that only held 5,200 people, but we had good hockey fans, a good hockey town. John Harris was the owner and we had passes to all the clubs and were living pretty good. This would be 1947. We had a very good year.

I think I was Rookie of the Year. I scored 32 goals and was called up for the playoffs to Toronto. Toronto was very strong down the

middle with Syl Apps, Ted Kennedy and Max
Bentley, had a very good defense and Turk Broda
in goal. I played on a line with Max Bentley
and Flem Mackell and also with Joe Klukay and
Todd Sloan. I think I only played eight games
because we beat out Boston in four straight and
then beat out Detroit in four straight for the
Stanley Cup.

Some of the incidents I remember. We were
coming back from Detroit after we won. I was
the rookie and was told to be the guard. There
was supposed to be no drinking on the train, but
Broda and the boys were in the rest room having
a few and they told me to be the guard. I
didn't pay any attention and Hap Day, the coach,
came by and found the boys drinking and he really gave them hell. He grabbed ahold of Broda,
gave him a shot in the cheeks, poured the booze
down the toilet and told them to smarten up,
that we were going on parade to the city hall.
Turk didn't hold any grudges but he really gave
me hell for not keeping guard at my post. Another thing I remember is Max Bentley. Max was
a horseman and he was always booking bets on the
train. I didn't know buggerall about the horses
but the first time I bet I picked a 100-1 shot
and naturally the thing came in. Max had to pay
me $200. I said, "Max, you're smart enough but
I know horses better than you do."

The second year I came back and I was enjoying the game, but as far as my heart, it
wasn't in it. I started with Toronto and things
were going pretty good. I think it was about
the 17th game, we got beat by the Rangers 6-2,
so Connie Smythe called Flem Mackell and myself
into the room and said, "Okay, guys, what the
hell are you doing out there? You're not
backchecking!" So Mackell who was even yappier
than I was said, "What do you mean? We got our
goals, Max got a goal, Costello got two assists,
I got the other goal, we played really good out
there." Smythe said, "Look, I had this ticket
for Costello, but seeing you're doing all the

yapping, you get the hell out of here." He sent Flem down to Pittsburgh. It didn't make any difference, I was sent down three weeks later.

I went down to Pittsburgh, still enjoying the game, but something was lacking. Most of the boys were falling in love, I was best man at Flem Mackell's wedding. The game seemed to lose a little of the fun for me. In other words, they told you what to do with your personal life and so forth. It was just the idea, "Well, am I going to do this all my life?" We only played 50 games a year and had passes to all the night-clubs and shows. My life was a little bit hedonistic, in other words, a little pleasure but not much else. My goal production went down, and also my interest in the game.

The Maple Leafs called me up for the playoffs again. I had the best seat in the house sitting on the bench. In fact, the night Gordie Howe got hurt I was sitting on the bench, saw it all. It was an accident. Guys like Mackell, Phil Samis and myself had a little ritual. We'd eat the steaks and all before the game, but never played. We'd wake everybody up during their pre-game naps and they'd be mad as hell.

The next year I went back down to Pittsburgh. I had a pretty good year but in the back of my mind things were different. A lot of us were discussing education. Phil Samis went back to school at Duquesne University, eventually became a dentist. Cy Thomas was another and he went back and took engineering. I always had figured that if you're going to do something in life, you should do it for somebody else and kind of forget about yourself. I had been thinking about the priesthood and decided I'd better go back to Toronto and university and give it a chance. Smythe and the guys were very surprised. It wasn't that I had anything against hockey, it's not that I didn't appreciate the game, it was just that I figured there was something else. There is a saying in the Bible, "You have not chosen me, I have chosen you." There was just something lacking, something tugging at my heart to give something else a chance.

Q. Did you enter the seminary right away?

I went to the seminary over on St. Mary's Street while I went to the University of Toronto. I got a BA there and then went to St. Augustine's Seminary for the next four years. I don't know if it was God's plan or what but I gave it a try. The first year went by and I really enjoyed it because of the people I met. I met guys that were crazier than hockey players in many ways. And good athletes too. Fr. Brian McKee who founded the Flying Fathers, Fr. Bill "Skinner" Scanlon and Fr. Pete Valleley, who was a demon on blades, and could skate all day and never get tired. Things went so well that before I knew it, the seven years went by and I was called to the priesthood. I don't regret it, I've had a lot of wonderful times in the priesthood.

My hockey didn't stop when I was ordained. I played wherever I was assigned. First of all, intermediate hockey for Kirkland Lake, then senior hockey for the Timmins team and then for the Rouyn, Noranda Allouettes. It was Senior A, that's good hockey.

Q. You were ordained in 1957. Will you talk about being a priest?

I was ordained in 1957 in my hometown of South Porcupine. I was first stationed in Kirkland Lake, then to Timmins, back to Kirkland Lake. I then went to Noranda, Quebec, from there to Cobalt, Ontario, then back to Timmins and then I came to Schumacher where I am now. I've been affiliated with the north for about 30 years. I chose the diocese of Timmins because I'm a northern boy. I was born in South Porcupine, I like the northern people, I like to work in the North. I like the four seasons. Most of the priests in the north are French-speaking. There are only a few English-speaking priests. We have good rapport between us so we pretty well pick and choose where we go. It works out well unless the Bishop has something else in mind.

My parish is an English-speaking one. Every parish I was in, whether it was Holy Name in Kirkland Lake or Blessed Sacrament in Noranda or St. Patrick's in Cobalt or Nativity in Timmins or here at St. Alphonsus, the people are good. They are very generous, very easy to work with. As long as they figure that you are trying to serve the people, then they help. As far as parish work is concerned, I like parish work and the reason is because it is a small parish. There are about 250 families.

My favorite saint is St. Martin de Porres. Now, where did he come into the picture? Usually a priest has a favorite saint. I first read about St. Martin de Porres when I was a seminarian and then I followed his career after I became a priest. And he was a bastard, the illegitimate son of a Spanish nobleman and a mullato woman. Nobody wanted him, so God gave him the power to heal both physically and spiritually. I liked his work because he was dealing with the sick and the poor. So every parish I went into I had a good rapport with the poor and decided to do something about it. I got into what is known as the St. Martin de Porres Apostolate which is food, furniture and clothing for people who are in need of these things. Right now in our society they say there are no poor, but there are a lot of poor. The rents are high and by the time people pay the rent, they don't have a lot left. We have people coming in for food, furniture and clothing every day. I like that. People are very generous. They give a lot. We

get a lot of contributions too. My buddy, Fr.
Dan Bagley over in Timmins, looks after the soup
kitchen. We're looking after the poor. As far
as the sick are concerned, I'm not a chaplain at
the hospital but I'm very close to the hospitals, nursing homes and especially the sick at
home who don't get too many visitors.

I liked to coach youth hockey teams. When
I was in Noranda, I even tried to speak
French and my French was so terrible that the
young French guys on the team told me, "Hey,
Costello, smarten up. Speak English for Christ
sakes, we can't understand your French anyways."
I like working with the youth. There's enough
work with marriages, baptisms, counseling, in-
structing converts. The different priests help
each other with confessions. My hours tonight
are 7 to 9:30 at Nativity in Timmins. Each guy
goes into the sin bin for a certain length of
time. There's plenty to keep me busy.

Q. Can you comment on the priesthood today?

The priesthood has changed to the extent
that once the priest looked after his parish by
letting the people come to him. Now the priest
gets out and goes to the people. The priest now
circulates in such a manner that he doesn't stay
in the rectory but goes out to where the action
is. I think the changes are for the better.
The mass is in English, the priest faces the
people, there are many new groups in the church,
the Charismatics, the marriage encounter,
cursillo, youth encounters, marriage preparation, and renewal, so I think the church has
changed for the better. They say we're neglect-
ing the youth, but up here we're very lucky because we are able to deal with the youth. Why
is there no interest in the priesthood? I don't
know. It's hard to figure. We've got only one
vocation coming up, one guy in our diocese is
interested in the priesthood. I think God is
still calling the kids, calling young people to

the priesthood, but I think the world has changed so much. There's so much pleasure and they have so much that they don't want to give it up. What about the future of the church? Who knows. People are always saying the churches are dying, going down, but in a lot of churches the youth are coming back. They're taking an active participation in the church, in choirs, altar boys reading the Gospel and giving communion, and active lay encounters. I think the church is here to stay for awhile yet.

Q. What about the Flying Fathers?

We formed the Flying Fathers around 1962. It started out as kind of a lark, playing against guys who were in worse shape than we were, like media guys, cops, firemen, and so forth. Found out it was better than bingo. So we decided to play a few games. The first game was for a kid who had lost an eye. That year we played about 5 games, the next year it was about 10 and pretty soon it was about 50 games a year. Finally, the Bishop kind of clamped down, said we were traveling too much so we cut it down to 25 games. We have been going for about 25 years, in fact it will be 25 years next year. We've played all over the place. We've played in Europe about five times, all over Canada, in the States. I think we have raised about 4 million dollars so far. The charitable work has been good for my priesthood. Besides, I've seen the world playing with the Flying Fathers. We usually have a meeting in June to decide what 25 games we want to play next year. Since this will be our 25th year, Fr. Tim Shea and Fr. Grant Neville are trying to get us scheduled in all the big centers of Canada. So far, we've lined up Halifax, Quebec City and Montreal. We're working on the others.

All the money we raise goes to charity. It goes to people who really need it. And it's good, cheap, family entertainment. Where can you find good, cheap entertainment today? People come and have a lot of laughs, see a little bit of good hockey, and seem to go away satisfied.

Q. The hockey has continued to be a positive force for you, would you agree?

A priest has to have his own side interests besides book work and his parish work. In today's world there is so much stress and tension. There's stress and there's tension so our job as priests is to mingle and try to bring joy and happiness into the world. The Flying Fathers help us do this. It's not that the games are hard, it's the parties afterwards. Ha. But here's where you meet the people. It's surprising how many interesting people you meet and how many people bring up problems at the parties. It's good for the priest as well. A lot of us spend a lot of time alone and it gives us a chance to share ideas and experiences.

Now as far as hockey is concerned, it's still a very dynamic game. What's the difference between today and the '40's and 50's? They are skating faster today, generally, they are shooting harder. There were a few who could really skate and shoot in my day, like Ken Reardon, Rocket Richard and Bill Brilko, but now all the players can do it. Is it dirtier, rougher? Debatable. Who's tougher or stronger than Gordie Howe, Ted Lindsay, Gus Mortson? See, we didn't have television in our days, and there were some dirty bastards in our day. We had guys every bit as tough and dirty as guys today, it was just that people didn't get to see them. I think one thing that has disappeared from the game is bodychecking. The guys are skating so fast, how are you going to hit them? Today, a lot of the hitting is done after the whistle. There is too much stick work, interference, too many head hunters today. As far as Gretzky is concerned, no doubt about it, one of

the greatest players of all time. He's got so
many moves and they say, "Why don't you put
someone on him?" Sure, but he's got so many
moves and is real tough to hit. The equipment
is lighter, the sticks are lighter so the players are wheeling around more. The game has improved, but it can improve more. It can improve
in the passing and stickhandling end of the game
and get rid of the interference and checking
with the stick in the guy's ear.

Q. Do you have any thoughts on the life you chose?

I think that as far as life is concerned,
God has a plan for everybody. They don't seem
to know sometimes, but he definitely has a plan
for everybody. As far as my plan is concerned,
I'm very thankful I had the opportunity of playing juvenile in South Porcupine. Very thankful
I had good parents. I was influenced by my parents toward religion. My dad was always up at 5
a.m., no matter what time he came in, for mass
and communion on the first Friday of the month,
and I was with him. I was influenced by his
honesty and sincerity in the home. Then I went
to St. Michael's and had the opportunity of
meeting some excellent priests and people. Fr.
Hugh Mallon, Fr. Regan, Fr. Lee and Fr. Dave
Bauer. These guys got me to thinking that life
could be short and the best thing in life is to
be concerned about others. As far as my life in
Pittsburgh is concerned, I think it enlightened
me to the fact that if you're not careful, you
can get seduced by the pleasures of hockey. In
some ways it could be a useless life. I'm not
comparing myself with the other guys. God
picked them to play hockey, get married and
raise children and most of them did very well.
The three years as a professional were good for
me. I wanted to find out what was going on in
the world and I certainly found out what was going on in the American and Canadian cities.

I didn't know at the time I went back to Toronto that I would really mature as a priest. I had it in the back of my mind, I thought God wanted me to give it a try. Once I got to the seminary I liked it. The priests I met, Fr. Bill Scanlon, Fr. Pete Valleley, Fr. Brian McKee, had qualities I had never seen in other people. Ask for a book, they'd run up a flight of stairs and come back with the book. Well, I couldn't believe that. In other words, they were concerned with other people, they were good and wanted to more or less implant their philosophy on me. As far as the priesthood is concerned, you're a rookie and don't know what to expect. You've just got to go out and work, you baptize, you marry, you deal with people. You work day in and day out. Just like my dad did for 40 years. But in the meantime, I had variety in my life. I could visit jails. I knew all the hard rocks in the jails in Noranda. You visit hospitals and have the opportunity to go into schools. There is always a challenge, always interesting. You can tell if a guy likes the priesthood by the joy and happiness he brings to his career. The priests I chum with on the Flying Fathers all seem to like it. They are interested in others and are concerned. I've been a priest nearly 30 years, I enjoy it very much and I don't think I've made a mistake in my vocation, but maybe the people do.

As far as the philosophy that God has chosen me, I hope I haven't picked this myself and I hope that God has chosen me for this career. I'm very satisfied and I hope I can improve at it. Who knows what the future will bring?

Pretty soon I'll be out of hockey. I had an accident a few years ago in the bush. I went hunting and I didn't intend to get lost but I got lost. I froze my toes and had seven toes cut off. Now it takes me two weeks to count the collection! That really didn't interfere with the skating too much except the doctor said, "Hey, slow down. You're coming to an age that if you go out there and really give it all, you're going to be in trouble." So I'm still out there fooling around, but I always have fast wingers with me, like Fr. Dan Bagley and Brothers D'Arcy and Mike Quinn. Nobody runs you, who's going to take a run at a priest, except some silly Protestant from Northern Ireland? There's still a little bit of hockey and it's a lot of fun. So I say to all young guys, if you want to play hockey and have fun, bring joy and happiness to other people, travel around the world and meet interesting people, become a priest and join the Flying Fathers.

CONNIE BRODEN

Thomas Connell (Connie) Broden was born on April 6, 1932 in Montreal, Quebec. He grew up and attended school in the Montreal area. He received a college degree from the University of Loyola (Montreal) in management and business administration. The degree actually was completed while he played for the Cincinnati Mohawks of the International Hockey League. As a player, he spent two years playing with the Montreal Junior Canadiens while attending Loyola. He played professionally five years in the Montreal organization. His time was spent with the Mohawks and the Shawinigan Falls Cataracts as well as the Canadiens. He originally retired from hockey in 1957 but came back and played for the Whitby Dunlops in the 1958 World Championships in Oslo. Following Oslo, he joined the Canadiens who won the Stanley Cup in 1958. Connie was the only player at the time to have to played on a World Championship and Stanley Cup team the same year.

An employee of Molson's Brewery since 1958, Connie has held several top executive positions including president of Molson's Alberta; brewmaster of Molson's Quebec; and vice-president for distribution and purchasing of Molson's Canada. Connie and his wife, Elizabeth, have raised four children, Barbara, Tom, Margot and Nancy. They live in the Toronto area.

* * * * * *

Tom Savage, a Montreal businessman:

"He is well-liked, a competitor in everything he does. I'm not surprised at his success in the business world because of his professionalism and dedication to everything he is involved in. Connie is the type of person who has not forgotten the people he met along the way now that he has obtained a high level in the business world. He often returns to the old neighborhood to renew old friendships."

Sam Pollock, former Montreal Canadiens General Manager:

"Connie Broden was a top hockey and fastball player right from minor hockey and high school days. He always was an important player on any team he played on, right through to the NHL. As a center, he displayed great hockey knowledge and coach-like instincts. Played on Stanley Cup teams and was on the 1958 World Championship team for Canada in Oslo. After his hockey career, he was employed by Molson Breweries and has been a senior executive for the past several years."

* * * * * *

I met Connie for dinner prior to a Boston Bruins-Toronto Maple Leafs game, and we discussed the interview. A few weeks later, we did the interview in the dining room of his house in suburban Toronto. His story is unusual for a former professional player from the '50's because of his college education. He had a college degree during an era when few players continued with formal education. It was this education that proved to be a strong motivator in his choosing to leave the game on his own when he was 26. It was a time when most players simply stayed with the game until the game said it was time to leave.

We met a second time over breakfast to finalize the interview. He wanted to clarify some statements he felt were unclear or misleading. His approach to the interview was professional. He had made notes prior to our meeting and actually led the interview. He sees his life as an on-going process and is making plans on more formal education following his retirement from Molson's in a few years.

* * * * * *

Q. How do you view your playing career?

I accomplished quite a bit. I played junior for five years and got to travel throughout Canada as a teenager, which was pretty good at that time. I played in the Montreal organization for five years, although most of the time I was in the minors. I still play old-timers hockey, which allowed me to travel to Europe a few times. Hockey gave me the opportunity to travel, to see things.

I spent five years with the Montreal organization and at the end of five years, I wasn't protected by them. Montreal was the best organization in hockey and if they didn't think enough of me to protect me, then perhaps it was time to get on with using the education I had. I was never a great hockey player, not particularly gifted. I was a hard worker and a good skater. The other thing that hockey provided me was that it really stood me in good stead for the working world. Hockey and the business world reward discipline and hard work. These traits pay off in sport. They really pay off in the business world.

I never lost the love of playing the game. I'm still playing and I'm not alone. There are guys in the Toronto area who have formed a team for players over 50. So, I still have hockey today. Since I retired in '58, I kept playing at least two or three times a week. You don't lose the love for hockey. It just becomes a smaller part of your life.

Q. Did you ever spend a full season with the Canadiens?

No. I was back and forth most of the time. The Canadiens had two farm teams at that time, the Montreal Royals and the Shawinigan Falls Cataracts. I spent most of my time with Shawinigan in the minors although I did spend a little time in Cincinnati. The thing I remember about being called up to Montreal was I got $100 if I dressed for a game, but I got $125 if I played in the game. I can remember I was always ready to jump over the boards if someone got hurt or something. I remember Toe Blake saying, "That's what we need, guys who are ready on the bench." I didn't think he realized my pay went up 25 percent if I played.

Q. Your career originally ended in '57 and then you came back and played in both the World Championship and Stanley Cup. Is it true you were the only one to play on a World Championship team and a Stanley Cup winner the same year?

That's right. In 1958 I played on the World Championship team with the Whitby Dunlops and with the Stanley Cup Champions, the Montreal Canadiens. I was the only one until Ken Morrow did it in 1980 with the U.S. Olympic team and the New York Islanders.

The World Hockey Championships was really something, it was a career highlight. Historically, Canada always won the World Championships. Then something happened. In '56, an Olympic year, a team from Kitchener-Waterloo got thumped by the Russians and in '57, the team representing Canada lost again to the Russians. So, '58 was a big, big emotional thing. I think Canada had already started to have all kinds of reasons ready why we wouldn't do well, like, "We didn't send our best players over while the other guys are sending their best." I think if you look back, it's the last time Canada went

through the World Championships unbeaten and un-
tied. And what made it meaningful to me was
that I really contributed, I was the leading
scorer in the tournament. When I came back to
Canada, with all the publicity I had received
during the tournament the Canadiens asked me to
play with them. They didn't really need me, but
it was a great way to end a pro hockey career.
The late Frank Selke gave me this opportunity.

**Q. If this was the high point, what was the low
point of your career?**

The high point was the World Hockey Championship. The low point, I guess, was the way I
first found out that hockey would no longer be
the major part of my life. It's probably the
same in business, but certainly people in hockey
were not direct, honest and open with me. I
found out that I wasn't protected when I was
painting the house I was moving into. It was
the summer of 1957. The radio was on and it
mentioned I was drafted by Eddie Shore's American League team. That's how I got the message.
No one talked to me previously. Remember, this
was after being in the Canadiens' organization
for five years. That's probably the low point
but it's part of growing up. It's at times like
that that you take a look at yourself. You have
to be honest and objective in assessing your
abilities.

Q. How about good and bad memories?

The good memories are the people I met
along the way. The friendships that I've made
have lasted over the years. In my work now I
have moved right across Canada. I worked in
Newfoundland with Molson's and even there I met
old friends, like George Faulkner, whom I played
with in the Montreal organization. When I was
in Edmonton, I met guys like Glenn Hall and Jerry Melnyk whom I'd played against 25 years earlier. These are the good things that have

stayed with me over the years.

Q. Can you talk about your transition period?

It started for me the day when I heard that I wasn't protected by the Canadiens and I was drafted into the American League. I more or less made up my mind to quit. However, when I told the Canadiens' Kenny Reardon I wasn't going to play anymore, he suggested that I go to Springfield's training camp because that was Boston's farm team. There was a good chance that I'd end up with Boston, staying in the National League. I went to training camp and when they told me I was going to start the year in Springfield, I decided that was it. I had told myself before camp that if I didn't make it -- if I wasn't going to play in the National League -- I was going to get on with the rest of my life. What I didn't know at the time was the money Eddie Shore paid to draft me wouldn't have to be paid if I didn't go to training camp. So, simply by getting me to go to camp, the Canadiens would be getting the draft money. Ironically, they had to pay back the money when they got my rights back from Shore so I could go over to play in the World Championships with the Whitby Dunlops.

When I came home from Springfield, I had to get a job. I had worked summers in a sporting goods store for Gerry Snyder. I hung around his store and I made applications at Shell Oil and Tooke Shirt Company. My brother worked at Bell Canada and he said I would get a job with Bell. They were hiring anyone with a college degree. I went down to Bell Canada, was interviewed and anxiously awaited the letter of acceptance. I got a letter and it started off with, "We know you are going to be successful but, unfortunately, it's not going to be with Bell Canada." I was heartbroken, having been guaranteed a job by my brother. I was married with one child and was in a complete panic for a while. Snyder suggested I talk to a friend of his at Molson's, Zotique Lesperance. I went down and applied for a job and told them I'd like to get into sales. It was suggested, with my lack of fluency in French, that I should try something other than sales. "How about production?" I said, "Sure, I'll take anything."

That was the fall of '57. I had made up my mind I was done with hockey. Even though I ended up with the Whitby Dunlops and the Canadiens in the spring of '58, I knew I was done. They asked me to attend training camp in the fall of '58 but I had made up my mind.

Q. Did being a hockey player help you get a job at Molson's?

It got me an introduction, a foot in the door, that basically was it. Once I got into Molson's, it was up to me to develop different skills. There I was in the production area. What the hell did I know about production? Within three or four years, I became an assistant brewmaster. I was prepared to work nights, weekends, and shift work. Being a foreman, being in charge of people, getting work done, certainly the training in hockey helped because it's a team effort. Some workers are laggards, some are star performers, they all have to be treated differently but they're all on the same team and have to be going in the same direction.

Another thing is one can always find time to continue formal education at night. I took business administration courses at McGill and science courses at Loyola. Molson's was super. Anything you aspired to do they encouraged you. It was simple. Talk to them, come up with an idea and they wouldn't say, "Why?" -- they'd say, "Why not?" That was the type of company it was and is.

Q. You had an education, wasn't that unusual for a hockey player back then?

It was pretty unusual back then. People like Elmer Lach and Buddy O'Connor, stars in the NHL, thought I was crazy playing pro hockey with a college diploma. They couldn't understand why I would want to play hockey when I could just go out and get a real job.

Actually, it was my parents who instilled it in us, my two brothers and me, the importance of getting an education. My dad was a super individual. He was forced to leave school at a young age. Both my parents were of Irish stock. As soon as they were old enough, they had to get jobs and work. They weren't allowed to get an education but they were going to make sure that their kids got an education. The other thing was that I enjoyed school. I performed well in school. I think everyone wants to gain recognition. You can gain it in a number of ways, you can be good at sports, you can be good in school. I was pretty good in school without too much effort, so I got praised for my school work. I liked it. I breezed through grade school and did exceptionally well in high school. It wasn't the same when I got to college. I was playing junior hockey at the same time. Now I had to have good work habits. I hadn't developed these habits because everything came easy to me. I tried to cut as many corners as possible -- borrow other guys' notes, cut classes. But it catches up with you. I thought at the time I was going to play hockey and didn't need any help. I didn't need an education. Some of the priests at Loyola made it extremely difficult on me, wouldn't give me a break in any way. They didn't care about me or about hockey, at least that's what I thought. The surprising thing was that once I kind of matured and got thinking about it -- I was now playing in Cincinnati and I went to Xavier University to make up a couple of credits I needed

for my degree -- the people that had made it
hardest for me when I was going through school
were also the most complimentary and went out of
their way to pat me on the back for having suc-
ceeded in getting the college degree. They continued to point out to me that the college degree was going to last a lot longer than hockey
would. And when you analyze it, it's true. The
one thing that continues to get better with age
is the mind. All the other things, like your
body, start to wear out as you get older.

Looking back, I remember the pressures that
came from playing hockey. I would be real nervous before a game, something that disappeared
when the puck was dropped. The day of a game
was a real hassle as far as I was concerned. I
thought it was only me, but as you grow older
and talk to other players you find out that for
most players there was a certain amount of pressure. I looked around and I saw my brother with
a college degree. He seemed to have everything
that I wanted. He had a home, a wife, a family
growing up. He could sit in front of the TV on
Saturdays and Sundays and watch sporting events.
Meanwhile I was on buses and wondering, "Why
this hassle, why don't I jump into that type of
life?" I didn't realize at the time that in
business there are just as many pressures.

**Q. You have spent your entire business career
with Molson's, how do you view that?**

When I started with Molson's, I didn't really have a clear idea of what I was going to
do. I was just happy to have a job. Once I got
into Molson's, a lot of opportunities were presented to me. I was in the production section
and I was doing office or clerical type work.
It didn't take me long to figure out that guys
who were in the plant, people like the foremen,
made a hell of a lot more money than people
working in the offices.

I was given an opportunity to work as a foreman, a supervisor in the brewing department, which meant working nights. The money was good and it gave me a chance to practice the skills with people that I had observed in hockey. How do you lead? On any one shift you have 25-30 people, some of them good, some of them bad, but you still have to get the work done.

Molson's encouraged me to continue my education at the same time. I started to make good dough, continued my education at night, and was given a chance to work with other people and develop my leadership skills.

I continued in the production area and became an assistant brewer. I went down to Newfoundland and worked in a small brewery. The advantages there were that you do just about everything. Now, I not only got a good working knowledge of brewing, but also the packaging of the beer, and brewing engineering. I even got a chance to act as plant manager.

I came back to Montreal and was named brewmaster. The brewmaster is responsible for bringing in the raw materials and making the liquid right through to the finished product that goes into either bottles or kegs. It was a big responsibility. The Molson brewery in Montreal was the largest Canadian brewery. I also went to brewing school (United States Brewing Academy) which added to my technical skills. Becoming the brewmaster is just working up through the ranks. He's the one person responsible for the total brewing. What they have in the smaller breweries is a person who would be both brewmaster and plant manager. The brewmaster is a title and there's only one per brewery.

Q. Is the brewmaster the top job in the production section?

No, the brewmaster is the top job just in the brewing section. Now that I was back in

Montreal as the brewmaster, I wanted to expand my area of responsibility. I hadn't been exposed to any part of marketing. Since it was Quebec and most of the marketing is in French, I was put into another section of marketing, distribution. Distribution is getting the product from the brewery to the consumer. In that capacity, I reported to the vice-president of marketing in Quebec and was able to travel throughout Quebec getting exposed to a lot of the marketing and sales people. As a matter of fact, one of the guys at that time who was also reporting to the head of marketing was Ron Corey. He was doing public relations work. Corey is now the president of the Montreal Canadiens. I spent seven or eight years as brewmaster and one year in distribution. I was then asked to go to Toronto.

The fellow who was president of Molson's in Ontario, John Rogers, whom I had known in Montreal, offered me a position in Toronto as director of production in the Toronto brewery. Now I was responsible for all production functions, and the head of quality control reported to me. I had the job from '76 to '79.

An opportunity was then presented to me to go to Alberta. Molson's has two breweries in Alberta. I was now in general management acting as president of Molson's Alberta. Not only did I have the production function but also the financial and marketing people reported to me. I was there for four years and then moved into a head office job. That's the type of work that I'm now in. I'm vice-president for distribution and purchasing.

Q. Is there anything about your career that you think stands out?

The one thing that I had experienced throughout my hockey and my brewing career is the number of people, leaders, that I was exposed to. As a matter of fact, one of the accomplishments I'm pretty proud of is that I developed a talk around it, about leadership. I used people both from my playing and working careers to emphasize certain points. I've even given this talk over in Europe. I called the talk "So You Want To Lead A Band." It came from a TV show that took people from the audience, put them in front of a band and gave them the baton. To me, the show showed the ability to lead was important. The guy with the baton was important. It was not as easy as it looked.

Q. What does make a good leader?

You have to have the respect of the people and you earn that, it's not given to you. You also lead by example. There's no question that you have to have discipline and I think the best leader is the one who gets the results through people and, at the end of it, the people wouldn't even know that you were the leader. In other words, a good leader makes everyone feel they were responsible for it and did it themselves. Those are the true leaders and through time, you can pick up different things from different people. Some of them have one skill while others will have different skills. The other thing is you learn some of the things from the worst people. You have to make up your mind if you are ever put in that position you're certainly not going to treat people in that fashion.

Q. Who would be a real leader you played with?

There's no question about it, Doug Harvey is the best leader I played with as a player. For whatever reason, he had the ability to get everyone up. It didn't matter the temperament of the people, he could blend everyone together. He was able to bring out the best in everyone to help the team. He kept everyone in tune. Everyone liked him, everyone wanted to be liked by Doug. Players would do anything to gain his respect. The Rocket (Maurice Richard) was captain but the leader was Harvey. He made the lowest player on the team, like me, feel like a million dollars. He kept the really good players, like the Rocket, from being too big-headed, kept them in line and down to size. The players and Toe Blake knew he was the leader but the people running the organization didn't trust him as the leader.

He was genuinely good, wanted the best for everyone. He had the time for anybody or any group that needed his help. He never associated with players from the opposing team, but once you were on his side, he treated you like an equal. He was definitely an us-versus-them type of leader. He was a real competitor and it showed in everything he did. I played fastball with him, he was a hell of a player, and he couldn't wait to hit against a good pitcher. He wanted to show everyone that we could hit the guy.

Q. Have you had any disappointments during your business career?

I should mention in all this, it's kind of an ego trip. You keep doing things and you think you're doing them for your family. I thought that when I played hockey, when I was going to school at night, I was doing all this for my wife, Liz, and our children. When you really analyze it, you're really doing these things for yourself. During all this, a lot of resentment built up within my wife. We had some tough times and were separated for a brief period of time. It became quite apparent that she wanted to do things that she could be proud of. So she went back to school. One of the happiest times for me was when she got her degree. We were living in Alberta when she graduated. She had taken courses throughout the years when we lived in different places across Canada. She was in her late 40's when she graduated and now has her own career. She works for Norman Jewison, the film producer and director.

Q. Would you say you are satisfied with the way things have gone?

I'm very happy with what I've done and the way things have gone. I think if I went back, I wouldn't change anything. One of the big disappointments certainly to my parents and perhaps to me was when I first started out in college I was going to be a doctor. I pulled out of that because of hockey. But guys that were in my class and who are now doctors don't seem any happier and probably have traveled less and met fewer people than I have. I feel fortunate and satisfied with my life. I'm not an old man, but I can see I have gone about as far as I'm going in the business world. It wasn't perhaps as far as I would have liked. I'm thinking of retiring in a couple of years. I intend to spend a lot of my time during retirement going to school. Maybe I'll take law. I'll do things that I want to do, and play a hell of a lot of golf and stay busy. Molson's is going to provide this. Basically, I can be retired at 58-59 and if I can live as long as my father, I'll have another 23 years. It should be pretty good.

TED IRVINE

Ted Irvine was born on December 8, 1944, in Winnipeg. He grew up and attended school in Winnipeg. He played his junior hockey in Winnipeg from 1961 to 1963 with the St. Boniface Canadiens and the Winnipeg Blues. He started his pro career in the Boston Bruins organization in 1963. His first four years were spent with their farm teams in Minneapolis and Oklahoma City. He joined the Los Angeles Kings organization the year of expansion (1967-68) and spent two seasons with them. The next six years (1969-70 to 1974-75) were with the New York Rangers. The last two years (1975-76 and 1976-77) were with the St. Louis Blues after being traded there by the Rangers. Ted retired from hockey following the 1976-77 season.

Ted returned to Winnipeg to live after his retirement. He went into the life insurance business almost immediately. Today, he and his wife, Loretta, operate T.L.C. Irvine Insurance Services, an insurance and investment business in Winnipeg. They live with their son, Chris, in Winnipeg.

* * * * * *

Emile Francis, the Hartford Whalers general manager and Ted's coach and general manager in St. Louis and New York:

"Ted was a real tough player. He always put the team first and himself second. He usually played on a checking line and was glad to do it. As a player, he took orders real well, very coachable. He was good with his teammates and was usually the organizer for team-related activities. I always figured he was getting ready for after hockey because he took courses during the off-seasons. He could have stayed with the Blues another year, but

I'll always remember him saying to me, 'Hockey's been real good to me. I want to walk out with my head high and be remembered for getting a day's pay for a day's work.'"

Brian Sutter, a former teammate with the St. Louis Blues:

"Ted worked hard as a player. I realized he was preparing himself while he was playing for what he is now doing. Most players think the hockey will go on forever. Ted was intelligent enough to realize it wouldn't. He has helped myself and my brothers a lot with good advice. Because he knows what a player goes through, he is able to get us to understand the importance of preparing for when the hockey career is over. He is a fine man, very trustworthy and honest. I respect him more now that I see what he has accomplished away from the game."

* * * * * *

I had only met Ted once prior to the interview and that was one a post-game radio show he hosts after the home Jets games. We met at the Viscount Gort Hotel in Winnipeg during training camp to do the interview. We met a second time later to finalize the interview. His comment as we started was, "Maybe I should be on a couch to answer these questions." It was clear he had spent some time preparing because he expressed an interest in speaking more about his post-playing career than his playing career. Following the interview, Ted simply said, "I'm glad I got a chance to say this stuff, I was never sure I would."

It seems apparent to me that Ted Irvine is immensely proud of playing in the National Hockey League. It meant something to him personally to reach the top of his profession. It was also apparent that he is proud to be doing what he is now and to have achieved the level he has and with the potential growth for his company. He did not reach this level quickly or easily. It took a while. The confidence he maintained with himself because of having been a successful player was instrumental in his growth away from the game. Ted's interview is a good example of how former players can call upon their playing experiences to help themselves in life after hockey.

* * * * * *

Q. How do you view your career?

When I look back now, the big thing is I made it. I turned pro when I was 18 and I made it to the minor leagues. Then I made it to the NHL for 10 years. I feel it is an accomplishment that from all the guys who played in this area (Winnipeg), I was the one that made it. I view it as a success that I reached my goal because I worked hard and I was prepared to accept some challenges from management and the game.

I started off as an offensive player and then became more of a checker. When I got to New York with the Rangers I was made into a defensive player. While I was a junior I was more of a goal scorer. I received some awards as a player that are important to me. I received the Charlie Conacher Award for Humanitarianism which was very important to me. In New York the players voted me as their selection as a player. It was the Player's Player Award. Another year in New York the media gave me the Good Guy Award.

Q. What is the Charlie Conacher Award?

It was given for humanitarian reasons, to the player who did charity work away from the rink. I started working with mentally retarded

children while I was in New York. I just started out being the Rangers' and NHL's representative at the World Special Olympics. I also represented the Special Olympics here in Manitoba.
The award was a big thing. It was given to me
at a dinner in Toronto by King Clancy and Harold
Ballard, old teammates of Charlie Conacher.
That was either in '73 or '74.

I continued working with the Special Olympics after I was traded to St. Louis. In 1977,
after I was done playing, Harry Red Foster approached me and asked me to start the Manitoba
Special Olympics here in Winnipeg. I did that
with another fellow, Dan Johnson. Manitoba has
one of the best Special Olympic programs in
North America today and I'm very proud of that.
It's a high-powered, classy organization with
people like Dr. Wayne Hildal and Dan Johnson.
In fact, I was just honored at a Jets dinner
with the first annual Harry Red Foster Award.
It is an off-ice activity that I have continued
on with after I got done playing and I'm very
proud of that.

Q. What were your high points, low points?

There were several high points. Winning
the Central League championship two years in a
row with Oklahoma City while I was in the Boston
chain was a high point. Those were fun years
with some great players, Gerry Cheevers, Bernie
Parent, Wayne Chashman, Bill Goldsworthy, Ross
Lonsberry and J.P. Parise, to mention a few. We
had a great bunch of guys there and it is still
a high point. Being drafted by Los Angeles and
starting off in the NHL was a high point the
first year when I played in every original city,
the six cities. I had watched games from those
buildings and it was a high point because of the
history of the buildings. Another high point
was the five years I spent in New York. I just
found that with the fans and the press, playing
with that club, being competitive with the

pressure, it took me a couple of notches higher as a player. Everyone treated me great and I enjoyed everything about the city.

Low points. I didn't play up to my potential in St. Louis. That was the lowest point I had in my NHL career. From a personal point of view, never winning the Stanley Cup, because I now realize what the ring means when you quit the game. I'll never forget Don Awrey of the Boston Bruins shoving the ring in front of our faces and saying, "This is what you guys lost." But, the Bruins won it, so good for them. In a sense a high point was playing in the Stanley Cup finals and, at the same time, a low point by not winning the Cup.

Q. Trades are part of the game, what was it like being traded from New York to St. Louis?

As far as being traded, I always had the attitude that, "Well, if I had been doing my job, I wouldn't have been traded." I was caught up in the athletic fog that it was a great thing because St. Louis wanted me. So, when I was traded to St. Louis, it was very easy for me to go. I thought it was normal, St. Louis wanted me. It happened so quick and we (Bert Wilson and Jerry Butler) went right to St. Louis and I never really had a chance to think about how good I had it in New York. But, about halfway through the first year I realized we were not a very close team. It wasn't the same type of atmosphere. I then realized that I had been traded. I realized that playing in St. Louis as compared to New York wasn't any fun. We were treated fair by the club. I simply realized that I wasn't doing my job and my career was starting to come to an end. I wasn't hitting, playing with the drive I had in New York. I didn't feel I had a role on the team and I needed one. This was around Christmas time my first year in St. Louis (1975). I played one more year after this.

Q. How about good or bad memories?

I don't have many bad memories, at least
personally, from my hockey career. During the
13 years I played pro hockey, I don't see any
real bad times for myself. I enjoyed it all.
I'm smart enough to realize that any bad times I
had I was responsible for and I can't blame anyone else for them.

Good memories were the guys I played with.
I met some dandy people. Players from the Boston, Los Angeles, New York and St. Louis organizations are the biggest memories. The fans I
met off the ice, an extra part of hockey was the
reward of meeting people. Now that I look back,
I wish I would have paid more attention to them
and learned more about them. But, I still have
fond memories of a lot of nice people around the
League.

**Q. Can you define your transition period in
terms of time?**

I don't think I handled the transition from
hockey as well as some might have expected.
Mentally, I don't think I got over the hockey
until about three years ago, probably around '83
or '84. I thought I would just step right out
of hockey and walk right into the business world
brilliantly. I realized after those six years
of transition that it was poorly done on my
part. I don't think I really accepted the fact
that I was out of hockey for those six years, I
just wouldn't let go of hockey. I thought it
would be an easy transition, just go and get a
job. I didn't realize what the transition meant
as far as financial, lifestyle and family responsibilities. How did I handle it? Obviously, very poorly in my mind. Now, when I look
back I wish I could have hurried up what I
learned because I wouldn't have had wasted those
years.

I never thought I was taking advantage of being an ex-player, but obviously I was. People would talk hockey to me and I would fall into the same old trap of talking hockey with them. I no longer talk hockey in my business until the business is done. I don't dwell on hockey any more. I used to use it as a crutch to break down any barriers in a sales conversation. I did it because I didn't want any rejection. I used my playing status as a camouflage for myself in a business situation.

Q. Did anyone in particular help you with your transition?

I think the only person who helps you is yourself and it's no different in hockey or business. How did you get there? Well, you did it yourself. I had help along the way, but I had to make my own decisions and decide what price I would pay to play. I think a lot of people were patient with me during the transition. No one said, "You got to get along" or anything like that. Mentally, I said I had better smarten up. I didn't want to embarrass anybody. I have a high regard for the NHL and the people I met after the game. I didn't want to be perceived as a drunk, I didn't want to be perceived as financially broke, I didn't want to be perceived as a poor family person, I didn't want to perceived not to be a community supporter. I simply said to myself, "Hey, I don't want to embarrass myself or anybody else and I'd better get cracking on what I have to do."

Q. Would you characterize your transition as rough or smooth?

When I look back I say it was rough. At the time, I was just doing it, I didn't know if it was rough or smooth. I survived it but there is no doubt it wasn't done properly. A better way of putting it is it was a learning experience. I'd say I was very immature during the transition period. It was just an extension of me as an athlete. When you quit the game you should be accountable to your family and your business. I wasn't accountable during the first five or six years when I quit the game. I was still going under the facade of being a professional athlete. I didn't have to answer to anybody, I was just going along my merry old way.

Q. What do you think you learned during this period?

I think the biggest thing was responsibility. When I look over my NHL career, I had to be responsible for two things. They were to keep myself in shape and try to win. That's what I thought an NHL career was. I didn't perceive myself to be responsible for a family life or making a livelihood after the game of hockey. I did what I thought I was supposed to be, an NHL hockey player who went to banquets, signed autographs and did charity work. I never accepted responsibility when I quit the game because I didn't know what responsibility was. I didn't know how to get up every day and go to work. I felt that if I worked one day and sold something, I took three days off and patted myself on the back. I didn't know how to handle being out of hockey and working every day.

In hockey, you got the thrill and charge from the game and would read in the paper the next day how you did. In business there is no thrill, there's just responsibility. I wasn't prepared for the difference. If I had to go through the transition again, what would I do differently? I would go back to when I was 18 and accept some responsibility educationwise, jobwise. Everything I did was related to hockey. I would come back in the summer and get a job at a liquor store because that's what everyone, all the hockey players, did when the season was over. Towards the end I thought I was cute. I got an insurance license. I had good intentions. I took a real estate course. I paid $500, got all the books. Peter Stemkowski and the guys laughed at me, I was a real estate dude, I read one chapter and that was it.

I remember even in Oklahoma City buying things like mutual funds. Why, I don't know, because I dropped them. But somewhere there I feel I knew I wanted to get involved in this area but didn't know how to do it. Maybe if someone would have gotten ahold of me and impressed upon me to do something responsible, my transition would have started earlier. I got caught up being a professional athlete and enjoyed being held at a certain level and didn't want to relinquish it. Another thing I would do differently is not get caught up in the glory. I remember the year in St. Louis when we lost to Buffalo in the quarterfinals. We were still sitting in the bar celebrating how well we did four, five weeks later. One day Jimmy Roberts walked in. He played with the Canadiens and they had won the Stanley Cup. We asked him what he was doing here. He said, "Look, we're expected to win up there (Montreal), that's our job, we have a nice dinner and party a little. But I'm home now and it's time to go on." Well, we were still sitting there thinking we had done great. What I learned from that, looking back, is that you have to be responsible, the game's fun but you can't party your life away.

Q. You and your wife are in business today, how did that come about?

When I quit, I had my insurance license. I'd gotten it around '75 because of the urging of Jean Ratelle. It was a natural. Great West Life called and I went down and joined a branch called Corporate Planning which was personal and corporate planning. I walked right in and thought I was a businessman. Told them I wanted to make $40,000 a year. Took all the aptitude tests and they said I'd be able to do it. Then

reality set in. I didn't have a clue to what
they were talking about. I would be the first
one in the morning, last one to leave at night,
but, I didn't know how to do anything. They
thought I was wonderful because I sat at the
very end of the office, never bothered anyone
and didn't cost the manager anything because I
didn't have a draw. I kept up my production because I kept on selling to myself.

The manager eventually left and took me
with him. I took some different courses like
the Wilson Learning Program which dealt with
people skills. I was leader trained, even
trained other agents. I was still going absolutely nowhere. I thought I was a businessman,
dressed like a top executive, drove a big car
like the top executives. But, I was living off
my hockey savings and not my business career. I
began to realize this and started to educate myself. I started to read a lot of books, not so
much technical books in our industry, but people
skills. How to sell, why the products would
sell, understanding the clients. I was turned
on more and more and began to narrow my market
and concentrated on money products. I was never
intimidated by how much people made, I was intimidated by their technical expertise because
of my limited background. The more I read, and
I was thankful I was a big reader, the more comfortable I started to feel. I started to believe in myself. So, I started to get into the
money or investment business about '82. By this
time I was comfortable with it for a couple of
reasons. First, I knew the product well and
second, people like to talk about their money.
And that's when I went strictly on my own and my
wife, Loretta, joined me about a year later
(1983).

She was with another firm and left. We
thought we would design programs for the family
markets -- 90 percent of our business is the
family market. We thought we would decide what
was important financially for the family and go

and get the products that would serve them. I reached a point where I knew I would have to specialize. When I first started out, I thought I had to know about everything, land shelters, film shelters, R and D, oil and gas, flow-through shares. I didn't know anything about them and was embarrassing myself. I guess my lack of education made me feel I had to know about everything. I thought I had to have the answers for everything. From all this I learned I had to specialize. We do limited things but we do them well.

Q. When you first started your own business, how did it go?

The first week I was in my office in St. James. I looked out the window, drank coffee and read the sports page saying, "This is all right, I'm on my own." But then it clicked, it was no different than being traded from New York to St. Louis. I started to realize that I need-ed to change things, that I was accountable for myself. I began to explore different concepts, drafted or designed different financial pro-grams. I went and did them. It began to be fun. When I first sold insurance I'd say, "No-body wants insurance," or "There are other prod-ucts around." I was just ducking my responsi-bilities. It became apparent that I couldn't blame the customer, the boss, or the product. It was up to me to do it. By going on my own, I found that I had to be responsible and account-able. Once I did that, things were easier to do.

Q. How have you used hockey to develop the business?

Hockey taught me to stand on my own two feet. I learned in business that I have to do things on my own. I realized that is what I did as a player. I was able to relate things in the business world to the hockey world. If you're out of shape, what do you do? A lot of guys blame the coach if they're out of shape or over-weight. What you do is work out and get in shape. I knew that. It dawned on me that the business world wouldn't be much different than the hockey world. The positive things from hockey, the different teams I played on, the re-wards I received, became confidence factors for business. Hockey and the relationship it has to my life after hockey is a big thing in my life.

Q. How do you evaluate yourself today?

My wife and son paid the price for my hock-ey career. I was irresponsible as far as lead-ing a family life. I'm getting closer to my son and now we relate to each other more and more. My family life is better. Because of the confi-dence I have in the business, I am able to spend more time doing things with the family.

Our business is gratifying. We want to get bigger, to expand, to have more space. People tell us not to do it. Why shouldn't we? My wife is involved in this. Right now she is ne-gotiating for another office for us. We listen to each other. I appreciate her talent, she ap-preciates mine, we understand each other more. I find now that I'm enjoying things more, the only problem is how do you recover 20 years of stupidity? I can't recover those years, all I can do is try to make it better for the future.

I view myself now and say, "Boy, I've got a great opportunity to make things better." It's not just financial because we've learned that's not the criteria for happiness. We can spend more time with our son, understand his life bet-ter. We are now able to challenge ourselves. Our future is exciting. We can expand our busi-ness, take on more agents. So, life after hock-ey is starting to be fun. Somewhere there is a price we paid for the hockey career. But, we came through it and things are now fun and ex-citing.

GARY DORNHOEFER

Gary Dornhoefer was born on February 2, 1943 in Kitchener, Ontario, and raised and educated there. He played his junior hockey with the Niagara Falls Flyers from 1961 to 1963. A member of the Boston Bruins organization, Gary spent his first three sessions with the Bruins and their farm clubs in Minneapolis, San Francisco and Hershey. An original member of the Philadelphia Flyers after expansion, he played the rest of his career with them. He retired from hockey following the 1975-76 season, after playing key roles in the Flyers' Stanley Cup championship seasons of 1973-74 and 1974-75.

Following his retirement, he remained in the Philadelphia area and worked for a car leasing company for one year. He then moved back to Kitchener and worked for Hockey Night in Canada as a color commentator for several years. He currently is associated with Mutual Life of Canada and works part-time with Hockey Night. He and his wife, Cheryl, live in Cambridge with their children, Stephanie and Stephen.

* * * * * *

Bob Clarke, former teammate and current general manager of the Philadelphia Flyers:

"Gary Dornhoefer is one of those guys we were like. He rarely drank or swore. He worked hard all the time and was a good family man. He has all the qualities you look for in a person. As a player he was really hard-nosed and very skilled. He enjoyed the physical part of the game more than the finesse part. He really paid the price physically to play the game. I think he received more satisfaction from a good bodycheck than from scoring a goal."

Keith Allen, former general manager of the Philadelphia Flyers:

"Gary was certainly a character guy. He paid the price to play the game. A hard-hitting player who took a lot of punishment to play, he never backed off. I knew he would always succeed in whatever he did because of his determination and drive. He was a person of high morals, a good family man and a clean living player. He was the type that set a good example for younger players. Anyone who played with him had a lot of respect for him."

* * * * * *

I had met Gary once before our interview, when he was covering a Leafs-Jets game and I was coaching. I talked briefly to him on the phone about the interviews and we met a few weeks later in Toronto at the Airport Marriott. We discussed the progress of the project over lunch and then did the interview. With his TV background, Gary spoke in an organized and articulate manner. We completed the interview over the phone.

Gary achieved his dream of playing in the National Hockey League and on a winning Stanley Cup team and recognizes what he did, the price he paid and the consequences. In one of the last interviews, he expresses a different view, looking back on his career, than the others did. But it is a realistic perspective on his career, past and present.

* * * * * *

Q. When you view your career, what do you remember?

I can remember as a youngster the first practice I went to. I think I was 11 years old.

The next-door neighbor said to me, "When the coach blows his whistle and wants everybody to go on the ice, make sure you skate nice and slow around the outside so you don't fall down. He has to pick the team from one practice (40 players)." This was a big day for me. The practice was at the auditorium, which was indoors. I had only played indoors at the auditorium once before. The whistle went and everybody jumps on the ice and I take off like a steamroller, fall down, get up and fall down again. I got a pat on the back from the coach and he told me to leave the ice, I wasn't good enough. Even as an 11-year-old, I was so determined after that incident to be an NHL player. I was the first cut but it made me more determined that I was going to make it.

Going over my career, it certainly was enjoyable while I played. I liked any sport that was competitive, your ability against someone else's. I enjoyed the team concept where you and your teammates together could be successful. When I played with the Flyers, the team concept was very evident. The Flyers were an organization that was goal-oriented. They had good leadership from the top, the owners, management and coaches. You knew that the organization was going to be successful. That rubbed off on the players and, ultimately, we felt, as a team, that we were going to win the Stanley Cup.

From the players' standpoint, to win the Stanley Cup and reach the level that you're recognized as the best team is top priority and money is secondary. All the practices, traveling, injuries would make it worthwhile if you won. Unfortunately for me, I wasn't there when we won our first Cup. I had received a shoulder separation in the third game of the Boston series. I was sitting in the press box and as the seconds were counting down assuring us victory, I felt left behind. I didn't feel I was part of the team since I wasn't on the ice at the end of the game. I didn't get the thrill I thought I

would. Then, when we won the second Cup, it
was, "Well, we've done it again." There was
something missing for me when we won the Cup the
second time. As I think back now, I was so
tired and worn out that I was happy the season
was finally over. A few weeks later, it finally
hit me. The team had won two in a row.

I played Junior A with the Niagara Falls
Flyers. My last year we went to the finals of
the Memorial Cup but lost to the Edmonton Oil
Kings. That's where I suffered my first injury,
a broken leg. Pat Quinn nailed me. The next
year, 11 of us went to the Boston Bruins' camp.
Niagara Falls was sponsored by the Bruins. I
was a little intimidated playing with the people
I had heard about, Johnny Bucyk, Doug Mohns, Leo
Boivin, Murray Oliver, Tommy Williams, and so
forth. The one thing I know now that I didn't
know then was that the team is picked before you
even go to camp. In order to get a second look,
you had to be the outstanding player on the ice.
All of us left after camp and most of us ended
up with Minneapolis of the Central Professional
Hockey League. I had a good start with 20 goals
by the halfway point. After a game in January,
Harry Sinden, the playing coach said to me,
"You're going up to Boston. Tommy Williams
broke his wrist and you're replacing him." I
didn't really want to go because I was absolutely terrified and didn't think I was ready to
play in the NHL. Luckily, we played an easy
team, the Detroit Red Wings, who only had Gordie
Howe, Alex Delvecchio and Bill Gansby and so on.
I remember leaning against the boards during the
national anthem because my knees were shaking so
much. It was amazing, once the game started the
tension and fears left. I was able to play using the skills I had developed in junior hockey.
Things went well for me and I was even the run-
ner-up, for the second half of the season, to
Jacques Laperriere for rookie of the year.

For three years, it was a real struggle.
There were only six teams in the NHL and only

120 players would make it. I talked myself out of doing well after the first season. During the summer, instead of being positive, I kept worrying about what would happen to me if I didn't play well. I spent the next three years up and down from the minors to the NHL. Expansion in 1967 gave a lot of players, like myself, another opportunity. I was drafted by Philadelphia. We won our first game, in front of 8300 people, 1-0, on a goal by Billy Sutherland. That was the start and it's amazing how hockey caught on in Philadelphia. We were very competitive at home. The fans started to fill the building. One thing about the Philadelphia fans, they're Flyer fans more so than hockey fans. They really supported us. They had a way of picking out their favorites and getting on someone they didn't think performed up to their expectations. Larry Hale was a pretty good player but the fans just booed him out of Philadelphia. If you were having a tough time offensively, the way to keep the fans from getting on your case was to play aggressively. They seemed to enjoy the hard-hitting style and would leave you alone if you played that way.

Q. What about the Flyers' success?

Things changed when Fred Shero took over as coach. You could see the direction the team was headed, they made good player selections. Of course, once Bobby Clarke came, things started turning around. We got good leadership from older players, we played together as a unit and that was through Shero's direction. We didn't need a coach to discipline us, the players did that themselves. We had a lot of self-motivators. It was a very close-knit team. We stood up for each other on the ice.

I remember the year before we won the Cup (1973). We came back from Montreal during the playoffs, having split the first two games in Montreal, and the fans gave us an eight-minute

standing ovation. I have heard a crowd holler
and scream like that. The Canadiens were really
intimidated by the crowd but won both games in
Philadelphia and went on to win the series 4-1.
Even though we did not win the Cup that year, we
knew we had arrived and could compete with the
best teams in the NHL.

Everybody played the system. We worked on
that every day, how to protect in our own zone.
Once we had that down, then we worked on how to
prevent teams from coming out of their zone.
The speed and tempo of the game was not as fast
as today and there was not as much puck movement
either. But the way we played, the system was
perfect. I think everybody believed in Shero as
a coach. We were dedicated, everybody played
hard. I think a lot of it had to do with Bobby
Clarke, watching him practice and play. He
worked harder in practice than most guys did in
games. You felt embarrassed if you didn't put
out the way he did knowing he was diabetic. We
won the two Cups and then had an opportunity to
win a third. Probably the worst thing that ever
happened to us was when we beat the Soviets
(1976). We were going for three Cups in a row
and the team started to deteriorate after that.
We lost a little bit of discipline. Guys were
coming late for practice, didn't put in the same
effort, missed curfews because we got too cocky
having defeated the Soviets with ease. Against
Montreal in the playoffs, we lost a few key
players like Bernie Parent and Rick MacLeish,
but we still had the team to win. We didn't.
If everyone on the team had given a little bit
extra, myself included, I feel we could have won
that third Cup.

**Q. When you analyze your career, how do you see
it?**

When I talk to different professional,
school or church groups, I try to weigh the positive and negative of my career. The positive

side is that the money was decent, especially toward the end of my career. Being competitive was a thrill for me. Winning was the ultimate, succeeding with your teammate was important. Recognition is important to many people but that wasn't why I was playing. On the down side, it's not much of a life for a family. I'm very fortunate that I had a strong wife. Cheryl really had that stick-to-it-ness and hung in there, bringing up our children and being supportive of me. The injuries were numerous and I was never able to play a full season. Today, I have difficulty walking 18 holes of golf or playing tennis or racquetball because of my knees. Year after year, the knees get worse. So, looking at both sides, if I had to do it all over again, I wouldn't do it. It wasn't worth it. I knew going in the price I had to pay, and I was willing to pay that price. The experiences from 15 years of playing professionally I wouldn't trade. But if I had a choice of doing it all over again, I wouldn't do it. Maybe I'd try the golf tour; you don't break legs doing that.

The one thing that really stands out is the association with the Philadelphia and New Jersey area. We met a lot of friends outside of hockey that were important to our family. You develop relationships with your teammates but I find that they are very shallow. Once your career is over, everyone goes their separate ways. For the most part, the only thing you have in common is hockey. How often do you see your former teammates? Maybe once every year or two. When I look back, I have only one real friend from hockey, Garry Inness, who I see often and can talk to and feel I can depend on. I'm very thankful for all the friends our family made away from the team because we still keep in touch with them from time to time.

Q. Can you define your transition?

As a player, I was told during my career to make sure I could fall back on something when I was done. When I quit after the 1875-76 season, I really didn't know what I wanted to do or what I was good at. My education was grade 12. What was I qualified to do besides play hockey? My options were scouting, and I wasn't too keen on that. I was offered a job to coach the Flyers' farm team in Portland, Maine, but I wasn't interested in doing that. I looked at insurance, took an interview with ARA Services and I talked to a company that was putting together a program on alcoholism and drugs for other companies. This appealed to me, but it was going to be a year before it was operational. They suggested I work in one of their subsidiaries, a car leasing company. I did it for a year and almost went crazy. It was the type of job that you sit at a desk, make phone calls and try to generate some business. It was difficult for me. I became a 25-cups-of-coffee-a-day guy and went absolutely strange. After the year, I inquired about the alcoholism and drug program and was told it was still six months away from being ready to make presentations to companies. I said, "I'm sorry, I can't work in the leasing company any longer and will have to leave." I handed in my resignation.

I decided to audition for a sports reporting job at a TV station in the Philadelphia area. I wasn't very good in the audition and the TV station never called back to let me know their decision. I called three or four times and the person in charge was always detained or out of the office or whatever. For a guy who had played pro for 15 years, I could accept no as an answer. I was disappointed in the station that they couldn't at least give me an answer one way or the other. The decision was then easy to make where we were going from there. We returned to Canada and I took the job with Hockey Night in Canada.

I had done some games for the Flyers while I was leasing cars. I enjoyed it. So I would say my transition lasted until I made the decision to return to Canada, a little more than a year after I quit playing. I knew during my last year as a player that I would retire from playing. My final game was in Boston and I had tears rolling down my face after the game. The next day I was fine. I knew it was time to get on with my life. I didn't want to just hang on and play sparingly. That's what I did my last year, play a few games, sit in the press box, play a few games. Saying good-by to hockey was very easy because the last two years were not much fun with injuries and less playing time.

Q. How did the job with Hockey Night in Canada go?

I started doing Hockey Night on a full-time basis and most of my work was out west. I would leave on Tuesday, go to Edmonton to work a game on Wednesday, fly to Calgary for a game on Thursday. Friday would be a day off and Saturday I would do a game somewhere out west, Calgary, Edmonton, Vancouver or Winnipeg. I wouldn't get home until Sunday afternoon. I would do this three weeks out of the month. I was home only 12 days a month. The rest of the time I was on the road. Here I was retired from hockey and I was traveling like a player. I would do only three or four games a month in Toronto, the rest were road games. I did this for a few years and then there was a change made within Hockey Night in Canada. My schedule was going to be cut down to 30 games a year. I couldn't live on what they pay for 30 games so it was time to make a change. One thing about the people with Hockey Night, they are loyal. If you do your job, they'll keep you. I found that out. Four years ago (1983), I decided to do Hockey Night on a part-time basis and look for something else.

While I was working with Hockey Night, the manager of Mutual Life in Kitchener would call and take my wife and me out for dinner at least once a year and talk to us about the business. One thing about him, he was persistent. Every year, like clockwork, he'd call. When I made the decision for a change, I went right to Mutual Life. I didn't even consider any other insurance companies. I took the examinations and got right into the business. It's been successful right from the start. I'm involved in a number of products, life insurance, disability insurance, annuities, RSP's, investment funds and financial planning.

Q. How do you like the insurance business?

I've loved it. I think you have to be goal-oriented in this business, which I was in hockey. The biggest thing is how you handle rejection and being a hockey player, you get that from all ends. You have to be committed and dedicated. You have to grind it out to be successful. A great thing about business is that you get paid for the work you do. If you don't work, you don't get paid. I think a lot of what I learned in hockey has helped me tremendously in the business at Mutual Life. I work a lot with Roly Thompson, who represents NHL players. My goal when I'm working with his players is to make sure that when their careers are over, certain areas of their financial planning will be taken care of. We want to make sure they have an insurance policy that will be paid for when their career is over, maximize their RSP every year and make some investments that, over a period of time, will accumulate in value. I am able to say to the players, "I made plenty of mistakes when I played, spent a lot of money, didn't save a lot, and I want to show you how to save."

Q. What adjustments did you have to make?

I was a loner, kind of shy. I really didn't enjoy talking to people that much until I got to know them really well. Most people always wanted to talk hockey and that was what all the conversation would be about. I've learned how to listen, to listen to what people's problems are. This was a big adjustment. During my fifth year with Philadelphia, I rededicated my life to Christ, being a born-again Christian. It's very important in our family life and has helped me through some difficult times. Cheryl and I teach a Sunday school class for young teenagers. It's been good for us, to be able to communicate with young people and be a friend to them. We're very active in our church work and it has helped me a lot in all aspects of life.

Q. Would you have done anything differently?

Some of the advice I give to players now is, "You're just a young player, you're playing for an organization, you want to get out and meet as many people as possible. If there's something these people do that interests you, pursue it and let them know you're interested. During the summer, gain all the knowledge that you can even if it means starting from the ground floor. It's only going to benefit you once your career is over." Unfortunately, when I played, and I think players today think the same, I thought my career was going to last forever. One good bodycheck and the career can be over. Then what do you do? During the off-season is a great time to study, get involved in a business and know the operation. Once your career is over, you get into that business and the transition would be easy because you've laid the ground work. Also get as much education as you can and perhaps playing college hockey instead of Junior A.

Q. How do you view yourself today?

I think a lot of people associate success with the amount of the paycheck you bring home. I really don't view it that way. I think it's having a control of your life and also by having harmony at home. There isn't anything of value outside the home if you don't have success at home with your family. We went through some difficult times and are still going through some difficult times with the children. We're just trusting God to give us some direction in how to handle these problems.

In the insurance business, it's normally a five-year program and I'm approaching that. I feel very comfortable doing what I am and I think the difficult period of the business is past me. I'm still taking courses to gain more experience and knowledge. My wife and I have an excellent relationship. Our kids are getting to the stage that they're going to be on their own shortly. Stephanie is in her second year of journalism at college with one more year to go. Stephen is out in the work world looking for his own apartment. We're coming to another sort of transition world with our kids going off on their own and then Cheryl and I will be by ourselves. The door will always be open for the children and you hope that when they have problems, they're going to rely on their parents for advice just as we did.

What's in store for me, only God knows. I like the direction that I'm going. The friends we have here are important to us. We had planned to stay in the Philadelphia area and never thought we would move back to Cambridge. It's really good to be back and I finally feel comfortable being back home. I feel pretty good about my life right now.

GERRY HART

Gerry Hart was born in Flin Flon, Manitoba on January 1, 1948. He grew up and attended school in Flin Flon, reaching Grade 11. He played his junior hockey with the Flin Flon Bombers. His professional career started with the Detroit Red Wings in 1968. During four seasons in the Wings organization, he spent time with the parent club and its farm teams in Fort Worth, Baltimore and Tidewater. He then spent seven seasons with the New York Islanders from 1972-73 to 1978-79. The last four years of his career were split between the Quebec Nordiques and the St. Louis Blues. He retired after the 1982-83 season.

Gerry is involved in two separate businesses on Long Island, insurance and real estate development. He lives in Lloyd Harbor, N.Y. with his wife, Maria, and two sons, Jordan and Robert.

* * * * * *

Bob Nystrom, a teammate with the New York Islanders:

"Gerry was the first to take me under his wing when I went to the Islanders' training camp. I remember him saying, 'No matter if it's practice or a game, give it 150 percent.' That is the type of person he is. He gives it his all, be it hockey, business or whatever and lets the cards fall where they may. He doesn't let little things become roadblocks. I admired him while I was playing because he was involved in business while a player. He's become a role model for a lot of us who are now finished playing. His success shows us that there really is life after professional sports."

Doug Kelly, a real estate partner:

"The thing that impresses me about Gerry
is he is basically self-educated. Not
only is he articulate for an ex-athlete,
he is articulate for a businessman. He
is well informed on local issues and government policy. He communicates well
with people. The self-confidence of a
professional athlete has helped him become a successful businessman. A good
trait he possesses is that he is not
afraid to admit he doesn't know an answer
to a question. Gerry donates a lot of
time to charities and community activities and believes it is important to be
active in the community."

* * * * * *

I met Gerry for the first time the day we
did the interview. We had talked on the phone,
and he was especially interested in the topic
because of his involvement with a former Island-
er teammate who had been recently indicted for a
serious felony. We had lunch, talked about the
project and then the hockey business. He was
intrigued with the differences between his businesses and the hockey business. We did the interview at his home in Lloyd Harbor. He rewrote
parts of the interview to clarify sections he
felt were unclear.

I quickly realized that this was a player
without a high school degree who earned himself
an informal advanced degree in business while
playing. He learned the real estate business on
the job. Upon his retirement, Gerry put his education quickly to good use. His story is a
journey from Flin Flon to Long Island and the
Hamptons, with hockey as his vehicle.

* * * * * *

Q. How do you view your career?

When I look at hockey as a career, I think
of the impact that it has had on my whole life.
The opportunities it has afforded me, that included more than playing in the NHL and making
lots of money. Growing up in a small town like
Flin Flon presented many limitations and hockey
was the vehicle that gave me the opportunity to
see the rest of the world. It was a whole educational and learning process. What I missed as
far as a formal education, I believe I more than
made up for through the various kinds of friends
and individuals that I came in contact with
throughout my career in many different places.
This all became very important to me in terms of
what I wanted to do with the rest of my life.

My hockey career was something I had to
work very hard at. Over the 16 years that I
played professional hockey, there were only a
few moments that I felt secure with my position
on the team. Every training camp was a fight
for survival. I believe now, looking back at
it, that pressure was what helped make me
reasonably successful today. I was never com-
placent with anything I approached. That struggle every year was a character builder. It
taught me that if you are on target with your
goals and objectives and you persevere through
the tough moments, you can accomplish almost
anything in life.

My hockey career was never really an event-
ful one, in that I played on a championship team
or won any personal awards. I am proud of the
fact that my playing career was a lengthy one.
I feel that with the limited ability I had, I
hacked out a formidable career.

Q. What kind of player were you?

That question is best answered by asking
myself how I think my opponents viewed me as a
player. I used to hear over and over again

how certain individuals hated to play against
me. I didn't particularly have a lot of
God-given talent, but I was a tenacious checker
and a grinder. I was a strong defensive player,
played my position well and knew enough little
tricks of the game to be effective. It was often said my name was synonymous with how I
played and that was with a lot of heart.

Q. What about high and low points?

The high point of my career came during the
1975-76 season playoffs. I was with the Islanders at the time and we weren't expected to get
past the first round of playoffs. We beat the
Rangers at Madison Square Garden in overtime in
the fifth game. We then dug ourselves a hole by
falling behind Pittsburgh by three games and
proceeded to come back and win that series to
set up a semi-final showdown against Philadelphia. By this time, we had caught the eye of
the hockey world. Again we got ourselves behind
by three games, but by then we felt we could
overcome any deficit. We went on to win the
next three games, and in the sixth game, I
scored the winning goal. After scoring only a
few goals all season, it was certainly a moment
that will capture my thoughts probably for the
rest of my life. Philly beat us in the seventh
game at the Spectrum, but that playoff series
brought respectability to the franchise for the
first time and I believe really set the stage
for a dynasty that was about to be born.

The lows of my career were more a series of
events than a particular incident. The worst
experience probably for any athlete is that
feeling of rejection, of not feeling a part of
the organization and not being able to contribute. The amenities and privileges that go with
being a professional athlete are really an im-
mense ego trip. When the bubble bursts, you become very quickly just like everyone else. It's
a feeling of having your feet hacked out from

under you. It happened to me a couple of times, once in Detroit after I suffered a severe shoulder injury. I had a very respectable year in Detroit my first year and really felt I had a future with the organization. I had made a lot of friends and got a lot of attention and recognition everywhere I went. This was the first time I experienced that kind of sensation. Then I separated my shoulder one night late in the season. I tried repeatedly to come back into the lineup prematurely and each time discovered that I couldn't play at the level I needed to. Before I knew it, I was being shuffled off to the minors. My world came crashing down. When I returned to Detroit in the off-season, it wasn't the same; phone calls didn't get returned, so-called friends were too busy with their own problems, recognition and the privileges that went with it were gone. I was suddenly just another guy on the street; the doors that were once open were closed; and I discovered the reality of life. It was a hard lesson to learn.

A similar experience happened years later when I left the Islanders. This time, however, I was much older and more mature. I had financial stability and coped with the situation much better. After being with the team for eight years, sitting in the stands and watching them win the Stanley Cup was an emotional experience. I went into the dressing room to congratulate everyone, but I couldn't handle the way I felt. I left and rarely go back to Islanders games even though I'm now living in New York.

Q. What about good and bad memories?

The good memories come with the camaraderie that existed on a hockey team. Hockey was more than a profession, it was your social life. The friendships, attachments and feelings towards each other is something and very hard to find in the outside world. This was especially so on a team like the Islanders that was deep in character.

I don't really have any bad memories. There were situations that were difficult, but they were character builders, they made the good times even better.

Q. Can you define transition?

It became apparent to me early in my career that my playing days could end at any time, not only because of an injury, but just general attrition, someone better could come along. Hence, my transition began early into my career. I learned to manage my money intelligently. My rule of thumb was: for every two dollars earned, save one and blow one. By following that principle I could be frugal and still have fun. I aligned myself with people that were successful and found myself gravitating towards the real estate business. My first significant investment was my own home when I was 25. Along with a friend, I began to acquire an investment portfolio in real estate. My friend was very astute in the business and I admit I merely hung onto his coattails the first few years. Our investments were conservative, mostly residential, and I felt very secure laying out my money. We established a partnership and I personally was on the deed to each and every property we either purchased outright or developed. The transition of hockey to business was an ongoing experience throughout my playing career. Toward the end of my hockey days, the real estate investment business was as much a profession as hockey was. When I experienced successive problems with knee injuries the last year of playing in St. Louis, it was easy for me to make the decision to put my hockey career behind me. There was a diminishing feeling of enjoyment for the game and I felt my time would be better utilized back in New York involved in managing my investments. I was 35 at the time.

Q. What did you learn from your transition period?

The single most significant thing I learned about making the transition was the importance of aligning myself with successful people; and even more important, that these people have the same high moral standards that you expect of yourself. The reason I always felt the necessity of these business associations was simple. I was a hockey player, not a real estate or investment entrepreneur, so why not invest my money right along with another individual that has a proven track record and knows the business. If he felt comfortable risking his money, I would put mine up right alongside his. I believe that in today's competitive market you cannot do real well being a part-timer. And let's face it, hockey is a demanding full-time profession. By the time I got out of the game, I knew enough about the business I wanted to be involved in, and I had the confidence and track record to move ahead on my own.

Q. Will you talk about your real estate business while you were playing?

My venture into real estate was very basic in terms of our strategy. Most of what I had ownership in were two-family homes. I was not looking to get into limited partnerships on large developments that were designed more as a tax shelter than an investment. The small apartment complexes were very liquid and easy to leverage; meaning we put as little cash into each deal as possible. This allowed me to buy more properties, and I wasn't worried about a positive cash flow because I had a decent income from hockey to carry them. Naturally, these highly leveraged properties, along with depreciation and maintenance, generated tremendous losses that were tax deductible. I was able to take my hockey contract to the bank and borrow against it to continue the acquisitions. Again there was very little risk in doing this because at any time I could spinoff one or two small dwellings for sale if the need for cash would be critical. I was also very lucky because at the time interest rates were low and property on Long Island was really starting to appreciate.

When my hockey playing days were over, the pay checks stopped and I became a little concerned over the amount of debt I had to service. I liquidated some of the properties within the partnership to pay off some of the loans. This wasn't so bad, because I was now paying tax at the long-term capital gains rate versus ordinary income rates on money that I had sheltered with the huge tax losses the properties were generating.

In hindsight, I wish I had hung in there a little longer because the rate of appreciation on properties on Long Island has been nothing short of phenomenal.

Today, of course, there is not the same tax advantage of doing what I did. However, real estate continues to go up in value and, for my money, it is still the safest and best place to place some of your money earmarked for investments.

Q. If your transition ended with your retirement, what adjustments did you have to make?

When hockey stopped, so did the bi-monthly pay checks. Real estate, especially highly leveraged, of course, does not spin off any real cash flow; therefore, I had to look for something else to do. I got involved in an insurance brokerage business that I was very active in. I had a partner in this business as well, and fortunately, I had the financial strength to stay with this venture because the first few years were very lean. I learned some hard lessons in this business. I had been away from the New York area for a few years and I soon found

out that people were not knocking the doors down
to do business with Gerry Hart the ex-Islander.
But I learned a lot about managing a different kind of business, employee-employer relations, financial planning, sales, and so forth.
The business in the third year started to make
money. In the fourth and fifth years, the
business really started to blossom, and then
another major setback. I decided that my partner and long-time friend was not someone that
could be trusted and I wanted out of the relationship. As I indicated earlier, it's the importance of the people you have business relationships with and this one was the most difficult business experience I had ever encountered.
Since it was a friend that was involved, it became emotional and ended up in litigation. Fortunately for me, again because of my real estate
investments, I had the financial stability to
see the situation through and to stick in there
for a fair solution.

**Q. What are you doing now in terms of employ-
ment?**

I am still involved in the insurance business in the marketing of extended warranties on
automobiles. I service two large national accounts and I see the potential for tremendous
growth not only in the auto industry, but in
light manufacturing as well. The industry is
still young and in its infancy and I'm enjoying
the diversity it offers.

In addition, I am once again very active in
the acquisition and development of real estate
projects. My partner and I are focusing on the
eastern portion of Long Island where there is
still plenty of opportunity for the development
of large open tracts of land. We are encouraging the participation of outside investors as
there are more opportunities than we can handle
ourselves. I hope, in the very near future, to
begin to offer our services and expertise in

this area of investment to other present and
former athletes that would actively like to participate in these opportunities. We would encourage only those that want to get involved and
learn something about the business. I think I
would get a lot of satisfaction out of being
able to offer something back to a sport that has
been very good to me.

**Q. What is your level of satisfaction with your
life today?**

I feel very fortunate that I am able to
provide my family with the quality of life-style
that we experience today. I am grateful for all
the opportunities I've had come my way, but I
also feel the gratification of having earned it.
I put in the time, whether it was in the
off-season or resisting the temptation for a few
beers and a long lunch every day after practice.
I think the success I may have attained today is
the culmination of a lot of years of putting in
that extra effort.

I also get great satisfaction out of having
resisted the temptation to stay in hockey in
some capacity. Even though I have aspirations
of getting back into the game again some day, it
has been very important to me to prove to myself
that I could make it in the real world. Today,
five years out of the game, I feel I have accomplished that.

**Q. Are you glad you stayed in the New York
area?**

New York is a wonderful place to live if
you can afford to do all the exciting things
that a big metropolitan area has to offer. However, I don't think the quality of life is as
good in New York as it is in some other areas of
the country or Canada, for that matter. The
congestion, the traffic, the competitiveness of
everything put a lot of pressure on life. To be

productive in this environment, you've got to out-hustle your opponent. In a sense, just like hockey. The upside to all that is that, this is where the opportunities are. If you're willing to pay the price, one can make it very big in this type of environment. Today this is where I want to be, but in the foreseeable future I dream of migrating back to Canada and settling in the Okanagan area.

Q. Has hockey been a force in your life?

I don't think I could have said all I did without realizing that without hockey, possibly none of it would have happened. Hockey has taught me some very essential lessons in life: competitiveness, that if you want something bad enough and are willing to make the necessary sacrifices and pursue it in a very tenacious manner, you can have it; teamwork, in hockey you not only had to pull your own weight, but you had to learn to trust and rely on your teammates to come through, business has been just that for me; setting attainable goals, training camp was always that awful time of year when team and personal goals were established. The individual who was focused and put out the effort in training camp seemed to always get the best jump on the season and on his way to attaining his objectives.

JOE CAVANAUGH

Joe Cavanaugh was born on April 13, 1948, in Providence, Rhode Island. He grew up and attended school in Cranston, Rhode Island. Following graduation from Cranston East in 1966, he enrolled at Phillips Andover Academy in Andover, Massachusetts, for one year. He attended Harvard University from 1967 to 1971 and then went on to Boston College law school, graduating in 1974. He played three years of varsity at Harvard, earning All-American honors. Always one of the top scorers in college hockey, he is still remembered as a great college player.

Following law school, Joe returned to the Providence area and went to work for the law firm, Edwards and Angell. He remained with them until the spring of 1986 when he and John Blish formed their own firm, Blish and Cavanaugh. He and his wife, Carol, live in Warwick with their seven children, Mary Caroline, Joey, Paul, Sarah, Tommy, Carol, and David.

* * * * * *

John Blish, law partner in the firm of Blish and Cavanaugh:

"We first met when Joe joined Edwards and Angell. I had seen him play hockey in college. I went to Brown, so I rooted against him. I have been with Joe since he was a rookie lawyer. His competitiveness was apparent immediately. We worked well together and eventually formed our own law firm. He is exceptionally competitive, has tremendous character and is willing to put out for a client to the limit. As a trial lawyer, he handles the jury well, very well. He is at the top of his profession as a trial lawyer. He has great mettle, great faith. He is a very religious person, a real credit to the community."

Gene Kinasawich, Joe's freshman hockey coach at Harvard:

"It was a total pleasure to work with him. He was the team's captain and a superlative leader. I taught a course at a private school in the Boston area, "Sport in Society" and had Joe as a speaker a few years after he was practicing law. His influence on the students was profound. He personally had kept his accolades and success in perspective and was able to pass this on to the students. Sport was important for Joe, but only part of the individual. He has very high moral standards and values. His individual qualities far surpass his athletic qualities."

* * * * * *

I met Joe for the first time when we did the interview at his office in downtown Providence. It was the Sunday night of the NCAA championships in Detroit. He had taken two of his sons there for the weekend. I had explained to him on the phone that he was to be part of the group of people who played elite hockey but chose to pursue another career. He was flattered to be considered. I knew nothing of Joe Cavanaugh, the person, other than he was a great college player who attended one of the world's top academic institutions. I did not expect to find a typical jock. I didn't.

We looked for an alternative group to illustrate that it was possible to be an elite hockey player and leave the game to pursue an alternative career. Joe's story does just that. His desire to be a trial lawyer, to have a law career and raise a family, won out over any possible hockey career that may have come about. He uses keen personal judgement in making the decisions that he did. A good question to ask yourself as you read this is, "Would you have this lawyer defend you in a trial?"

* * * * * *

Q. Maybe you can start by talking about going to Harvard, how you decided to go there and what it was like.

A significant time in my career was when I graduated from Cranston East. I had an opportunity to go to Boston College on a full scholarship, but at the same time I wanted to attend an Ivy League school. I had applied to Brown here in my hometown. I didn't get into Brown. I was put on a waiting list at Harvard. I was always close to my father and he always told me if I had the chance to go to Harvard, I should really think about it. My father had nine kids and I was the second oldest. Without hesitation, without thinking about it financially, I decided to go to prep school and try to get into Harvard the next year. Now that I have seven kids and I think about how my dad took care of our education, I often remember this.

I passed up the scholarship to BC and went to Philips Andover. A friend still tells me the reason I went to Harvard over BC was because of the nice tennis courts at Harvard. I was All-State in tennis in high school and played on the Harvard tennis team. The year at Andover was good for me because I had another year to mature academically and physically. We played against a number of college freshman teams. I had come from playing on a high school team that lost maybe six or seven games in three years. Curt Bennett, who later played pro, was on the team. Anyway, I look back on that now and realize it was a turning point for me. I think that if I had gone right to BC out of high school, a lot of things would be different in my life now.

I considered going to Yale after Andover, but decided to stay with Harvard because I wanted to play on a good team and was pretty sure Harvard would be. Harvard had a good hockey tradition. I played freshmen hockey, which was a great advantage for me. I remember scrimmaging against the varsity and hardly touching the puck. The next year I was on the varsity as a sophomore and found it pretty easy. I'll say one part that I wonder about never playing pro is that I always found I got better with better competition. I remember scrimmaging with the '72 Olympic team my first year in law school and I felt I got stronger each day. By not playing pro, I do wonder if I could have improved enough to play well at that level.

Q. What was it like playing hockey at Harvard?

How did I find hockey at Harvard? Hockey was a large part of my life. That's how I got into Harvard. As I understood it, the admissions' department looked for people who were outstanding in one area. For me, I was a good athlete. One of my great memories was during my senior year. A guy named Norm Letvin, who is now a practicing doctor and also a teacher at Harvard Medical School, was in my class, a good friend of my roommate. Norm came to a couple of playoff games and later in the week he was analyzing the game to me as a scientist would analyze the game. Here's a guy who had never gone to a hockey game, yet he was so bright he was telling me things that were so accurate and perceptive just from observing a few games.

It had to do with the way our team was forechecking. He noticed that on certain lines the wings would go in the corners while on other lines the wings wouldn't go near the corners. What was impressive to me was that he would look at the game in that way, a game which I'd played all my life and he picked up subtle points just by going to one game. It was fascinating to me that I lived with that type of person for four years. It made my realize more and more that, "Gee, beyond our little world of eastern hockey, who cares? This guy doesn't care, he doesn't even know we're in the Nationals." That brought

me back to reality. I think my life was more
realistic at Harvard than it might have been if
I had gone to another school where athletes were
treated differently. Just this week at the Nationals in Detroit (1987), I looked around and
saw how involved the Michigan State fans were at
the games. I said to Mark Fusco, who also
played at Harvard, "These people are more intense and involved with their hockey team that I
was," and I was captain of the Harvard team. It
just shows the different levels. To us, hockey
was important. But because of the environment
it wasn't that important. I think there were
times that I found this frustrating while I was
a player, but overall, I think it was tremendous. In retrospect, the Harvard atmosphere was
the best situation I ever could have been exposed to.

**Q. Looking back, did you have any thoughts
about playing pro hockey?**

My mom was always interested in and influ-
ential with our sports. She was always talking
to me about being a hockey player, but just for
fun. We'd go to the Providence Reds (AHL)
games. She'd say something like, "You'd never
want to do that, play pro hockey." And without
really thinking, I would say, "Yeah, that's
right, I would never want to do that." This was
when I was a little kid and never really considered pro hockey. There were probably two reasons why while growing up I never thought about
pro hockey. One was my background. I'd always
thought of it as a game and my parents were always saying, "It's only a game, there are other
things that are more important." And two, American players like myself were not playing professionally. It's different now, many kids
think about playing pro right from bantam hockey. Their parents probably do, too.

I learned in my junior year that the Bruins
had me on their negotiation list. People

started to ask me if I was going to play pro.
My last year at Harvard I was beat up. I lost
my four bottom teeth. I had already lost the
top four. I broke a finger and had a bad shoulder. I pulled a groin just before the Nationals
in Syracuse. It was easy for me to make the decision in the spring of my senior year. I was
very tired, a little bit sick of hockey, and I
was getting ready to graduate. I had the tennis
season coming up. I was waiting to hear from
law school. The combination of all these things
with one other factor contributed to my decision. I had met my wife, Carol, in the fall of
my senior year. She went to Wellesley and was
from Baltimore. She knew nothing about hockey
and I was sure she didn't want to be married to
a pro hockey player because of the life and the
traveling. All this made it easy to decide to
quit playing hockey and go to law school.

Q. Was this it, did you quit hockey completely?

A lot of people told me I should play on
the '72 Olympic team. Bill Cleary, who now
coaches Harvard, and Jack Riordan, the athletic
director, urged me to think seriously about
playing. Some Harvard alums suggested I play,
clerk at a local law firm for part of the year,
and then go to law school the next year. I
don't know for sure what it was, maybe my background, but my instinct was that I should not do
it. And I decided not to. I didn't even in-
quire at Boston College Law School as to whether
they would defer my acceptance for one year.
However, in the fall, when the Olympic team came
through the east, I skated with them. Our amateur team (the Braintree Hawks) played against
them. I also played with the Olympic team
against Boston University in the Boston Garden.
Murray Williamson was the coach and he told me
if I took six weeks off from law school, I could
join the team and go to Sapporo, Japan. I
talked with the law school people and decided to
join the team. This showed me hockey was still

in my blood and I wanted to try to do both.
However, around Christmas, in the third period
of an amateur game, I tried to go by a guy and
he hit me. I broke my wrist. I remember being
in the Braintree Hospital and the nurse saying
when they held up the x-rays, "I hope it isn't
broken because you won't be able to play for the
Olympic team." And I can remember before she
put them up, I was so tired, from school, from
playing hockey, planning my wedding, and worrying about taking the time from school, and saying, "I hope it's broken." It was. I never
played another game.

Q. Did you always want to be a lawyer?

The first reason that I decided to go to
law school was because my dad was a lawyer and I
had a great deal of respect for him. He had
graduated from Providence College and then the
Harvard law school. He had his own firm. I
knew he had been very successful and enjoyed his
practice as a lawyer. It became almost second
nature for me to try that profession. Having
come from Harvard where I think 20 percent of my
classmates went on to law school helped make it
a natural for me to try it. I never really
thought of doing any other type of law than trial law. My father was a trial lawyer. I didn't
consider corporate law or tax law or any other
kind of law that didn't relate to the court
room.

Law school is quite an academic experience.
You don't really have much trial training or experience. I found law school to be a challenge.
I knew it was going to be a challenge. As much
as Harvard is a challenging school, I think it's
more difficult to get into Harvard than it is to
stay in Harvard. I worked at Harvard but I had
been schooled at Andover and had been a good
enough student in my earlier days that I knew
how to get by at Harvard. That's why I was able
to play two sports. When I started law school,

I was concerned that I wouldn't be prepared and wouldn't do well. That was why I didn't think I could afford a year off to play hockey. It turned out that law school was not that diffi- cult; I found I had talents that I didn't real- ize I had. I developed those talents. After the first year, my wife and I were married. In any event, I liked law school, I learned to think like a lawyer and clearly loved the law. I remember my dad would want to talk about ten- nis, but I only wanted to talk about cases and issues. I was really into it.

After law school, I came back to Providence and started right away in the trial department in a large firm. Trial work is very competi- tive; it's almost like a game when you go on trial. It's clearly preparation that wins tri- als, but it's also an opportunity to maintain your cool under fire, to be able to take some momentary losses, and to know there's a whole game (trial) to be played. My experience in hockey and sports has helped me so much in my trial work and as a lawyer. The ability not to get flustered, or not to get mad at the judge, the other side, or a witness, is important. It's very similar to hockey when you can't say something to a referee, not lose your cool in a game, or not get upset when you lose one game because you know you're coming back to play an- other one. I know a lot of good trial lawyers who never played sports, but personally, my ex- perience playing in sports situations has helped me immeasurably in the legal profession.

Q. Do you enjoy your work?

I enjoy it. I have specialized in media law, handling libel, privacy, and first amend- ment issues for newspapers, and radio and TV stations. I have also developed a personal in- jury practice. I'm dealing with interesting people although I do represent some big corpora- tions. But, even then, there are always people

involved whom I get to work closely with. I
have had cases that are personal to me because I
have had a special relationship with the client.
I want to win those cases for those people because I know what they've gone through, a personal injury or a contract situation where
they've been treated badly or whatever. What is
most interesting about my job, I've learned, is
that the clients expect you to explain to them
in an easily understood way how they stand le-
gally. Do they have a strong position, a weak
position? That, I see, is my main job.

The best service I can give a client is to
tell him right up front, once I've analyzed the
situation, whether or not he or she has a strong
or weak case. Sometimes it's difficult for trial lawyers, particularly young trial lawyers,
because people come to you thinking you're going
to be a gun slinger, be their champion, go in
there and teach the other side a lesson. But
really our first job is to look at the facts and
then decide how the law will be applied to those
facts. Many times there's not a strong case and
the hardest thing to do is to tell a client
right up front that he or she does not have a
strong case. This part has been a learning experience for me. Initially, the tendency was
for me to take on all the cases. The client
wants to hear, "Yes, we'll take care of that,
don't worry about this, we'll do it." I have to
be objective, tell them, "No, that's a problem.
Why? Because if that truth comes out, you're
going to lose."

In one sense, a trial lawyer is a hired
gun, although you are hired to objectively analyze the case and tell them the strengths and
weaknesses of the case before the trial begins.
If clients know this and they still want to go,
then I go with them. I think I would have difficulty in a criminal context, but in a civil
case I can do that.

Q. What made you start your own law firm?

The firm I used to be with, Edwards and Angell, is an excellent firm. It has some of the best lawyers in Rhode Island. I received great training there. The problem was the firm was becoming more and more like a big corporation. When I started there in 1974, there were 45 lawyers. When I left last year, there were almost 100. I was treated very well; I was doing well. I was on the executive committee, but my sense that I was getting away from being a lawyer and becoming more of an administrator was becoming stronger and stronger. I just wanted to be a trial lawyer. If I went out on my own, I could be my own boss. I could decide what cases I would take and not worry about the other lawyers. It was becoming clear to me that in this big firm the administration was becoming a big part of my practice.

We started our firm in May, 1986. John Blish, who also was at Edwards and Angell, is my partner. He's been a trial lawyer for 21 years. We think a lot alike on most things. We share the same philosophy about how to treat clients, and why we're in business, which isn't necessarily to make a pile of money. We like each other. Our motives and values are similar. We thought if we started together, we could form the type of law firm we both would be comfortable with. So far it's been terrific. The first year has gone better than we had hoped. We've gotten more business than I thought we would get as a new firm. It's also been ideal as far as getting back into the practice of the law and away from the administrative problems.

The only problem for me personally during this time was that my dad passed away. He passed away in September of 1986, so I made the change and went through with this transition without his input. When I think about it, I realize I had had his input on every major decision I ever made. He had brain cancer and was unable to communicate for his last year. He could not talk, couldn't write, couldn't even signal what his thoughts were on any matter. That was a low period for me during this last year.

Q. How do you evaluate yourself, both personally and professionally?

What I haven't mentioned is that a major force in my life has been that I'm a practicing Catholic. I've often thought that everything that I do, and I was taught this way as well, related to talents that I've been given by God. The full development of these talents should be used to make a contribution to the people you live with, your family, the people you work with. I suppose one of my reasons for not going on with sports was what I had been taught: I had a sense that that would be, for me, limiting in terms of my abilities to influence what goes on now, and perhaps later in life, to have more of an impact on the community I live in. I don't mean that to sound elitist. I mean it on a very personal basis. A sense of my vocation back at that time that I had to make a decision whether to play Olympics or pro hockey was that I was called to do something else. I was not supposed to be a professional athlete. The question is what was I supposed to be? What I think is that I was supposed to be a guy who had played sports but also could go on and do well academically and then do well in my profession.

I would like my children to know they have a father who will be like my father was, and who was someone who tried to do his best, tried to be honest and was always trying to do what he thought God wanted him to do. That's what I'm trying to do. How do I evaluate my life? There are ups and downs. I begin every day, have some failings, but my goal is to try to find on a daily basis what God wants me to do, as a lawyer, as a father, even as a pee-wee hockey coach, and try to do that in a natural way. I think I'd be remiss or not honest if I didn't say that my faith in God has always been a key factor in my life. I really can't evaluate my life, because I don't know how I'm doing. I'm trying to do what I think God would want me to do as a father in a community trying to be a successful lawyer.

Q. Any thoughts on your family?

Having a big family, I always lived in an environment where that's what a family was. That's what a marriage was. I have many friends who don't have kids or only a couple of kids who are real happy and terrific couples. But, for me and my wife, we have found that a big family has been great for us. Obviously, you make sacrifices. The kids make you give in ways you wouldn't normally have to give, of time, money, passing up opportunities to do other things. Again, I suppose it goes back to why I decided to go to law school. I sensed that if I went the other way, I might just kind of go astray. With the kids, they keep me in line. I have so many obligations to them and it makes me, I hope, a better father and a better person to be giving to them. Hopefully, they'll live in an environment which will be healthy for them. It's no big deal. I've done financially well enough to have seven kids. The person who is a real hero to me in that respect is that person who doesn't have a lot of money, but still has a big family and makes real sacrifices.

CESARE MANIAGO

Cesare Maniago was born on January 13, 1939, in Trail, British Columbia. He grew up and attended school in Trail. He played his junior hockey with St. Michael's in Toronto. His professional career started with the Toronto Maple Leafs in 1960-61. The previous season he played with the Chatham Maroons of the Ontario Senior League and they were the Allen Cup winners that year. As had many players from the six-team NHL era, Cesare played with a number of minor league teams. These include Sudbury, Vancouver, Spokane, Hull-Ottawa, Quebec City, Buffalo, Omaha, Baltimore and Minneapolis. Nine years, from 1967-68 to 1975-76 were with the Minnesota North Stars. He had previously played for the Montreal Canadiens, New York Rangers and the Maple Leafs. His last two years, 1976-77 and 1977-78, were with the Vancouver Canucks. He retired in 1978.

Cesare operates Maniago Sports, a wholesale sporting company, in Vancouver. He lives in Vancouver with his wife, Mavis, and three daughters, Jodi, Carolyn and Donna.

* * * * * *

Lou Nanne, a former Minnesota teammate who became general manager of the North Stars:

"Cesare was one of the brightest players both on and off the ice I ever played with. He was extremely hardworking. As levelheaded as any goalie I've known, with no superstitions or idiosyncrasies we normally associate with goalies. He would get nervous and intense just prior to a game, otherwise he was very relaxed. He played with a great deal of emotion. As a player, he was always preparing to do something after hockey. Every summer he worked at some type of business. A

very honest, loyal, bright and fine person, I'm not surprised by the success he
has had since quitting the game. He is
still the same person today that he was
when we first met."

Emile Francis, Cesare's coach with the New
York Rangers and later Hartford Whalers general
manager:

"Cesare was a hardworking player, great
concentration. I was always impressed
with his work habits. I think he made
himself into a top-notch goaltender. Off
the ice, he didn't waste his time, he
was always reading, preparing himself
for other things. A popular player and
person, he mixed well with people. I
remember that with the fan club, unlike
most players who only came to the get-
togethers because they had to, Cesare
enjoyed it. He enjoyed being around
people and people liked him as well."

* * * * * *

I met Cesare for the first time when we did
the interview. It was at the Hotel Vancouver
prior to an exhibition game between the Canucks
and the Jets. The interview went well. He was
prepared and knew what he wanted to say. My
first impression was that this was an intelligent and secure person, at ease while talking
about his career and comfortable with the decisions he had made that led him to his present
career. I believe the interview is a reflection
of such a person.

Cesare's story is a good example of a player who never lost sight of the idea that there
is more to life than hockey. It becomes quickly
apparent that he worked during the off-seasons
for a couple of reasons. One was that he was
always planning to do something whenever hockey
would end. The second was that work and doing

things along this line came naturally to him. It is doubtful he ever thought or ever wondered about taking a summer off to simply play golf and hang around. Cesare is a good example of a player who planned for life after hockey, thus making his transition a simple and smooth process.

* * * * * *

Q. How did you end up in the sporting goods business?

Talking about the career I have today, the transition was very easily made. I was quite fortunate. Near the end of my career I was looking for something in the business that I have now, involved in the wholesale sporting goods business. That came about during my last two years in Vancouver. Before my total career in hockey was over, I had to face reality that I'd have to get involved in something else, once I was through with hockey. There were several avenues that were open to me because I worked in several areas during the off-season. I got involved in the stockbrokerage business, in real estate, and in the construction industry as an estimator. I think keeping contact with other people outside of hockey all of those years helped me to achieve a smoother transition.

It started when I was still with the North Stars. Lou Nanne was an advisor with the Northland Group at the time when they reorganized into the Northland Hockey Stick Company. I approached them and we discussed the possibility that if I came back to Canada that I would have the line for Canada. As it turned out, about four months later I was traded to Vancouver, so I brought the Northland Line to Vancouver with me. Walt Stohlberg, who was in the business and looking for a hockey line, contacted the Northland people and found out that I had the line for Canada. He called me. It was ironic.

He was a fan who used to have a small sporting
goods store in my home town in Trail. After
meeting with him, I started working with him and
shortly after that he asked if I wanted to get
involved in a partnership. I agreed. After a
couple of months, he had a stroke, followed by a
few other successive strokes, and he passed away
about a year after we started working together.

I'm still playing at the time. Probably
the most difficult task I've ever had was the
final year in Vancouver. I had purchased the
business from Mr. Stohlberg's widow. I had individuals working for me, but I realized that I
really couldn't devote 100 percent to either the
business or to hockey, and I felt that I wasn't
being fair to either one. I knew that I had to
make a decision, that I really had to call hockey a career and to pay attention to the new
business. And that's what happened. The transition was very, very easy.

**Q. Your transition period then began with the
meeting with the Northland people, when did
it end?**

I think a real load came off my shoulders
when I met with Jake Milford, who was the general manager for the Vancouver Canucks at that
time. We had discussed the possibility of my
playing one more year. This was right after the
season was over and I asked Jake to give me a
couple of weeks to think about it. I discussed
it with several other people outside of the
game, including my family. Some of them felt
that I should continue to play at least one more
year, but I knew what I was going through that
last year, not being able to devote 100% to either the game or to the business. I finally
made the decision, on my own, that I had to call
it a day. I informed Jake, wanting to give them
ample time to prepare and get another goaltender
into Vancouver. He expected that decision. I
think once it was made, I felt totally relieved
that I finally cut the ties.

Q. You played your hockey with St. Mike's. How important was that?

I felt fortunate that I was able to make the decision to leave hockey quickly and easily, and I was happy with it. I was never fearful of getting out of the game because I had been in the stockbrokerage business, real estate, and worked construction. I knew a lot of individuals that prolonged their careers because they're afraid of that transition. I was preparing myself, and it was when I was at St. Mike's, right out of junior hockey, and I think Father Bauer was the most convincing individual at that particular time. I didn't know whether to continue on with my education, or to at least give professional hockey a try. He strongly advised me. He said, "Hey, listen, go with your wishes, where you feel very strong. If you feel that you don't have a chance in hockey, then make up your mind and pursue an education." He said if I wanted to try to pursue professional hockey as a career, to give it two years. If at that time I felt that I wasn't making any strides, then call it a day. It wouldn't be too late to go back to school.

I took that advice for what it was worth. I felt that there was progression at the pro level and, fortunately, I got some breaks along the way. One thing I strongly believed in was to always create an alternative to the game. In other words, if the hockey career was over and done with after the third, fourth or fifth year, there would be something that I could slot myself into outside of the game. And I did. I had worked in construction since I was about 13 years old, in masonry. My brother, Dino, was in the business so I worked with him just about every summer. First as a common laborer, then I went into the office and started estimating. At this time I was making contacts with key business people, meeting what we would call the generals in the construction business. I was making contacts with those people so I wasn't afraid of getting involved with people in the business world. I stayed with him for several years, and then another opportunity came along. I got involved with a local firm, Midland Doherty, which is now a large Canadian national firm. I'd received my brokerage license and was to go to a small town in British Columbia and run that office. That happened right at the time that expansion took place in the NHL. I was playing with Minnesota.

I felt that the stockbrokerage business gave me a bit of strength because in those days I would negotiate contracts on my own rather than having agents like a lot of other people had. I felt that I had some strengths there and that if I couldn't come to terms, I had something else to fall back on. That probably was one of the proudest moments in my life, in negotiating a contract that I felt was what I was worth. If I hadn't been accepted, I would have had to start with something new. I was confident enough that I could, and if I wasn't going to continue on with hockey, then I could go immediately into a job where I could work independently. I felt that that gave me a sense of pride in that I knew that I was capable of doing a lot of things outside of hockey.

Q. Do you think this confidence made you a better player?

Yes. Many of the players were insecure, they felt a lot of pressure from a performance standpoint, it was as if, "My God, if I don't perform well and if they don't want me, what am I going to do with my life?" I was a more relaxed type. I'd go out there, try my best, work with the skills I had. It wasn't the end of the world if my God-given talent wasn't enough to play professional hockey. I had something else to fall back on. I think that really made me a better player.

I think players today, particularly the ones who have had some education, are in a little better shape than those, both years ago and today, who don't have any. They know they've been to school, they've lived a student's life, which is counter to most hockey lives, and they can say, "I've got an education, when I'm done with the game, I can get a job."

I think if I was a general manager of an NHL team today, education is one aspect of the individual I would look at. It's not just how talented you are on the ice, but also the amount of education you have. I think the better educated you are, the stronger your ideas and the better you'll be able to perform as a player. I think you create more ideas in the sense of what you're capable of doing on the ice. I'm a believer in that. Whether it actually will happen or not, I don't know.

Q. How did a player from Trail, B.C., end up at St. Mike's in Toronto?

An executive with Cominco, Mr. Pete McIntyre, took an interest in me. Cominco was the mining company my dad worked at. Mr. McIntyre was a personal friend of Conn Smythe. It's funny in a way. He called my dad into the executive offices one day. My dad, being an immigrant and having never been in the front offices all the years he worked there, was real worried. He was afraid he had done something wrong and was in trouble. Pete McIntyre asked my dad what plans I had for my future with regards to hockey. We, my dad and I, talked it over and I decided I wanted to play junior hockey and to continue my education. Pete said he would call Conn Smythe and set it up. It turned out I had a choice between the Toronto Marlies and St. Mike's. I decided on St. Mike's.

Q. What kind of a player were you?

I would say that times during my career I
had doubts whether I was capable of being the
best in any particular league that I played in.
I think that whole attitude changed because out
there (British Columbia) growing up as a kid you
really had only one dream, and that's playing in
the NHL. You want to be the best at whatever
you do, at least that was my philosophy at the
time. Yet once I got into junior hockey and saw
other goaltenders that I really admired, I knew
I was capable of playing as well as, say, Bruce
Gamble, who was playing at that time. I think
it just came to me with a different type of attitude, in that I wanted to try and be the best
in any particular league that I played in. Even
though it didn't actually happen that way, I
thought, "Okay, well fine, I'll play my best and
we'll see what the results are like," and fortunately enough, it happened the first year out of
junior hockey by winning the Allen Cup. I felt
that I had a tremendous season and if any one
season gave me the attitude that I was capable
of playing in the NHL, that was it. It was
probably the first year where I felt that the
players were so dependent on my playing well
that they basically gave me more credit than I
thought I was worth. And that was probably one
of the nicest feelings that I could get from
teammates.

You can go through life and it's no different now being in business than, say, playing
hockey. And hockey was probably the greatest
disciplinary thing that I could have had because
it has continued on in life, too. When you've
done a job well, you feel extremely good about
it. That's what happened in hockey, too. To
sum it all up, I thought I was better than an
average goaltender, not the best, but I'd classify myself as probably in the... maybe with a
total of 12 teams and 24 goalies, I'd classify
myself in at least the top 8. I feel good with
that analysis. I really do.

Q. What about high points?

At various points of my life, as a player,
starting out as a young kid being able to go to
Toronto St. Mike's. I think that was maybe a
stroke of luck going to the best junior league,
at least at that particular time in Canada, and
being able to play with Toronto St. Mike's. One
thing that I wanted to pursue, was to try to
continue on with an education. It seemed that
St. Mike's was the only team in Canada that really offered anything like that. We lived on
campus, there was strong discipline with the
priests and the people that were running the
school, and I was able to pursue my education
with few problems. I think that added a lot to
the success of my career. Naturally winning the
Allen Cup was probably the stepping stone in
getting involved in professional hockey.

Q. What about low points?

I think it's almost hitting the bottom of
the pit where you're almost at a decision of
calling it a career while you're playing the
game. It happened a couple of times. Once when
I was totally discouraged when I was playing in
the minors with New York. I was in Baltimore at
the time, and I was having to shuffle back and
forth from New York to Baltimore, on the train.
It happened that I went back to Baltimore on the
train after a Sunday game, and there was a heck
of a snowstorm and we were late getting back to
Baltimore. And I can only get a cab to within a
mile and a half of the apartment that we had.
This was about three in the morning. The cabbie
dropped me off, and I started walking. All I
had on was a raincoat. I thought I was going to
freeze to death. I got to the apartment, in
fact, I flagged down a sand truck that was plow-
ing one of the roads and I literally stood right
in front of the truck. If he had to run me down,
he was going to run me down because I thought I
was going to die anyway. The fellow picked me

up, and I finally got home. My feet were almost frostbitten, my hands were just as bad. I'd made up my mind then that I was going to call Emile Francis in the morning and give him an ultimatum. I had been in New York for almost a month now, commuting back and forth. Either he makes the decision that I stay permanently in Baltimore the rest of the year or I move to New York immediately with my family. And if he wasn't going to make a decision on either, that I was going to quit the game right then and there. It kind of makes me laugh now that I think about it, because Emile and I are fairly close. He said, "Well, why didn't you ask before? Definitely, move the family up." It makes me think about the cat and mouse game, so to speak, with general managers. This definitely was a low point.

I would say after that there was only one other time and that was in Minnesota my first year when I got off to a horrible start at training camp. I really didn't know whether I was capable of continuing on. I thought I had completely lost it. Anything that I tried just absolutely backfired. You have disappointments along the way, but nothing to the point where you're saying, "Hey, I've had it, I'm going to quit the game."

Q. Looking back, do you have good and bad memories?

Good memories, a lot of the individuals that I played with. I like to think that one of the nicest years was the first year of expansion, again, with Minnesota. The group that we had there came from all different organizations and we just molded together as families, as players. There was no such thing as a clique. We moved together as a team. If there was a get-together after the game, it was the whole team. If we were on the road, it was just common knowledge that if we were going somewhere, everybody was invited. It was healthy, really healthy. And we had a successful year, I think, because of it.

We weren't critical of each other, we weren't nitpicking at each other. If we played a poor game, we blamed ourselves as a unit, and not as individuals. It was a strong feeling of unity, and I think that probably gave me more insight in how to run a business and how to work with people than anything else. And that, to me, was a strong basis of teamwork.

Naturally, you know, you can talk about memories, winning the Allen Cup, which was ironic. I was playing with the Chatham Maroons and we ended up in my hometown, playing the Trail Smoke-Eaters and we won the Allen Cup right in Trail. Just to see the mixed reaction of friends that you grew up with who really didn't know whether to cheer for Trail or you and give you credit because you're playing with the opponents. But winning, it was an exciting moment. I've always said that even once I've gotten out of hockey, and being involved in sales, there is nothing more exciting than winning a big game. People often talk about getting the chills up and down your spine and I literally used to get that periodically playing hockey. There was no greater excitement, and I haven't had that feeling since. Even though a lot of pleasant and exciting things have happened since being out of hockey, there's just not anything quite as thrilling as that. And I do miss that, if anything, that real thrill.

Bad memories. Probably one of the saddest times that I ever had in hockey was when I was involved with Minnesota and Bill Masterton was given a bodycheck. We knew it was very serious at that particular time, but we had to leave right after the game, go on to Boston. We were all quite concerned about his injury, and then when we got the word earlier in the morning that he didn't recover. It was probably one of the saddest moments in my life, because as I had mentioned before, we were very close as a team.

We were particularly close with his family. In fact, just the night before, we had them over to the house for dinner to celebrate both our birthdays. That's probably one of the lowest and saddest moments that I ever had as a player.

Q. Were you able to take advantage later of your playing status?

I think being involved in the sporting goods business, being a former player helped me tremendously, especially when we got involved with hockey equipment. It made it easier to make the sale, and that definitely did have a bearing on our successful years in business. The transition was very smooth, I had no problems whatsoever. There's nothing that I would do differently.

The type of work I got involved in, during the off-seasons, helped me to get organized. Now, once hockey was over, to literally run your own business, with people working for you, there had to be some type of organizational patterns and also, as far as treatment of employees is concerned, I honestly felt that they should know exactly what my thinking is and what I would expect out of their performance. The key to all that is communication.

I think my most successful years were when the coaches were involved and that they communicated with their players. It has to be a one-to-one basis, I can't see it being different from running a business. If there are problems, you have to take them (players/employees) aside and discuss them at length. These are adjustments you make, but I think that hockey was a good training ground for it. That's my personal belief on what I feel should be happening out there, is to at least communicate with people. I think this could be more of a downfall than anything else with a lot of individuals. I think this is why we have a successful company, at least I'd like to believe that that's part of the answer.

Q. Did anyone help you once in business?

I was fortunate. I'm very, very conservative. There are a few people who have been instrumental in guiding me in business. My brother, who had been in business all of his life, and a close friend in town who had a car dealership, Gord McLennan, helped. I'd always gone to them for advice when I first got involved in business, whenever I had to make a major decision. We would discuss the problem, they would make recommendations, and maybe the final decision was done on my own, but I think they were the ones that really got me rolling in the right frame of mind on how to operate a business.

Q. How do you view yourself as a professional businessman?

I look at myself as being a successful business person. One thing that I've learned about business, and unfortunately you don't have any prior training for this, is that while you're playing hockey, you have very little distrust in anyone. You take everyone as being honest and trustworthy. When I got involved in business, I started off with the same attitude. Well, unfortunately, in business, it didn't work that way. It made me a harder person, my personality had changed from what I was as a player, to a businessman. And unfortunately it's a harsh, cruel world in business and I had to adapt to that.

That's one of the sorry things that I see in business, in other words while you're at work, your personality changes. You accept the responsibility that goes with the job you're doing, and once you leave work, your personality changes again. Now I've got to go home and I can't let the problems at work be carried home. I found that a bit difficult at times. It took me a couple of years to adjust to that. One thing I'm thankful for is the understanding from my wife. It started very early in my career as a hockey player. She naturally was interested in the game and any problems I had she liked to share in those problems. But it got to the point after awhile, where I didn't want to discuss my problems at home. It only brought out the anger I had and made it more depressing. I felt that whatever problems I had, I wanted to leave them at the rink, or if I wanted to discuss it, I was the one that would bring it up. We've applied that right through to running a business.

You almost have to look at the total career and say, "Hey, I've played for a lot of teams and we were on the move fairly often." Even with that, that was an education in itself, having to adjust even though we were kind of in our own environment as hockey players. Our whole family had to adjust to different surroundings. I think maybe I've been fortunate in that the only position I've had outside of hockey is having my own business and not having to work for someone, and not being transferred from one job to another and going through the whole scenario as I did as a hockey player. I've been fortunate that way. But I don't think I'd find it devastating if I had to, say, move to Toronto tomorrow and take on another company. I wouldn't care to do it at this point of my life, but I think I could if I had to.

And that gives me more satisfaction than anything else. I guess I've always been that type of individual that wanted to make my own decisions. I wanted to try to be the best at whatever I was doing. And playing the position of a goalie, you're always looking at it as if, "Okay, I'm part of the team." But there's only one person for that position. And I think it carries on into business too. I know one thing that I've learned and this is maybe through my brother. We had always discussed the possibility of partnerships and he'd been in partnerships and none of them worked out. He literally said

to be skeptical of getting involved with other
people in business. So I've had that outlook as
far as business is concerned. If I'm going to
run it, I'll live and die by the sword. I'll
live with my decisions or I'll die by my mistakes.

I feel a real strong sense of being inde-
pendent in my own way, that I'm not answerable
to many other people. I do have good people
working with me, and I take a lot of their input
which I feel strongly that I need. I don't
think that I could make decisions without consulting with them, regarding prices or looking
at a new line. I wouldn't make that decision on
my own without consulting with my people. I try
to get as much feedback as I can from my staff
and I think that's important. But yet invari-
ably, the final decision is mine and I have to
live with that decision.

RON ELLIS

Ron Ellis was born on January 8, 1945, in Lindsay, Ontario. His father was in the Canadian Air Force and he moved around quite a bit during his childhood. Most of his youth hockey was played in the Toronto and Ottawa areas. He played his junior hockey in the Toronto Marlboros organization from 1960 to 1964, one year with the B's and three with the A's. His entire professional career, 15 seasons in all, was spent with the Toronto Maple Leafs. After 11 seasons, he retired for two years (1975-76 and 1976-77) and then returned for four more. He retired in 1981. Ron was a member of the Team Canada for the Super Series in 1972 with the Soviet Union.

Following his retirement he taught physical education for one year. Later he ran a general insurance business in Orangeville, Ontario for three years. He currently owns and operates Ron Ellis Sports in Brampton. He and his wife, Jan, and two children, Kitty and R.J., live in the Brampton area.

* * * * * *

Paul Henderson, a former teammate with the Toronto Maple Leafs:

"Ron was a dependable guy to play with. As a linemate I always knew he would do his job. As a player he was steady, dependable and disciplined. He was a team player who saw his success tied to how the team did. Our families are best friends. The adjectives I used for him as a player fit him as a person, quiet, dependable, steady, dedicated and disciplined."

Mel Stevens, a friend and former sports chaplain:

"The dominant characteristics of Ron Ellis are his consciousness and determination. He is always striving for excellence. A highly respected gentleman in Canadian sports and hockey, he deserves that reputation. Today, this is exhibited through his Christian commitment. As a player, he was never totally satisfied with himself and found himself with his commitment to Christ. He has great concern for young people, he spends a great deal of time working with youth organizations. It's a pleasure to know him."

* * * * * *

I met Ron for the first time when we did the interview. The interview was done in his store in Brampton during the Memorial Cup playoffs being held in Oshawa. He had been contacted only four hours prior to our meeting about the interview. He looked at the questions for the first time while I described to him the project. His comment before we started was, "I've thought about these questions a lot." He spoke in a deliberate manner, as though he wanted to be sure what he said reflected what he meant. We completed the interview over the telephone.

After the face-to-face interview, I had a distinct impression that Ron is a person of high personal standards who works hard at meeting them. His life has been a journey to find the meaning and purpose for his existence, a quest on which he has centered much of his adult life, and on which he will focus the rest of his life.

* * * * * *

Q. When you look back, how do you view your career?

When I look back on my career, I consider myself to be very fortunate. I played on a Memorial Cup team with the Toronto Marlies, played on a Stanley Cup team with the Leafs in 1967. I was able to play with Team Canada in '75 -- which was quite an experience, probably the highlight of my career -- and I was able to play with the Toronto Maple Leafs for 15 years. The Leafs were the team I wanted to play with when I was a youngster. I never played in the minors and I was never traded. It was really more than I could have hoped for.

Q. How would you describe yourself as a player?

I think I was the kind of player that had to change a little when I turned pro. In junior hockey I always played center and was fairly effective, not only as a scorer but also a checking centerman. My last year with the Marlies, Jim Gregory, who was the coach, asked me if I would consider moving to the right wing. I had never really played right wing before and it actually was the break that made it possible for me to play in the NHL. The Leafs were very strong down the middle at that time with Bob Pulford, Dave Keon, Billy Harris and Red Kelly. I played right wing the year we won the Memorial Cup (1963) and led the team in goal scoring. Because I hadn't played right wing before, I had to be very careful how I checked my opponent. I worked as a two-way player. I hope that's how people remember me. "Yes, he could score goals but he could also be counted on to check a big line or to play in the last few minutes of a close game." Certainly in Toronto I wasn't known as a flashy player. In some cases people thought I played a robot style of hockey, but the people that were paying my salary and the coach and general manager as well as my opponents appreciated and respected my style.

Q. You mention the Canada-USSR series of 1972 as a highlight. What was it like?

It was an exceptional series. It was the first time Canada was allowed to use its professionals against the Russians. We knew that the challenge match was not going to be a cakewalk. Maybe the Canadian press viewed and printed it that way, but not the players. I, for one, was very much aware that the Russians don't accept challenges unless they're pretty sure they're going to do well. They didn't come over to be embarrassed. In fact, I think they thought they would win.

Paul Henderson, Bobby Clarke and myself were invited to training camp in August of '72. They needed enough players for two teams since there was no opposition for exhibition games. The three of us were put on a line but I don't think the coaches thought we would play very many games. Everybody was promised to get into one game, that was the carrot they put in front of us to come and give up our summer. The three of us made up our minds that we were going to work hard. For some reason, we jelled as a line, possibly because we were two-way players. That's the way you have to play the Russians as they would counterattack so quickly. We became one of the more effective lines on the team and played in all eight games. Paul ended up being the Most Valuable Player and scored the game-winning goal in the last three games. That's what made it so special as we weren't supposed to make the team.

Another thing that made it such an experience was the storybook ending. We got ourselves in trouble to the point that we had to win the last three games in Moscow to win the series. Paul scored the winning goal with just a few seconds left in the final game. It was a thrill of a lifetime.

I think the '72 series showed that Canada was not the only hockey power in the world. A

lot of people believed that if you're a Canadian, you should be a better player than someone
from another country. Consider a country like
the USSR. With their population and the number
of players at their disposal, they're going to
have a few superstars of their own. I think it
made Canadians realize, "Hey, our players our
good, but they're up against top competition."
Winning a Stanley Cup was a great highlight of
my career, but playing for my country in the '72
Series is even more memorable.

Q. How about high and low points?

My career was sort of spotted with high and
low points. I mentioned some of the high
points. I was the type of player that tried to
control my emotions. I tried not to overreact
because, in hockey, you can be a goat one night
and a hero the next. It's a tough life from
that point of view and can be difficult to handle.

I did have periodic times of depression
during my career. After I had played several
years, I began to wonder if this is what I was
supposed to do, if this was the real purpose of
my life. I think all hockey players, all professional athletes, ask themselves the same
question. I would wonder if chasing this little
black puck around was my purpose, if I was really doing what I was put on this earth to do.
This happened even when I was playing well. It
was hard to explain.

Q. How about good and bad memories?

The good memories, just the tremendous people that I've met and have been able to have as
teammates. I made some great friends playing
hockey. There is something unique about going
through experiences as a team that pulls you
together and molds you into a unit. The Stanley
Cup team brings back happy memories and special
relationships. Another team that keeps coming

to mind is the '78 Leaf team when we beat the
Islanders in seven games. Lanny MacDonald
scored the winning goal in overtime on Long
Island. That team was very close and I'll
always have a special feeling for each guy that
took part in that great series.

There is a low side. Hockey can be very
hard on the family life. I think the wife of a
player has to be a special person. Fortunately,
for me, my wife understood the demands of the
game. She kept the house quiet on game days and
put up with my request to have meals at certain
times. There's a lot of time away from the family. Basically, your social relationships during the season are with your team members. You
see few friends away from hockey and this was
difficult, especially for my wife who is a very
sociable person. My kids were quite young when
I was playing so the fact I was away from home a
great deal wasn't a serious problem.

**Q. You had two different retirements. Can you
talk about the transitions?**

I had played 11 seasons prior to the first
retirement. Basically, I just came to a point
in my life where I was having problems justify-
ing the game of hockey as my purpose in life. I
had just signed a four-year contract and walked
away from it when I retired. The previous year
was my most successful season as far as total
points were concerned. I played on a line with
Darryl Sittler and Tiger Williams and that season we were a very effective line. I went to
training camp the following year because I wanted to be sure that if I retired, it was not because I wasn't able to get myself in shape. So
I attended camp, worked hard, played in all the
exhibition games and then shocked a few people
by retiring.

To take a step back, I had become a born-
again Christian during that off-season. Of
course, a lot of people right away said that's

why I wasn't going to play anymore. "He's a born-again Christian, he can't play anymore, they can't play hockey." But that wasn't it. I think the faith I had gained gave me the courage to make the decision to retire. I had always wanted to play 10 seasons. I walked in Red Kelly's office and said, "That's it, Red. I thought about it a lot and I feel I have to retire at this time." I didn't close the door forever, I just had to get away. Red was very understanding about it all.

I didn't have anything planned for the future. I had done a few things in the off-season as I experimented with different careers that might develop after retirement. Within a few months, I was working for McClintock Homes in Toronto. They were in the home building business and had some properties up in King City which had a golf course on it. Through an associate of mine I met the president and, to make a long story short, I joined them. My job was manager of the golf complex and I helped in the sale of homes they were going to build around the golf course.

I thought that was pretty exciting, being out of hockey and still staying in the sports world. I worked for this company for two years. Then something happened. In '77 Canada was going to use its professionals in the World Cup at Vienna for the first time. I called Al Eagleson and said, "Is there anything I can do to help? I've been through it before." He said, "Do you think you could play?" I decided to give it a chance and get in shape. I thought this would give me an opportunity to see if I could play and make a comeback. The first year out of hockey I didn't miss it. The second year the itch to play started to come back. I made the team after not playing for two years and probably played some of my best hockey of my career in Vienna.

When I came back to Toronto, Jim Gregory, who as the Maple Leafs' general manager, called me and asked what my plans were. I had a major decision to make but I really felt God saying, "I showed you, you can play hockey, play it for me." So I returned to the National League and played four more seasons. They weren't as productive as the ones prior from a production point of view, but they were enjoyable years. I think it was because of my Christian faith. I saw things from a different perspective. My life wasn't based on the circumstances around me, whether I was scoring goals or not, whether the team was winning or not, I went out every day and practiced and played as hard as I could, glorifying the Lord. All of a sudden the game had a purpose.

The second retirement was expected. I had even suggested to the Leafs that I should retire after the third season back (1979). But they said, "No, we have plans for you next year." I was preparing myself for retirement. I had tried a couple of things in the off-season. I worked for a few summers as a partner in a pen wholesaling business. As well, my parents and I were partners in a tourist camp located in the Muskokas. It was ironic, Punch Imlach, who was responsible for bringing me into the league was also responsible for me retiring. He asked me to go the minors about two-thirds of the way through the season. I hadn't played in the minors and I wasn't going to start. I said, "No, I'll retire." I was a little shocked, I thought I could complete the season, help some of the younger players. I wanted to finish my career in Toronto, it was very important to me at that point. The first time I retired I felt I could come back and play. This time I knew it was over. I think the real transition started and I didn't have any specific plans.

Q. What did you do for employment at this time?

Beginning in September, I taught for a year at a Christian school. It was a new school and they needed someone to help with the phys. ed.

department. I had the time, wasn't sure what I was going to do so I said I could help. It was an enjoyable year. I taught grades seven to ten. I realized I would have to go back to school and finish my BA. I had gone to school several off-seasons and was only a few credits short of a degree. I realized that year, though, that I didn't want to make teaching a career. The experience taught me a great deal but I realized it wasn't for me long-term. At the end of the year I informed the school they should find another teacher as I was not going to return in the fall.

We were living in Orangeville (Ontario) at the time where we had built a country home. A friend of mine had an insurance business in Guelph and had wanted to expand it to the Orangeville area. After some discussion I took the insurance course and started an office in Orangeville. I ran it for three years. It was part of the transition. After three enjoyable years, I had picked up a lot of skills. The business went very well. They were pleased with what I was doing but I knew it wasn't for me. I started to get restless again. It's hard to describe. After being brought up in hockey, ever since you were eight or nine, it's hard to find your niche in life that can give you the same feelings you had as a player. You can break out of a slump with two or three goals one night. It's not like that in business or life. Hockey is a world of its own. And I always believed there was life after hockey. Even though the insurance business was going well, I was looking for something else.

I started talking with two other men about putting up our own building and getting into a high-end sporting goods business. We didn't want the type of store that would be known as a "jock store." We wanted something a little different from the normal sporting goods store. This is where Ron Ellis is now. I still believe I'm in transition, trying to find that final niche. I've got good people with me and we think we can do some great things. I'm hoping to use the store as a vehicle to help other players that are going through post-hockey adjustments. Possibly we could conduct seminars or develop a retreat facility. Something that would assist the hockey player make the transition to real life.

Q. Can you characterize your transition?

I think it's been long. God willing, I'm nearing the end of it. It has been difficult. Not financially, nothing like that. Just trying to find a part of me that enjoys doing something other than playing hockey. I need to find that thing that's going to give me that same amount of satisfaction, the same drive and willingness to get up each morning and work at it. The teaching and insurance jobs have been part of my development. I'm now using the skills I acquired in those jobs.

Q. What adjustments have you made?

I was a very disciplined person as a player, never late for a practice, game, so forth. So I'm never late for appointments, meetings. That has helped in business. I believe in team work and everybody here has a responsibility to do their part. If we do our jobs well, we'll be successful, we'll succeed as a team. Putting in the time is not a problem. I've been prepared to always put in the time needed to get a job done, 10-12 hours a day, whatever. I think I get this from my parents who are both hardworking people.

Q. Can you evaluate yourself in terms of the progress you are making?

I'm content with the progress. I'm wise enough to know I have a lot to learn. I'm prepared to do what is necessary to learn.

That's why I have two partners. They are skilled in areas where I don't have expertise. One is in the financial end and the other is in the marketing end. I manage and operate the store. We make a good team that way. There's no question we have a heck of a challenge here. It's like being down 3-1 in a playoff series right now. We're a new business just feeling our way along, facing challenges as they come. We have a long way to go before it's a viable business. I've got a lot of faith and I know we're going to give it all we have. The business is very competitive and exciting at the same time. We have some concepts that are not quite the same as some of our competition and in time we will see some positive results.

Q. To what extent has hockey been a force in your life?

Hockey's been a very important force in my life. There's no question about that. I do not regret my years as a hockey player at all. I have learned a great deal about life through hockey. I know what it's like to win and to lose. I realized what it takes to be a pro athlete, the training that's involved, the mental anguish you go through. I think that prepares you very well for life after hockey. The experiences I had will always remain with me. I've enjoyed it and I'm thankful for the head start that I got in life that I got because of hockey.

The transition from hockey can be very difficult. Mine, I believe, is near completion. According to my doctors, I have been close to a complete nervous breakdown on two occasions. My faith, family and friends have helped me through the dark times.

I believe the good Lord has a plan for my life. Up till this time, he has been preparing me for something special. It is my prayer that the work with other pros in transition will be part of his overall plan.

GLENN HALL

Glenn Hall was born in Humboldt, Saskatchewan on October 3, 1931. He grew up and attended school in Humboldt. He played his junior hockey in Humboldt for a year-and-a-half and in Windsor for two. He started his professional career in 1951 with the Detroit Red Wings. He spent five years playing with the Red Wings and their farm teams in Indianapolis and Edmonton. Traded to the Chicago Black Hawks in 1957, he played ten seasons with them. He moved to the St. Louis Blues with NHL expansion in 1967-68. He retired after his third year with the Blues in 1971. He was elected to the NHL Hall of Fame in 1975.

Glenn is a goalie consultant with the Calgary Flames. He lives on his farm in Stony Plain, Alberta with his wife Pauline. They have four children, Patrick, Leslie, Tammy and Lindsay, and five grandchildren.

* * * * * *

Al Albour, a former teammate with Windsor, Detroit, Chicago and St. Louis:

"You won't find a much better person than Glenn. He's just a great person. He was when he played and remains so today. He's a sharp individual. Glenn tries to camouflage it, but he is very bright. You look at the number of consecutive games he played and it tells you what kind of competitor he was, just unbelievable in that sense. When we won the Stanley Cup in Chicago, a lot of it was his doing. A true professional."

Cliff Fletcher, general manager of Calgary Flames:

"Glenn showed his true character when he was part of expansion and came to the St. Louis Blues. The team won the Vezina

Trophy, an unheard accomplishment when you realize the role of the original six teams. He showed his true leadership and competitiveness on a team that consisted mainly of career minor leaguers, older veterans and marginal National Leaguers. Glenn is one of the true throwbacks to the by gone era of hockey with his ability to enjoy the game in and away from the arena."

* * * * * *

I had met Glenn one day prior to the interview, when we rode to a junior game in Belleville, Ontario. We did the interview at the Ramada Inn during the Stanley Cup finals between Edmonton and Philadelphia. We had dinner before the interview and talked mostly about the game and, in particular, goaltending. Glenn outlined his answers before our meeting.

His interview is less about life after hockey as it is life with hockey. I came away from the interview thinking, "Here is one of the game's all-time great players. He maintains a real positive view of his game despite some of the things that happen to a player during his career." This is a person who views his career fondly and is content with his present involvement with the game.

* * * * * *

Q. How do you view your career?

I enjoyed it. I was reasonably successful and I think I got the most out of my talents. The teams I was on didn't win as many Stanley Cups as I would have liked but I sure treasure the one we did win. I played a long time and the game was very good to me.

Q. You won the Stanley Cup in 1962 with the Chicago Black Hawks; any thoughts on that?

There was a period of time that people thought we should win the Cup every year. But if you were on the inside, you knew there were weaknesses. We obviously camouflaged the weakness very well because they kept saying again the next year that "Yes, we were going to do it." We weren't capable of tightening up. We were explosive offensively, but we weren't capable of cutting that half a goal a game down that a team has to do in the playoffs. The other good teams in the league like Toronto and Montreal could do it. Against Toronto you would never get a rebound. Montreal had the skills in both ends of the rink, we had only the offensive skills.

Playing then in Chicago was something. The fans -- and the noise level was just great. Even today, the noise level is still impressive. I was there a couple of years ago and I was sitting with Al MacNeil in the press box. They sang the National Anthem and the fans started to yell and everything and Al said, "Kinda makes you want to join the Army." It gives you the goose pimples. It's quite a building, still probably the greatest building in hockey. But I remember when the building was empty, too. Then we got a couple of kids named Bobby Hull and Stan Mikita and we became a real respectable team.

When I first got to Chicago in 1957, if you ever saw a kid with a hockey stick it caused a traffic jam because people would be stopping their cars to look. It was rare. Once the Hawks got better, won the Stanley cup and, with Bobby's influence, a few rinks were built and hockey began to grow in the area. I think in some ways the Hawks of the early 60's helped spread the game west.

Q. Anything different during that era that you remember fondly?

A couple of things really. The first was the initial years and the idea you were brought up through the system as a junior. It was good for us. We were taught what was acceptable and what wasn't. You kind of learned on your own. But to make it to the NHL, you had to learn. Even though I only played two years with Detroit, I was in their system for 10 years, two years in junior in Windsor, one-and-one-half in Humboldt, four on their minor league teams and two with the Red Wings. I liked that development system, it was good for me.

The other was expansion. Without a doubt, it extended our earning years for a lot of us. I was ready to retire at 32 or 33. Nobody enjoyed the game more than I did. It became difficult to perform at the level which I demanded of myself, so I was probably ready for retirement when expansion came along. My career was extended with a lot of others and it brought us larger salaries.

We were treated unbelievably well in St. Louis. I felt happy with how we performed. Expansion was stupid. They didn't, the original six, give anything up. The new teams only got the players the six didn't want any more. What we did in St. Louis with guys like Doug Harvey, Al Arbour, Dickie Moore, the Plagers, Red Berenson, Noel Picard, Jacques Plante, Jimmy Roberts, Jean-Guy Talbot and Ab McDonald, was simply tremendous, with hard work and the fact that hard work brings good results. The young kids came in and wondered why we were working so hard. They learned to work as well. I'm sure the opposition wondered why we worked so hard as well. I think we represented our division very well the first year. In fact, we made the Cup finals the first three years. It shows that hard work makes up for a lot of weaknesses.

Q. What do you see as your achievements during your career?

What I feel very good about is that I was named, I think it's still a goalie record, 11 times to the All-Star teams in the National Hockey League, seven times to the first and four times to the second. I'm very proud of the fact that I played over 500 consecutive games, which was quite an achievement. Gretzky isn't even going to beat that one. I won the Red Tilson Memorial trophy in my last year of junior hockey. I felt good then and still do about it. That award was for the most valuable player in the Ontario Hockey Association. I felt very good last year (1986) being associated with the Calgary Flames when they beat Edmonton and eventually made it to the Cup finals.

Q. What kind of player were you?

I was always ready to play, nobody had to wake me up. I was totally ready to play. I was a pretty good skating goalkeeper. I think my skating was a real strength. I had good reflexes, good balance. My recovery was good and it was tied to my balance. Back then the goalkeepers always thought survival. The styles have changed so much since the mask came in. We tried to get our feet over in front of the puck and the head out of the way. It was survival, number one. We couldn't get ourselves in some of the awkward positions you see goalies in today. We couldn't afford the luxury of getting hit in the face or head like they can today. When we got hit, it was a real accident because we weren't trying to stop the puck. We got hit in the face because we were doing something wrong, in a bad position or one would get away from you. As a player, I enjoyed playing the game. It was fun to stop the puck. But then young players like Bobby (Hull) came in the game and the shooting started to change.

Q. What was it like having Bobby Hull shoot at you every day?

There's nothing that Bobby liked to do more than shoot the puck. He could really shoot the puck. I'll tell you a funny story about his shooting. The day after a game when we would be practicing, the cleaning crew, mostly women, would be working in the stands. He would see a lady bent over, maybe 35 or 40 rows up, sweeping. He'd bounce a puck off the seat next to her. He'd grin. Finally they refused to work while we practiced. He scored 50 goals with the conventional stick. I think the year he got 58, if he had been using the conventional stick he would have gotten 70 or 75. The curved sticks let the shooters like Bobby cut the puck, get it to work on you. In today's game I would have trouble looking at so many shots. I was more of a reflex goalie than an angle one. Today, the goalies just try to get out there and let the puck hit them.

Q. Any high or low points you might want to mention?

Not really any low points. The nice thing about the mind, it forgets the things that you don't want to remember. I do remember the sick feeling when we would be losing and we'd be trying so hard and nothing would happen. But, then it gave us something to compare with when we won.

We have fond memories about the places I played in. My wife, Pauline, really likes Chicago. She was really a Chicagoan. Through the people we met in Chicago, there was so much more to the city than just playing there. We still have very good friends there today. St. Louis was great. We were treated so warmly when expansion took us there. There's just something about Missouri that makes me feel good when I think about it.

Thinking back, it's much easier for the athlete than the wife. The players are always with each other during the season, traveling, practices, get-togethers. The wives, however, were often alone. But, for us, it helped us make good friends away from the team. They have been lasting friends, too.

Q. Can you define your transition period?

When I retired it was immediate. I just felt the weight of the world was lifted off my shoulders. I knew I could simply do what I wanted to and it felt great. I had made preparation for retirement. Our intention was to stay on the farm and work the farm. The first year, around training camp time, I remembered what training was like and knew right then that I didn't miss it. Training camp was putting on the wet equipment for practice number two. That and the other things that I remembered gave me a good feeling that I no longer had to do it.

I knew I had played too long, 20 years of pro, which is a long time. The skills were eroding, to a degree, that my total desire and love for the game were being pushed instead of being natural. The enthusiasm had slacked off. The treatment when we lost was getting hard to take. If we lost, I knew exactly what was going to happen. We'd get on the bus, they'd be mad at us, we'd go to the airport, fly home and get in maybe at 4:00 a.m. or whatever and we'd have a 10:00 a.m. punishment practice. I wasn't opposed to practices, I was opposed to the punishment practices. I remember Eric Nesterenko, in Chicago, saying, "We're sorry we lost, we didn't mean it, make us stand in the corner." The coaching staff had to prove that they were doing everything to get us on the winning track. I just felt it wasn't good for my game to be punished. I got to the point that I just didn't need it anymore. My transition was short.

Q. Speaking about training camp, what is the truth behind those stories about you painting your barn every year and missing training camp?

I missed training camp often because I didn't think training camp was necessary, essential. There was no learning process at training camp. It was simply to get in shape. And I didn't think I had to be at training camp for somebody else to get in shape. I could move as well on the first shot I looked at as the one I looked at at Christmas. There was no advantage to me to be at training camp. It just made me mentally tired and fatigued by the time the season started.

How that story started was I had advised Tommy Ivan, the Chicago general manager, at the end of a season that I was retiring and I wouldn't be coming back. I said to him, "You can do anything you want with that information, release it if you want." On July 1, I got the same form letter saying that training camp started on such and such a date. I ignored it. When training camp started, the press asked, "Where's Hall?" Tommy called and I said, "Tommy, remember I told you I was retiring?" Well, he didn't think I was serious. I then got a bunch of calls from the press and I said to my wife, "Tell them I'm painting the barn." After that, it simply got blown out of proportion.

Q. You grew up in Saskatchewan and now live in Alberta, both prairie provinces. Will you talk about being on a farm?

I grew up in Humboldt, but in town, not on a farm. Early in my career, I played in Edmonton in the minors. We decided to make our home in Edmonton because of necessity. There were no jobs at home and we had to work in the summer to survive. We had always looked for a farm to buy around Edmonton. For a long time it was the case that we couldn't afford the farm we liked and could afford the farm we didn't. We eventually found one in Stony Plain and bought it in 1965. I have been extremely fortunate. I couldn't believe when I first played pro that I would be paid to play the game I liked so much as a kid. After we bought the farm, I was able to farm a few years before I retired from hockey. So when I quit, I had prepared some for it. The farm is west of Edmonton and most of the farming is cereal crops. We grew barley. It's not a great farm, heck, it's an enjoyable farm. After I quit playing, we did a little cattle farming. I enjoyed the cattle. I then had the opportunity to get my foot back in the door with hockey.

Q. How did you end up back in hockey?

I was out of hockey about seven or eight years. I also worked with the Edmonton Oilers in the WHA for a short time. But I didn't like it. Not totally out of hockey, I did coach the junior B team in Stony Plain. It was a community-sponsored team and I thought I could help the community, so I coached a bit. It wasn't a relaxing situation because I found out that as soon as I'd walk into the arena, I'd be hyper like when I played. So it wasn't totally enjoyable. My son was playing at the time and I felt I owed something. It was a small town and I felt it was important to help out. The team directors were just creating an opportunity for the kids to play hockey and I suppose it was an opportunity to say thank you to the people in Humboldt who had given me a chance to play.

Billy MacMillan was the coach of the Colorado Rockies in 1980 and asked me to help out with the goalies. It was only part-time and I enjoyed it. When the club moved to New Jersey, I stayed involved. When Billy and Bert Marshall were let go from Jersey, I just felt, "Well, hell, I'm one of these guys, I'm in this group,

I should be let go." So, I guess I quit. A while after that, Cliff Fletcher called me and asked me to come down to Calgary. Cliff was with St. Louis when I played there. I eventually ended up helping out the Calgary goalies. It was an ideal situation. It's close to my home and they weren't looking for someone full-time. I enjoy working with the young goaltenders. I'm spending more time in Calgary than I did in Jersey or Colorado. The relationship I have with Calgary and the people that work for them is very enjoyable.

Q. Any thoughts on goaltending?

Goalkeepers are generally loners. I suppose I could become a hermit real easy. I enjoyed being alone. People look at you kind of crazy and say, "How can you enjoy being alone?" I can think things out very well when I'm alone. I enjoy the open spaces. I'll come into Edmonton for awhile but pretty soon I'll get claustrophobia and turn and head for the hills. People always say that we're different. Years ago goalies didn't have anybody to talk to. Now, with the two and three goalkeeper system, they are able to conserve. I suppose I would have liked someone to talk hockey with. When I was coming up, Terry Sawchuck and Harry Lumley were in goal for Detroit. If they knew anything about how to stop the puck, they certainly weren't going to tell me because they knew what my intentions were. It was definitely not to their advantage to help me. Back then, we didn't do those things. Even when I was in Chicago, Tiny Thompson was a scout and I never asked Tiny for help nor did he offer it, and this is one of the things that I now regret. With the goalies I work with now, they've been very responsive. I'm not very demanding but they've been very good working with me. I really enjoy working with them.

Q. I'm always upset when I hear hockey people today blame goalies for losses and why a team does poorly, any thoughts on that?

I've heard those statements and they bother me. I think all goalies have the same attitude as I did. I never let up on a goal that was scored on me. I felt bad when I was playing poorly or when I let in a bad goal, but at least I tried. I never set up a player for the future. There were times when we would be ahead or behind and I had chances to let a player think he beat me. This would have allowed me to set him up for the future. He'd always think he could beat me with the same shot. I never did that. I don't advocate it and don't think many goalies have done that. Anybody who scored on me didn't make me very happy. The same can be said for all other goalies. It's a tough position to play.

As a player I didn't pay a lot of attention to what a coach was saying. Five minutes before a game or between a period I didn't hear what a coach was saying because I was in total preparation. All I would be thinking about was what I had to do. During a game when someone got ready to shoot, I'd already had looked at the shot in my mind. Every option that was there I had tried to prepare myself for. You didn't have to be a Rhodes Scholar to know where the shooter was going to go. They'd give you the fakes here and there, but I knew where they were going to shoot the puck. All goalies go through this when they're playing. It's unfair to them for management to place the blame in their direction. The goalie is only part of the team.

Q. Has hockey been a force in your life?

It's been absolute, total. It's really the only thing I know. It's probably the only thing I've been interested in knowing, I've enjoyed it. If you enjoy it, you must like it. Not many people can say they enjoy their job and I can't think of anything worse than going to work and hating it. I've gone to work when I didn't feel like working, I was sore, I was hurting and everything else, but I went to work. Hell, the sun came up the next day and I was okay.

I don't know if it's important, but the best hockey player I've ever played with was Gordie Howe, the best I've played against was Gordie Howe, and the best I've seen is Gordie Howe. There are a a bundle of really great hockey players like Bobby (Hull), Stan (Mikita), the Rocket (Maurice Richard), (Jean) Beliveau, certainly Bobby Orr and Wayne Gretzky that I have enjoyed being associated with in the game of hockey.

DICKIE MOORE

Dickie Moore was born on January 6, 1931, in Montreal. He grew up and attended school in the north end of Montreal. He played his junior hockey with the Montreal Royals and the Montreal Junior Canadiens and was a member of the first two Memorial Cup Championship teams from Quebec. His professional career started in the Montreal Canadiens organization in 1951. He spent half of that year with the Montreal Royals in the Quebec Senior League prior to joining the Canadiens. He stayed with the Canadiens until his first retirement in 1963. During this time he played on six Stanley Cup teams. He came out of retirement to play with the Toronto Maple Leafs in 1965 and then retired again. He came out of retirement a second time to play for the St. Louis Blues in 1967-68, the first year of expansion. Inducted into the NHL Hall of Fame, in 1974, he twice led the league in scoring and is considered by many people to be one of the greatest left wings to have played the game.

Dickie owns Moore Equipment, Ltd. in Montreal, an equipment sales and rental business. A lifelong resident of Montreal, he and wife, Joan, live in the Montreal area. His two children, John and Lianne, work at their father's business.

* * * * * *

Henri Richard, a teammate with the Montreal Canadiens:

"He was a great team man, maybe the best I have ever known. A very hard worker, he would do anything to help the team. He was the same as a person, he will sacrifice anything to help his friends. He is quite successful in his business. He should be knowing the kind of person he is and how hard he works. He has done pretty well since he quit playing."

Sam Pollock, former Montreal Canadiens general manager:

"Dickie Moore showed outstanding ability and leadership qualities at an early age. He was an outstanding hockey player from minor hockey all the way to the NHL. He won the Memorial Cup twice and the Stanley Cup six times. He was not only a great player but a very popular and likable person. He was extremely well respected by his teammates. The left wing with Henri and Maurice Richard on one of the greatest lines to ever play the game. He has been just as successful in the business world as owner and manager of a large service company. A real top Hall of Fame hockey player."

* * * * * *

We met in his office at Moore Equipment. His office is a working one with hockey and work things strewn about. Amid the activity of a bustling business, we were able to get his story told.

As I drove to a junior game in Laval following the interview, my thoughts on Dickie Moore were clear. This was an individual who chose to play hockey. What comes through loud and clear is that he wanted to win. The theme of his story is that he wanted respect and he earned it.

* * * * * *

Q. **Will you talk about your early days playing juniors?**

Before juniors I had my own hockey team at 13. We used to get second-hand equipment from the Forum. I even got sticks from the Forum to supply to our team. Our team went on to the

city finals and did a hell of a job. In fact,
we ended up against Sam Pollock's team which
came from the west island of Montreal. We felt
that this was the rich area so we had a goal to
beat them. Our area was very competitive in
that way. From this, I went on to play junior
hockey in Montreal.

I was fortunate to be on the first Memorial
Cup winner from the Province of Quebec. I felt
it was a great honor. The games were played in
Winnipeg and Brandon, Manitoba. It was in
1947-48. In fact, I was just asked to return
for the 40th anniversary in Brandon. We thought
we were cowboys going out there. We bought the
10-gallon hats. It was a great series.

The Montreal Junior Royals won the Memorial
Cup. The next year I still had a couple of
years of juniors left and a lot of the guys
graduated to the Senior Royals or the Canadiens.
It turned out they wanted to break up the Royals. They, really Mr. Frank Selke, sent a lot
of the players to the nationals. He left me,
the black sheep, to go to the Junior Canadiens.

They were coached by Sam Pollock. I had
always wanted to play for the Royals because my
older brother, Jimmy, played there. Anyway, everybody went to play with the nationals. Boom
Boom Geoffrion was with them. They were trying
to build a Memorial Cup winner. Of course,
Beliveau was in Quebec City with the Citadels.
To make a long story short, we won the Memorial
Cup. We had a hell of a team, Pollock coached
and he went on to the top from there. It was an
honor to be on a second Memorial Cup team in a
row. But we were good, Ernie Roche, Billy
Gould, Kevin Conway.

The next year, I said I needed more money.
No one agreed with me. I was working at CPR
(Canadian Pacific Railroad), had worked there
all during juniors. I did that because I wanted
to have some security in case I didn't turn out
to be a hockey player. I finally got a raise

but I only signed for the season. When the
playoffs came I said, "That Beliveau is making a
lot of money, if I'm going to have to hit him
and chase him around, I wanted to be paid like
him." Pollock got mad at me, said, "No way."
Billy Reay was helping Sam coach and he got them
to give me a raise. But only to win. I said I
only play to win. Anyway, we went into the
playoffs against the Citadels and they beat us.
I was a little discouraged. I just wanted
equality, I never played for the money, only to
win.

After we were beat out, the Citadels called
me and said, "Dick, do you think you'd play for
us in the playoffs against Ontario?" I said,
"Sure, what an honor." Selke got drift of it
and called me on the carpet. He said, "Who do
think you are? You're a traitor." I said, "No,
they're from the same league, they just want to
beat Ontario." Selke hated the Citadels but I
thought it was an honor, helping our own. I
never got to do it, Selke didn't let me go. I
did go to the series and watched. The Barrie
Flyers ran them out of the rink.

It's still an honor to say that I played
with Gordie Knutson who has turned out to be one
of the top plastic surgeons in Canada. Gordie
was kind of an idol of mine, me not being that
good academically and him being my roommate. He
came to Montreal to take an exam from Brandon
that he had to write at McGill University. When
he came back to Brandon, I said to him, "How'd
you do?" He said, "Ah, 85 or 90 percent." I
was pretty close with Gordie. He was of Swedish
origin and my mother was Swedish so I felt a
closeness between us.

Q. Following your junior career, how did the
professional career start out?

The next year I had to make a decision
whether I was going to be a hockey player or an
employee of the railroad. While I was

contemplating what I would do, I received my letter inviting me to the Canadiens' camp. I tried my best but I could see I wasn't in their immediate plans. Mr. Selke called me in and asked me to play for the Senior Royals. I said, "No." I was disappointed. I was given the choice between signing with the Royals or going to Chicoutimi (Quebec) or Victoria (British Columbia). Mr. Selke offered me $2,800 for the season. I said I thought it was unfair. I didn't really understand the salary process. No one helped you when signing and I didn't have any idea what the salaries were. He promised I would join the Canadiens by Christmas. I said, "Why not now?" I ended up signing for a minor league for $2,800. He kept his promise and called me up on Christmas Day. I refused to sign the major league contract Mr. Selke offered. I was looking to protect my interests. But I had to sign an NHL contract to play and I eventually did. The offered me the minimum $7,500. It was a lot of money. I was making about $20 a week at the railroad. I had heard Beliveau was making $10,000. But Mr. Selke and I eventually came to an agreement after several hours of negotiations. I was surprised at the salary structure. We ended up agreeing to two years for $15,000 total with $2,000 for signing. I signed my first contract in his kitchen in Westmount. That was it. Once I signed I was happy. I don't hold grudges. That was Christmas Day, 1951.

I had a pretty good first half with the Senior Royals. I was playing with Cliff Malone and Les Douglas. I was lucky because I seemed to always be playing with intelligent guys. Cliff had gone to college and was one of the better wings in the league. I had 18 goals by Christmas. I was riding high. In fact, Frank Carlan, the coach, still calls me today. It's very flattering and honoring that he does. I only played 23 games for him.

The second half I was with the Canadiens.
I had 15 goals and 33 points in 33 games. Pret-
ty good I thought. It was a good start in the
NHL.

Looking back, I was lucky. It had to be
luck. I was on six Stanley Cup winners. I was
playing with a great bunch of guys. I'm a team
man but I'm still an individual. I felt I could
win. It was a great time to be with the
Canadiens.

**Q. You played in an era when most players
worked in the summers, didn't you?**

I always worked in the summers, the railroad, construction, sales rep, whatever. During
the first three years, I worked construction in
the summers. I worked with a friend of mine,
Larry Zeidel, an my brother, Jimmy. I was in
the ice cream business in 1956. I had a couple
of stores and it worked well. It was a summer
business and didn't interfere with hockey. I
bought a golf course in 1958. I found out there
was no money in that and got back in the ice
cream business. I was preparing for my future.
Let's not kid ourselves, I knew the day was going to come, that they were going to say,
"Goodbye, Dick." I started this business in
1961. I was pretty careful. I didn't want to
gamble my savings. In fact, my wife and I were
going to buy a house on the lakeshore, even made
the down payment. I thought, "What if I get
hurt and I can't meet the payments? This is
crazy. I'd better wait until I can buy revenue
property." I took that route. I bought a house
that I rented the upstairs and we lived in the
downstairs.

I spent 12 years with the Canadiens. I
didn't want to leave them. I was a true
Canadiens player. During the summer of 1963, I
was called into the office. I had prepared myself for the future throughout my whole career.
I was in this sales business when Mr. Selke

called and asked me to stop down and see him. I
told him he could tell me on the phone, but he
wanted me to come down to his office. I said,
"No, I've got a business to run, I'm busy." I
kept putting it off. He called a second time
and I told him I'd be down when I was free. I
didn't expect to be traded. I had 24 goals the
year before. But, it was winning the game that
was important.

I eventually got around to see Mr. Selke.
He told me, "We're thinking of trading you." I
quickly replied, "No, nobody trades me, I quit.
Thank you for everything, good-bye." I walked
out of his office, grabbed a phone and called
Red Fisher, the sports reporter. Told him I retired, he thought I was crazy. But I told him
to write it. I was lucky, it was 11 a.m., just
before deadline. I got it in the paper. I'm
laughing now, but then I was pretty upset, because I wouldn't play for anyone else. That's
what made the Canadiens what they are. The
pride. The playing for them. The sticking together.

So I quit. I was operating this business.
They never made the trade. A couple of months
later the Canadiens traded Donnie Marshall and
Phil Goyette to the New York Rangers. I put two
and two together and figured that must have been
me that was supposed to go to the Rangers. That
same summer I fractured my kneecap. I was testing a grinding wheel and the wheel hit the kneecap. The fragments were removed but I said
leave the cap. I wanted to play more. Mr.
Selke eventually asked me back for the playoffs.
I didn't go and was off the year.

**Q. How did you eventually come out of retire-
ment?**

The next summer I was drafted by the Toronto Maple Leafs. Punch Imlach called me to tell
me. As a kid I wanted to play for the Leafs. I
thanked Punch and told him I didn't know if I

could play because of the knee. He said, "Don't worry about it, we'll have to sign you." We negotiated a contract. Flipped a coin to settle a $1,000 difference. Punch was a helluva guy, super individual, very superstitious. I learned from him, it was an education. Back then, you didn't know the opposition, you never fraternized. But, Punch treated me very well and I still respect him for it.

I went to the Leafs camp. Punch told me to take my time and get in shape. I was a little embarrassed. My pride, I wanted to play. I would not sit on the bench. My family moved to Toronto and an awful thing happened. I was driving my kids to school and a little kid ran across the street and into my car. I was pretty upset. I went to the Garden and told Punch I was quitting. He told me not to worry, but I was upset. It turned out the kid was all right but we went back to Montreal. When Punch would come into Montreal with his team, he would call, he always had my paycheck. Late in the season he asked me to come back for the playoffs. I said, "Sounds good," and went back. We played against the Canadiens in the semifinals and lost. I didn't go back the next year.

I was out for about two-and-a-half years. One night, it was in 1967, I was playing Old Timers hockey in Lachine and Cliff Fletcher, who was scouting for St. Louis, asked me if I would like to make a comeback. I was 20 pounds overweight, running the business, having a bit of fun. Scotty Bowman then called me and asked me if I wanted to play. This was the first year of expansion and I told him, "Sounds good, depends if the money is good." We reached an agreement and I had to lose the 20 pounds. Couple of weeks later I headed for St. Louis. It was a great year. The Canadiens beat us in the finals for the Cup. We lost each game by a goal. Glenn (Hall) was the goalie and he played great. We had a lot of ex-Canadiens. I think it was the Canadiens' pride wanting to win, the will to win, caring about winning and losing, that made St. Louis a success then. We were determined to win. Even though we were always down by a goal, we thought we could win.

St. Louis asked me back the next year. I was 37 going on 38. I could have played again if I had good legs. My knee was bad. I had to exercise backwards by lifting weights to strengthen my legs to skate. I wanted to leave the game on my own. The Sid Salomon family treated me great. If it wasn't for my legs, I would have continued to play. They tried to lure me back for the playoffs. I said no. I knew that I did it twice but a third time, that I'd only be kidding myself. I did go down to watch them in the playoffs. They went to the finals, did a hell of a job. It was great, everybody was enjoying it. Again, it was the Canadiens' pride.

Eventually, the Blues called me and asked me to coach. I was sitting in my office and said, "Sid, sounds great, I'll make a deal with you. You buy my business and I'll coach your team." I couldn't just get up and leave the business. If I got fired, where would I go if I didn't have this business in Montreal?

Q. **Was it the right decision, sticking to business and leaving the game?**

The business is good. We're doing better every year. The business looks good now but back then we had the lows of any new business. We use the philosophy of sport here. We have a good team. One employee started Day One and has remained with me through today. It is the team spirit of individuals like Pierre Roy, Guy Gaudreault and Vince Fazzolari who have made the business grow into what it is. We all enjoy the team concept.

My hockey background has really helped us. People have been good to me. This is my hometown, people know me. It helped in the business. If I had to do it again, I don't know if I would be a businessman. Maybe I would have devoted myself to hockey.

My son and daughter work with me in the business. John went to Husson College in Bangor, Maine. When he first graduated he thought he would be a golfer and went to Florida for a while. He eventually came back and has worked here for seven years. Lianne also works here. At first it took a while for her to adjust. I told them it's hard to work for your father. But they have learned the hard knocks of the business and are very good at what they do. Our oldest son, Richard, worked here as well. We lost him 13 years ago in a car accident. The kid was very gifted, very intelligent. It was tough for all of us, but our family stuck together and we learned to live with it. It was a major tragedy for us.

I also have to thank my wife, Joan. As someone said, "A man is only as good as his better half." She has had to put up with a lot with me being away when I played. She has had to sacrifice the time it took for me to start and develop the business. She has been a great mother with the children for which I'm very proud.

Conclusion

Initially, we thought that the patterns of behavior would define groups according to "satisfaction level". The groups would have been: (1) Happy as a player and happy after hockey; (2) Happy as a player and unhappy after hockey; (3) Unhappy as a player and happy after hockey; (4) Unhappy as a player and unhappy after hockey. However, we found that the player's transition period better determined the groups. Everyone spoke positively about their playing careers and all have accepted their post-playing careers. The differences were in the transition periods. We developed four general groupings from this study.

The Smooth Transition Group

The largest group is called Smooth Transition. In this group are players who had a smooth transition and quickly got on with their life and a second career. The members of this group recognized the end of their playing careers and were prepared to begin to work outside the playing arena. They found jobs quickly. Members of this group either knew what they were going to do or quickly made the decision after retiring. In this group are: Connie Broden, Mike Eruzione, Gerry Hart, Glenn Hall, Cesare Maniago, John Mayasich, Dickie Moore, Morris Mott, Henri Richard and Don Saleski.

Players from the pre-expansion period before 1967 consistently made the transition well. This appears related to the fact that salaries were not large and everyone worked in the summers. Their adjustment problems were less severe than those of post-expansion players.

The Rough Transition Group I

The second group is called Rough Transition I. In this group are players who had a rough transition, got through it and got on with their lives. Members of this group characterize themselves as having required an extended time period to adjust to being out of hockey. For them, the transition period was an intense learning period. While the actual transition time varied, they each realized their need to get a job and put together the effort to begin a second career. In this group are: Gary Dornhoefer, Ted Irvine, Jean Pronovost and Tom Williams.

A prime characteristic of this group is that they have moved on and developed a second career. They each believe they enjoy their jobs, have achieved a level of success and recognition and are satisfied, for the most part, with the direction of their lives.

The Rough Transition Group II

The third group is called Rough Transition II. It is similar to Rough Transition I with one exception. Group members have yet to establish a second career. Still, they believe that their post-hockey lives are headed in the right direction. In this group are: Ron Ellis, Mark Heaslip, Ulf Nilsson and Gary Smith.

The Alternative Group

This group, as described in the Introduction, confirmed our expectations. They made the decision to leave hockey themselves and pursued what they thought were their real careers. The members of this group, Roger Bourbonnais, Joe Cavanaugh, Father Les Costello and Jerry Kruk, are now well established in their careers. Each recognized the importance of education and prepared himself for the day he left the game. They have controlled their destiny more than the players in the other groups.

The Hypotheses

Hypothesis 1. Players measure personal achievements in terms of team champion-
ships.

This hypothesis was confirmed. The players
spoke about the importance of playing on winning
teams. Players whose teams won championships
cite them as achievements. Nearly everyone interviewed played on a championship team at some
time. It is clear that, as professional athletes, they are competitively driven and measure
success in terms of winning.

Mike Eruzione:
"It's the pride of knowing you accomplished something that you set out to
accomplish. My last seven years of hockey, four at BU, one of the years at
Toledo and the Olympics, I won six championships. I don't care what level you're
talking about, it's important to win."

Morris Mott:

"But, I wouldn't say there was anything
outstanding like a Stanley Cup victory
that I could point to and say, 'This was
the highlight of my career and I wouldn't
have been happy if I hadn't achieved
it.'"

Henri Richard:

"I guess winning the Stanley Cup is an
achievement. It's a team effort, of
course."

Mark Heaslip:

"The one real highpoint was winning the
Calder Cup."

Ulf Nilsson:

> "The good things that happened to me? We won two championships in Winnipeg and when we won in '77-78, the last game I played in Winnipeg, that's when I had the chance to skate around with the Avco Cup."

Hypothesis 2: Formal education is important in "life after hockey".

This hypothesis was confirmed. Many players said they came to realize the importance of education and wished they had a college degree. The players who had a formal education recognized its value. But formal education is not a requirement for a successful second career. Several players, Dickie Moore, Don Saleski, Gerry Hart, Henri Richard and Cesare Maniago, received a sound business education through their off-season jobs. Their on-the-job training provided the skills and confidence which formed the foundations for their second careers.

Roger Bourbonnais:

> "The law practice allows our family to live in a relatively good fashion. There is a sense of security in having a profession that provides a certain comfort level."

Connie Broden:

> "Another thing is, one can always find time to continue formal education at night. I took business administration courses at McGill and science courses at Loyola."

Mark Heaslip:

> "The fact that I didn't graduate from college came back to haunt me. The doors would open because I was Mark Heaslip,

because I had played hockey and I was a personable guy. But it's funny how they look for a degree."

Don Saleski:

"The only regret I have is that I didn't finish my college degree. I sure would like to have it now."

Fr. Les Costello:

"The next year I went back down to Pittsburgh. I had a pretty good year but in the back of my mind things were different. A lot of us were discussing education. I had been thinking about the priesthood and decided I'd better get back to Toronto and university and give it a chance."

John Mayasich:

"My aspirations as a youth were not to play pro hockey. It was high school, college and the Olympics, in that order."

Hypothesis 3. Some players would regret having spent so long playing the game, and would wish that they had never played professionally.

This hypothesis was not confirmed. With one exception, everyone was glad they had played professionally. It is clear that they loved the game, and that this love has endured. They continue to care about hockey and are proud of their playing accomplishments. The one exception was Gary Dornhoefer, who said he would not do it again. He did not regret having played, but is bothered by playing injuries that still affect him.

Glenn Hall:

"It's been absolute, total. It's really the only thing I know. It's probably the only thing I've been interested in. I've enjoyed it. If you enjoy it, you must like it."

Joe Cavanaugh:

"A sense of my vocation back at that time that I had to make a decision whether to play Olympics or pro hockey was that I was called to do something else."

Jerry Kruk:

"I loved the year-and-a-half of pro hockey."

Gary Smith:

"I ended up playing 17 years in pro and it seems to me that it was almost like someone else that was playing. I really enjoyed it."

Gary Dornhoefer:

"The injuries were numerous. I was never able to play a full season. Today, I have difficulty walking 18 holes of golf or playing tennis or racquetball because of my knees. So, looking back at both sides, if I had to do it all over again, I wouldn't do it. It wasn't worth it."

Hypothesis 4. Money earned as a player is not as significant a measurement of achievement as reaching the top of one's profession.

There was little discussion concerning the amount of money earned as a player. No one judged his success by the size of his contract. This does not mean that money was unimportant. It may indicate that players focus more on their athletic than their financial feats. Several players emphasized their pride in having reached the top of their profession. This is an accomplishment that does not appear to diminish with time or success.

Ted Irvine:

> "I feel it is an accomplishment that from all the guys who played in the area (Winnipeg), I was the one that made it. I view it as a success that I reached my goal because I worked hard and I was prepared to accept some challenges from management and the game."

Gary Dornhoefer:

> "From the player's standpoint, to win the the Stanley Cup and reach the level that you're recognized as the best team is top priority and money is secondary."

Tom Williams:

> "My top salary was $50,000 a year, so I never made big money. I made $300,000 in sixteen years, $18,725 a year. But money wasn't my main deal then and it isn't now."

Dickie Moore:

> "But only to win. I said I play only to win...I just wanted equality. I never played for the money, only to win."

Hypothesis 5. The effective use of the off-season during the career, either for education or employment, would ease the transition.

This hypothesis was confirmed. The players who characterized their transitions as smooth did, for the most part, make good use of their off-seasons. There was a contrast between players who did not and those that did. While the schedule may keep a player from outside activities, he does have the summer free. The off-season can be a period to gain experience and confidence.

Cesare Maniago:

"One thing I always believed in was to create an alternative to the game. In other words, if the hockey career was over and done with after the third, fourth or fifth year, there would be something that I could support myself doing outside of the game."

Don Saleski:

"I knew that hockey could end at any time. Therefore, I went to Villanova in the off-season. I had a hockey school in Philadelphia. I also worked for a company called Anchor Container as a salesman. The purpose was to prepare myself for retirement."

Jean Pronovost:

"But, as a player you don't really want to think about it or pay a lot of attention to it. I really didn't get myself prepared for the time I would be done playing. I thought I would play more and more."

Gerry Hart:

"I am grateful for all the opportunities I've had come my way, but I also feel the gratification of having earned it. Gerry Hart put in the time, whether it was in the off-season or resisting the temptation for a few beers and a long lunch every day after practice."

Hypothesis 6. A player's fondest memories, other than his athletic achievements, are of teammates and people met through hockey.

This hypothesis is confirmed. Everyone spoke fondly of their hockey associates. There is a real sense of camaraderie on a team. The travel, practices and games enforce the notion that "we are together". From this sense of unity and mission, friendships develop quickly. Locker room humor is real and effective. Shared experiences foster these friendships. It is, therefore, not surprising to find that the players' good memories are populated by their teammates and acquaintances.

Ron Ellis:

> "The good memories, just the tremendous people that I've met and have been able to have as teammates. I made some friends playing hockey. There is something unique about going through experiences as a team that pulls you together and molds you into a unit."

Henri Richard:

> "Being able to play with my brother, Maurice, is a good memory. I was only 6 years old when he started to play with Montreal in 1941. He got married and left. He was more like an uncle to me. And then being able to play with him for five years and we won five Stanley Cups those first five years. I liked that."

Ted Irvine:

> "Good memories were the guys I played with. I met some dandy people. Players from Boston, Los Angeles, New York and St. Louis organizations are the biggest memories."

Life After Hockey

There are a few apparent general conclusions to be made from these interviews. The first is that these players respect and love the game. Hockey continues to be a large part of their lives. To them, it is not just a sport, but the foundation for their present lives. These former players have a good sense of themselves. They know where they have been, what they have gone through and where they are now. It is also clear that the confidence they gained as top players remains with them today.

The second conclusion is that these are mature men. They have a positive outlook. The stories they tell are not about the bad things that happened, but the good. They can accept blame for their disappointments. They see their families as giving them focus and strength, more so than would today's players. They recognize their wives' contribution to their hockey careers. The satisfaction that comes from a good marriage and staying close to their children is evident. They realize life didn't end when they hung up their skates for the last time. In real life, unlike in the world of professional sports, there is no cheering, no trumpets blaring for a good day of work, no pat on the back for being on time, and no adulation from the customer. But they have come to accept that they're like other human beings, just trying to do their best.

Finally, we can conclude that there is "life after hockey." There certainly are former hockey players who have fared worse than those in this group, though that percentage of all retired players is difficult to say. But, for the many players who share similar experiences with our interviewees, there is definitely "life after hockey" and it is good.

At the end of his interview Tom Williams told me something that sums up "life after hockey." He spoke as we walked, "I had a long day today," he said. "I was up at 3:30 this morning to do something with one of my sons. I then drove to Binghamton and put in a long day.

I knew I said I'd be here at 7:30 tonight. If I
was   a   player,   I   never   would've   shown.   I
would've figured he can call me again. But, you
know, I'm not a player any more. I said I'd be
here, that meant I had to be here."